# THE DEATH PENALTY

Amnesty International Report

**AMNESTY INTERNATIONAL** is a worldwide movement which is independent of any government, political grouping, ideology, economic interest or religious creed. It plays a specific role within the overall spectrum of human rights work. The activities of the organization focus strictly on prisoners:

- It seeks the *release* of men and women detained anywhere for their beliefs, colour, sex, ethnic origin, language or religion, provided they have neither used nor advocated violence. These are termed *'prisoners of conscience'*.
- It advocates *fair and early trials* for *all political prisoners* and works on behalf of such persons detained without charge or without trial.
- It opposes the *death penalty* and *torture* or other cruel, inhuman or degrading treatment or punishment of *all prisoners* without reservation.

**AMNESTY INTERNATIONAL** acts on the basis of the United Nations Universal Declaration of Human Rights and other international instruments. Through practical work for prisoners within its mandate, Amnesty International participates in the wider promotion and protection of human rights in the civil, political, economic, social and cultural spheres.

**AMNESTY INTERNATIONAL** has over 2,000 adoption groups and national sections in 37 countries in Africa, Asia, Europe, the Americas and the Middle East, and individual members in a further 74 countries. Each adoption group works for at least two prisoners of conscience in countries other than its own. These countries are balanced geographically and politically to ensure impartiality. Information about prisoners and human rights violations emanates from Amnesty International's Research Department in London.

**AMNESTY INTERNATIONAL** has consultative status with the United Nations (ECOSOC), UNESCO and the Council of Europe, has cooperative relations with the Inter-American Commission on Human Rights of the Organization of American States and is a member of the Coordinating Committee of the Bureau for the Placement and Education of African Refugees (BPEAR) of the Organization of African Unity.

**AMNESTY INTERNATIONAL** is financed by subscriptions and donations of its worldwide membership. To safeguard the independence of the organization, all contributions are strictly controlled by guidelines laid down by AI's International Council and income and expenditure are made public in an annual financial report.

# THE DEATH PENALTY

## Amnesty International Report

Amnesty International Publications
10 Southampton Street, London WC2E 7HF, England

First published 1979 by Amnesty International Publications
10 Southampton Street, London WC2E 7HF, England

ISBN 0 900058 88 9
AI Index: ACT 05/03/79
Original Language: English

Printed in the United States of America.

CONSIDERING that every person has the right freely to hold and to express his convictions and the obligation to extend a like freedom to others, the objects of Amnesty International shall be to secure throughout the world the observance of the Universal Declaration of Human Rights by:

*. . .opposing by all appropriate means the imposition and infliction of death penalties and torture or other cruel, inhuman or degrading treatment or punishment of prisoners or other detained or restricted persons whether or not they have used or advocated violence.*

—from the Statute of Amnesty International

*Amnesty International does not approve of and would not defend any violent crime. However, it cannot regard the death penalty other than as an anachronism and an act of cold blood beneath the dignity of a modern state. . .*

*The limitation on the power of and potential for abuse by the state follows from the recognition of the sacredness of life free from the ultimate interference of a state-imposed death penalty.*

— from the *amicus curiae* brief submitted by Amnesty International to the United States Supreme Court in the case of *Gregg* v. *State of Georgia*, 1976

*. . .the main objective to be pursued in the field of capital punishment is that of progressively restricting the number of offences for which the death penalty may be imposed with a view to the desirability of abolishing this punishment.*

— from United Nations General Assembly Resolution 32/61 of 8 December 1977 on capital punishment

## EDITORIAL NOTE

Most of the information contained in this report covers the period 1973-1976. Where there is mention of earlier events, it is because it is necessary to put the law or practice of the death penalty in perspective. Some important changes in legislation, or significant trends in practice, occurring in 1977 and early 1978 are included for the same reason. Significant information which has been received after the beginning of 1978, and which can be given briefly, is incorporated in footnotes.

An addendum to this report, covering changes from 1977 to mid 1979 was prepared after this report was completed and appears at the end of this edition printed in the USA.

The contents list shows those countries which have totally abolished the death penalty for all crimes, whether committed in peacetime or in time of war. It is only such countries which can properly be classified as abolitionist. (Federated states in which some jurisdictions retain the death penalty cannot be classified as abolitionist.) This classification was correct as of 22 February 1979.

Regional surveys in Chapter III start with a short general introduction which, where appropriate, make mention of jurisdictions not covered by individual entries. This is particularly so with regard to the English-speaking Caribbean and the Middle East.

**CONTENTS**

* Totally abolitionist in law on 22 February 1979 for all offences, whether committed in time of peace or war.

## PREFACE

*by Thomas Hammarberg, Chairman, International Executive Committee, Amnesty International*

Amnesty International is committed by its Statute to oppose "by all appropriate means the imposition and infliction" of the death penalty, on the ground that it violates the right to life and that it is the most cruel, inhuman and degrading of all forms of punishment.

An international Conference, convened by Amnesty International and held in Stockholm in December 1977, marked the beginning of work on a world-wide scale for the abolition of the death penalty. This *Report* establishes a basis—a source of information—for that work.

It has been published to draw attention to the main points at issue in the debate over whether the death penalty should be abolished or retained, and to give detailed information about the extent to which the death penalty has been used in the period under review. This is mainly 1973-76, but the *Report* does also take account of the major trends in its use up to the end of 1977.

It considers both the judicial death penalty, decided upon by courts and enforced according to law, and extra-judicial execution—murder committed or acquiesced in by government. Although there are differences between the two, both involve the decision to deprive an individual of life. Indeed, as the Declaration of Stockholm points out, "The death penalty is increasingly taking the form of unexplained disappearances, extra-judicial executions and political murders." (The Declaration as a whole is Appendix A of the *Report*.)

Research for the *Report* involved work on both official and unofficial sources of information and met with inescapable difficulties. The official information which governments give to international organizations such as the United Nations is not always a model of accuracy or comprehensiveness: to counter this problem, Amnesty International wrote to embassies in London, asking if governments would provide information on the law and practice of the death penalty in their own jurisdictions. Not all of them replied. Among those who did, some stressed legal provisions, others actual applications of the death penalty or the granting of clemency, and still others outlined the context in which the death penalty should be seen in the country in question.

In short, the information available to Amnesty International was neither complete nor consistent in emphasis, and its shortcomings are reflected in the *Report* itself.

A further point in explanation: the *Report* argues the case for abolition; it does not enter into discussion about alternatives to the death penalty. This is deliberate, a recognition of the scope and complexity of the subject, not a refusal to confront it.

Attitudes towards every aspect of the death penalty—and towards what might replace it—are shaped and reinforced by religious, social, cultural, even economic influences, and many believe that their power and diversity rule out any world-wide effort to achieve abolition. This is, in fact, not so. In December 1977, the General Assembly of the United Nations confirmed its position on "the desirability of abolishing capital punishment"; it also called upon the Sixth United Nations Congress on the Prevention of Crime and Treatment of Offenders (to be held in 1980) to "discuss the possible restriction thereof". This step is most welcome, and Amnesty International hopes that it will lead to the United Nations stating unambiguously that "the death penalty is contrary to international law". In its Declaration, the Stockholm Conference recommended that this should be done.

The intention behind this *Report*—and behind the efforts to achieve abolition of the death penalty which will follow it—is to stimulate thought, discussion and action on the part of Amnesty International itself and other non-governmental organizations, governments, individual experts and members of the public *throughout the world.* In the past, debate and action over the death penalty seem, in the main, to have reflected the views and traditions of people in Western Europe and the United States of America. One of the main aims of this *Report* is to broaden the context in which the abolition of the death penalty is considered, so that it takes in the legal and social systems of Africa, Asia, Latin America and other parts of the world.

CHAPTER I

# IN SUPPORT OF ABOLITION

*"Everyone has the right to life, liberty and security of person . . . No one shall be subjected to torture or to cruel, inhuman or degrading treatment or punishment."* – From the Universal Declaration of Human Rights, proclaimed by the General Assembly of the United Nations on 10 December 1948

Amnesty International's main ground of opposition to the death penalty is that it is a cruel, inhuman and degrading punishment and a violation of the right to life. There are, of course, other major objections to it and they will be discussed a little later in this chapter. First, however, in order to put the abolitionist case into perspective, it is necessary to look at least briefly at some of the main arguments in favour of retaining the death penalty. It is also essential to make the point here that neither in this chapter, nor in the *Report* as a whole, is there any attempt to survey in detail all the evidence and argument involved in the issue of the death penalty.

The retentionist argument is often based upon the following points:

1. For particularly reprehensible offences, death is the only fitting and adequate punishment.
2. The death penalty acts as a deterrent.
3. Those who commit certain grave offences must be put to death for the protection of society at large.

Among the main arguments put forward by the abolitionist are:

1. The death penalty is irreversible. Decided upon according to fallible processes of law by fallible human beings, it can be–and actually has been–inflicted upon people innocent of any crime.
2. There is lack of convincing evidence that the death penalty has any more power to deter than–say–a long period of imprisonment. Its deterrent effect on rational offenders is highly questionable; it is even more so in the case of offenders who are mentally ill, or who are impelled by violent political motives.
3. Execution by whatever means and for whatever offence is a cruel, inhuman and degrading punishment.

To deal with these points in more detail:

### *1. The possibility of error*

In all legal systems, the essential requirement should be for proof of guilt beyond any reasonable doubt. In reality, it is possible for the outcome of any trial to involve error. A number of factors may contribute to this, separately or in combination:

#### *(a) Inadequate or incompetent legal representation*

Those who cannot afford to pay their own legal fees may consequently have to rely on the help of charitable organizations or on legal aid schemes which are at times inadequate. Many people accused of capital offences and unable to pay for a defence lawyer of their own choice have been represented by someone who is inexperienced or who has insufficient knowledge of the case.

*(b) The role of judge and jury*

Judges and juries are entrusted with two tasks: the determination of guilt and/or the choice of penalty.

When carrying out the first, they may, in capital cases, attach greater value to preserving the life of the defendant than to assessing facts accurately. In certain cases, juries have not convicted because they did not wish the defendant to be put to death. Such action can cause irregularities in the administration of justice because it bears directly on the method by which guilt or innocence is determined.

When jurors have to decide upon punishment, they are charged by law to do so without regard to personal sensibilities and prejudices—that is, in effect, to do the impossible. Whenever a jury is involved in a capital case, a chance set of reactions and prejudices influences consideration of the death penalty and may turn the outcome itself into a matter of chance.

*(c) The role of the police and of psychiatric and probation services*

In many countries, the resources of the police are so limited that their investigations may not be accurate, impartial or thorough.

This situation is often compounded by the absence of an adult probation service capable of gathering information about the defendant which might help the court at pre-trial hearings or on passing sentence.

In a number of countries, too, there are inadequate psychiatric services—or none at all—available to the court, even for cases in which a full psychiatric report is essential, that is, if (i) the fitness of the defendant to stand trial is to be correctly assessed, (ii) guilt accurately determined or (iii) the appropriate sentence imposed. Many retentionists support the view that no insane person should be sentenced to death, but in many cases the death sentence is passed by courts when they are in no proper position to decide whether the defendant is sane or insane. (On the other hand, when psychiatric services are available, the burden placed upon the witness called to give psychiatric evidence may often be much heavier than that carried by other expert witnesses. In capital cases, a defendant who is declared sane may be executed, and the determination of sanity may depend upon the evidence of a single individual—who, if a doctor, has taken an oath to preserve life.)

*(d) Procedural issues*

Chapter III of this *Report,* a survey, country by country, of the use of the death penalty, reveals the inherent arbitrariness of all the procedures by which the death sentence is passed. It also makes reference to those jurisdictions that have reversed the burden of proof for some capital offences so that it is for the defendant to prove innocence rather than for the prosecution to establish guilt. Chapter III shows that sentencing authorities adopt one of five different methods in imposing the death sentence, all of them arbitrary and discriminatory:[1]

(i) The *mandatory* death penalty provision: these laws provide for the imposition of the death sentence without exception upon all those convicted of specific crimes, often those committed by members of armed forces in time of war, or crimes against the state.

(ii) The *discretionary* death penalty provision: judges or juries have complete freedom to choose between death or imprisonment as punishment for the convicted offender. This type of provision may work against members of groups who are the object of racial or other forms of discrimination, and decisions about punishment may be influenced by the prejudices of those whose duty it is to pass sentence. Such wide discretionary powers can result in arbitrary and capricious sentencing.

(iii) The *guided discretion* provision: similar to the discretionary provision in that it gives the sentencing authority the power to decide who should die and who should be sentenced to imprisonment; differs from it in explicitly listing aggravating and mitigating circumstances to be taken into account in determining the sentence. One example of a mitigating circumstance is that the crime was committed while the offender was under the domination of another person.

Although the "guided discretion" provision gives guidance on deciding the merits of a particular case, it is not necessarily non-discriminatory. It is impossible to specify in advance all the characteristics of a given capital crime and weigh their relative importance. No legal provision can classify fairly the emotional, social and other factors which may have had a bearing upon the commission of a capital offence.

(iv) The *extenuating circumstances* provision (unless these circumstances exist, the death penalty must be imposed in all relevant cases): in practice, an alternative sentence based upon extenuating circumstances is passed only when the offence has certain characteristics similar to, but not confined to, the mitigating circumstances in the "guided discretion" provision. These characteristics may include certain psychological or pathological traits which the defendant was unable to control.

(v) This fifth provision is not specified by law and is therefore distinct from the other four. In countries that make a practice of condemning active political dissenters to death, imposition of the death penalty can amount to the carrying out of government policy by a court which is unlikely to have judicial independence. Moreover, the categories of crime for which the death penalty may be imposed could be drafted in such a way that almost any kind of political activity inconsistent with government policy becomes a capital offence.

In some countries the trial for a capital offence may be held in a general atmosphere of tension and excitement, and the attitude of court, lawyers and jurors (where they have a part in the proceedings) is directly affected by this.

There are also situations in which the authorities with whom the decision to inflict the death penalty finally rests may be influenced in that decision by domestic or international political considerations.

### 2. *The death penalty as deterrent*

The argument that the death penalty deters is founded on the belief that people who have it in mind to commit a capital offence may be dissuaded from doing so if they know that they will risk forfeiting their lives. The point at issue, however, is not whether the death penalty has a deterrent effect, but whether it is any more effective as a deterrent than—say—a long term of imprisonment. According to one line of retentionist argument, the belief that the death penalty is an especially powerful deterrent is based on commonsense—whatever that may be. It is, however, open to question whether commonsense can provide insight into the mind of a murderer, for example. Certainly it takes no account of the fact that the majority of murder victims are killed by someone who knows them[2] or by someone whose mind is disturbed. In either case, the murderer is unlikely to weigh up the risk of execution rationally beforehand—and equally unlikely to be dissuaded by threat of punishment.

Those who do commit capital crimes after "rational" consideration apparently believe that they have a very good chance of evading arrest or of avoiding conviction. Studies of the personalities of murderers give no sign that the death penalty has any significant influence on the behaviour of those convicted before they committed their offence, nor is there any satisfactory evidence that abolition of the death penalty for certain offences has been followed by an increase in the incidence of crimes which formerly carried the penalty.

A point to be made here is that, in most parts of the world, there has been a tendency over the last several centuries towards reducing the categories of offence to which the death penalty once applied.[3] For example, in the seventeenth century in many European countries, the death penalty could be imposed for a very wide range of offences – among them offences against property, violent non-homicidal crimes, sexual offences and offences relating to opinion and belief. It is apparent that most Western societies are satisfied with the present limitation on the number of capital offences. The range of such offences throughout the world is very wide, but there is evidence of a tendency, over the years, to restrict the number of capital offences. However, some countries now go against that trend by applying the death penalty for drug offences, economic crimes and certain crimes of violence.

There is information to show that, in two neighbouring countries or jurisdictions, one abolitionist and the other retentionist, where social and economic conditions are much alike, the murder rate tends to show similar fluctuations.[4] It seems probable that the former is less affected by the use of the death penalty than by social and other factors. There is apparently no connection between the number of executions in any one year and the incidence of murder in the years that follow. (In general, only a relatively small percentage of the total number of people convicted for murder is executed.)

### 3. *The cruelty of the punishment*

(a) Those condemned to death often suffer acute anguish—both physical and mental—before execution. This is so whether the prisoner is told beforehand of the date of execution or not. When the date is known, at least the fear of waking to face death without warning is removed. Even so, the stress which the condemned suffer can be great enough to cause psychosis.

(b) The methods by which executions are carried out can involve physical torture. Hanging, electrocution, the gas chamber and the firing squad may not kill instantaneously. Both hanging and garotting, which are meant to cause death at once, by breaking the neck, may instead kill by strangulation. Electrocution has on occasion caused extensive burns and needed more than one application of electric current to kill the condemned.

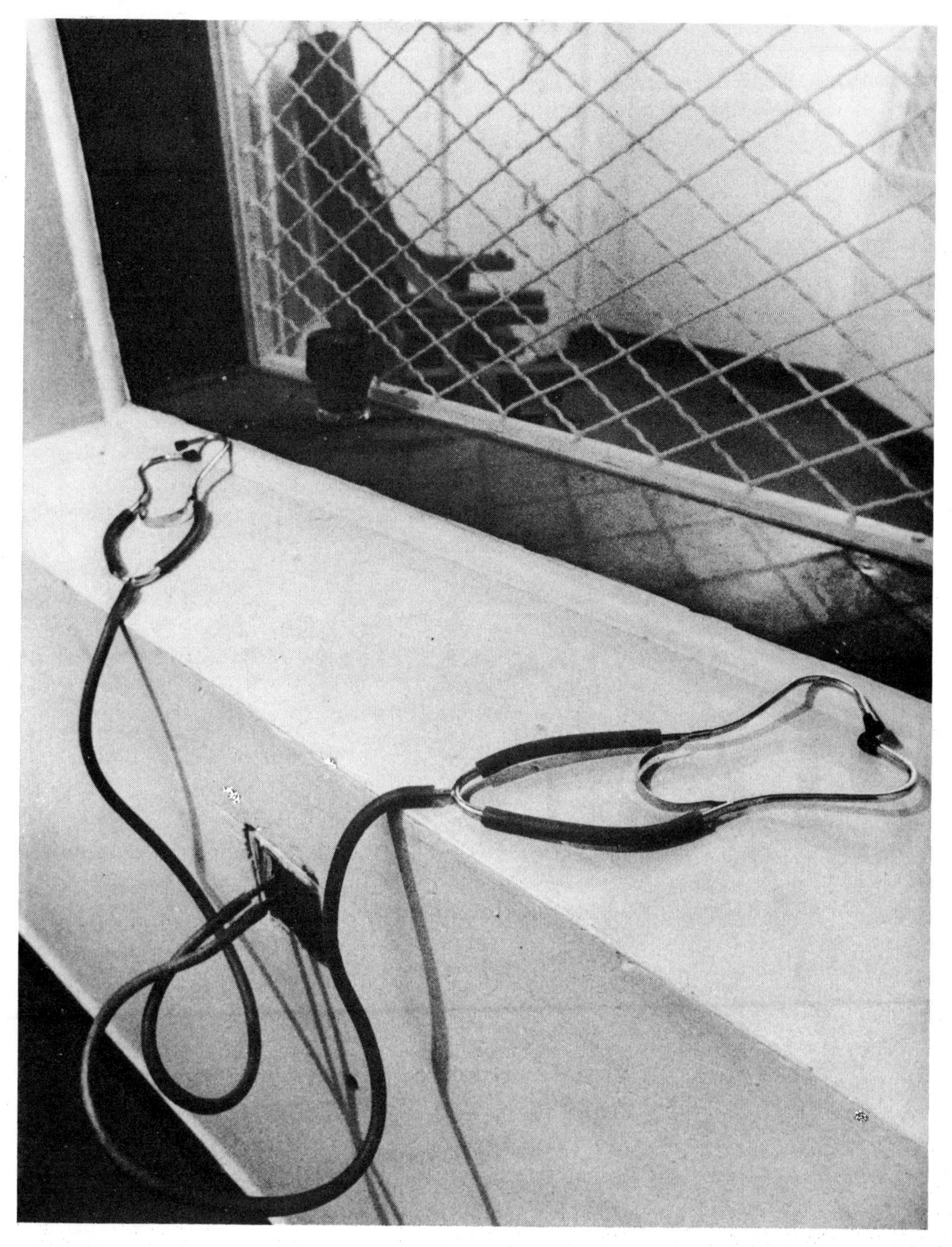

A gas chamber *Jackson Hill 1978*
Acid is placed in a box under the chair and a cyanide pellet released into it. Tubing from a stethoscope on the arm of the chair leads out of the gas chamber to where a physician monitors the heart beat. The prisoner usually loses consciousness after two to three minutes and is proclaimed dead in about fifteen minutes. The gas is extracted through a hole in the ceiling.

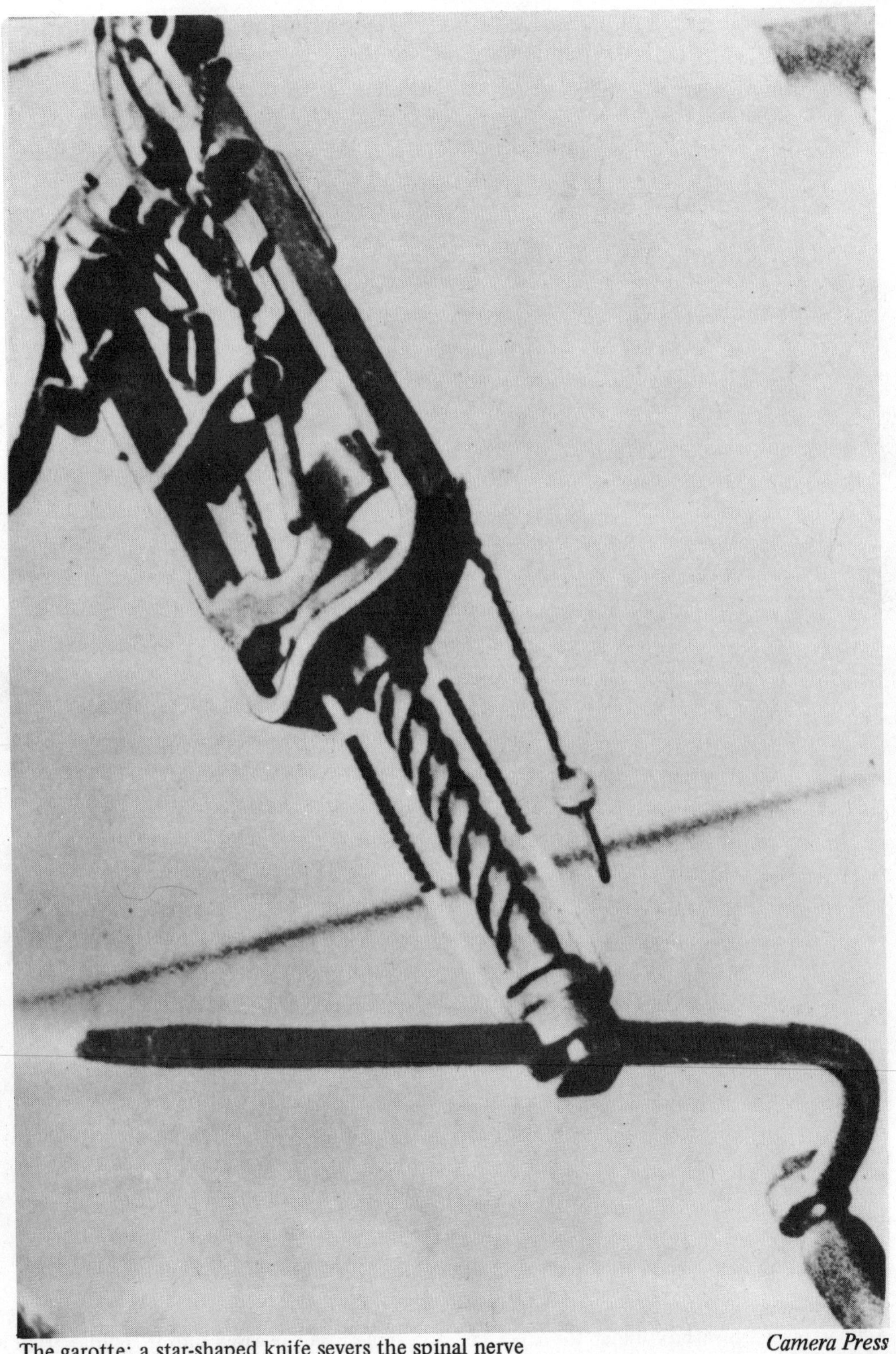

The garotte: a star-shaped knife severs the spinal nerve *Camera Press*

The guillotine *Popperfoto*

The electric chair *Camera Press*

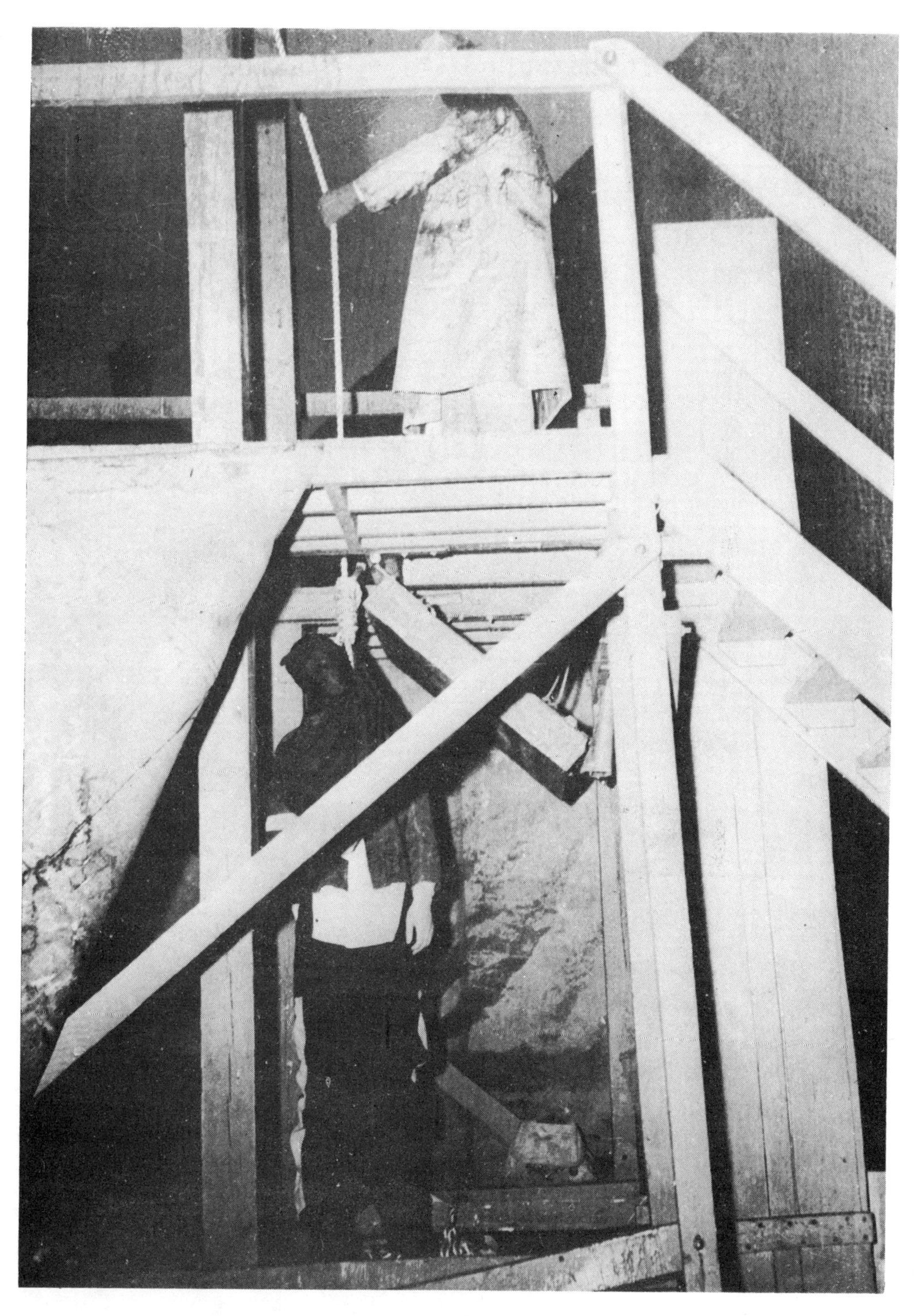

The scaffold immediately after a hanging *Keystone Press*

Execution by firing squad *Keystone Press*

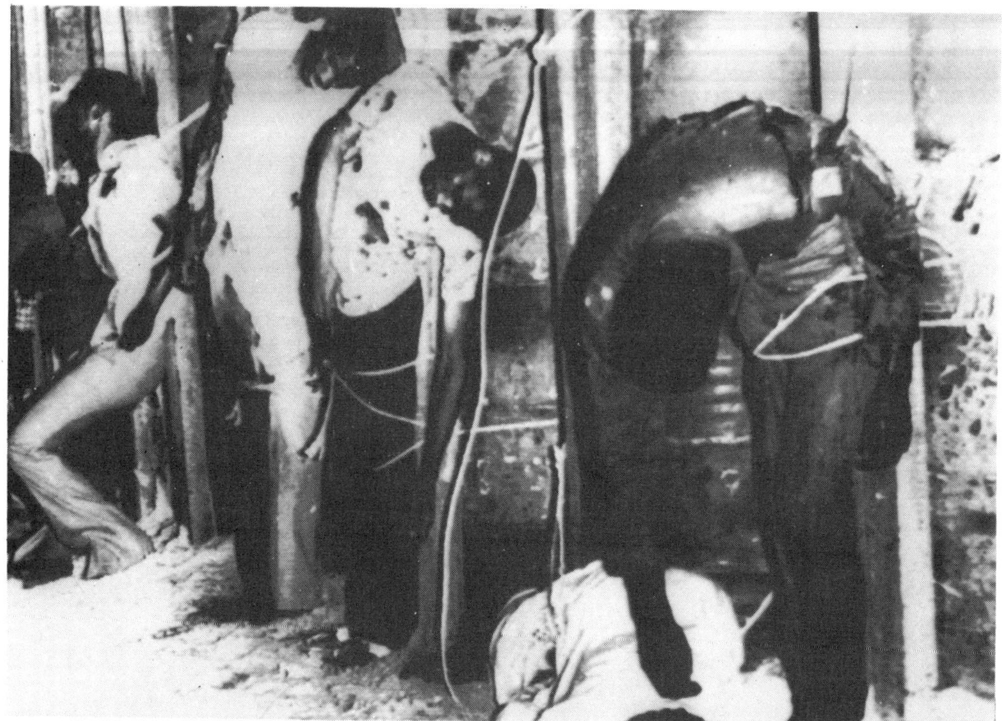

Executions by firing squad. *Universal Press International*

Executions by firing squad *Associated Press*

Public hangings

Public hanging

The death penalty *Camera Press*

Widespread concern about the use of the death penalty as a matter of principle is felt only in a minority of countries. In most of the world, the death penalty is not a public issue and there is little to suggest that many societies regard putting someone to death after judicial process as abhorrent. Governments tend to justify use of the death penalty on the ground that public opinion is in favour of it for certain crimes. They do not, in general, offer proof that the death penalty has validity as a deterrent: they simply reiterate the statement that it has.

Most of the published studies on the death penalty have relied largely on data from the developed world and have generalized from particular theories and practices which do not apply elsewhere. For the majority of people in the developing world the issue of the death penalty is likely to be of small concern in comparison with the social, cultural, economic and political problems that face them. When the matter is raised, it is mainly by vocal minorities, interesting themselves in specific cases: there is rarely wider discussion of the fundamental question of abolition versus retention.[5]

The view that no world-wide, corporate effort to achieve abolition of the death penalty is possible has much support. To test it, Amnesty International convened an international conference, held in Stockholm in December 1977. The participants–among them theologians, lawyers, judges, politicians, psychologists, police officers, penologists and journalists–came from fifty countries. Seminars arranged by Amnesty International in preparation for the conference were held in Colombo, Hamburg, New York and Paris; another meeting, in Port-of-Spain, Trinidad, was sponsored jointly by the Caribbean Human Rights and Legal Aid Company, the Trinidad and Tobago Committee for the Abolition of the Death Penalty and Amnesty International, and Amnesty International also took part in a seminar organized by the All Africa Conference of Churches in Ibadan. The agenda for this meeting and for the Port-of-Spain seminar was wide-ranging; the other four seminars worked to more limited agendas. All six reported directly to the Stockholm Conference.[6] Amnesty International has now issued a document entitled *The Stockholm Conference on the Abolition of the Death Penalty* (AI Index CDP02/0178). (The Declaration made by the Conference is Appendix A of this *Report*.)

It was abundantly clear from the Conference that there are people all over the world who believe that the death penalty should be totally abolished. There is also agreement among them that the death penalty is unique as a punishment, quite separate from all other punishments and not simply distinguishable from them in degree of severity. This point has a direct bearing on all consideration of alternatives to the death penalty.

Amnesty International's view, in brief, is that these should in no way constitute cruel, inhuman or degrading treatment and in no circumstances contravene the United Nations Standard Minimum Rules for the Treatment of Prisoners. Discussion of possible alternatives in detail, however, is not directly relevant to the intention behind this *Report*: to support the fundamental abolitionist aim of putting an end to a barbaric practice.

## *Notes*

1 "The history of capital punishment for homicides . . . reveals continual efforts, uniformly unsuccessful, to identify before the fact those homicides for which the slayer should die . . . Those who have come to grips with the hard task of actually attempting to draft means of channelling capital sentencing discretion have confirmed the lesson taught by history . . . To identify before the fact those characteristics of criminal homicides and their perpetrators which call for the death penalty, and to express these characteristics in language which can be fairly understood and applied by the sentencing authority, appear to be tasks which are at present beyond human ability." – *Opinion of Justice Harlan, McGautha v. California, 402 US 1831 (1971).*

2 The closeness of the relationship between victim and murderer is examined in the Canadian Murder Statistics Program, 1961-1974, for example. During that period, at least 69% of those murdered were killed by someone they knew: 28% of them by a member of their immediate family, 13% by casual acquaintances, 8% by close acquaintances, 7% by someone with whom they had a common law relationship and 5% by kin outside the immediate family. Of the rest, 5% were killed either by a lover or by someone involved with them in a love-triangle and 3% by someone with whom they had a business relationship.

3 UN General Assembly Resolutions in 1971 and 1977 have spoken of "the main objective" as being to progressively restrict the number of capital offences with a view to the "desirability" of total abolition. (See Chapter II)

4 See T. Sellin, *Capital Punishment,* Harper and Row, New York, 1967, and *Capital Punishment Developments, 1961 to 1965,* United Nations, 1967, p.39.

5 Attitudes to death–and to the taking of life–in any case have their roots in religion, culture and social tradition and consequently vary very widely. According to Muslim belief, for example, death may be an opportunity for expiation and cleansing; for the Hindu, death is the first step towards reincarnation; to the Buddhist, death may be the result of *Karma,* the inescapable force arising from actions carried out–consciously or unconsciously–in the past. The subject is a vast and complex one and all that can be done here is to acknowledge that fact.

6 Appendix D gives the agenda for each of the six seminars.

CHAPTER II

# THE DEATH PENALTY IN INTERNATIONAL LAW AND ORGANIZATION

### *The death penalty when imposed by courts of law*

Since most countries retain the death penalty for certain crimes, it is not surprising that international law does not prohibit its use. What may cause surprise is that, as recently as 1971, no less a body than the General Assembly of the United Nations affirmed "the desirability of abolishing [capital] punishment in all countries" (Resolution 2857 [XXVI] of 20 December 1971). The purpose of this chapter is to canvass the international treaty law on the subject, and then to trace the progress made, particularly at the United Nations, in establishing the trend towards abolition which is internationally approved.

The leading statement of law is to be found in the *International Covenant on Civil and Political Rights,* adopted by the General Assembly of the United Nations on 16 December 1966 and opened for signature, ratification and accession on 19 December 1966 (Resolution 2200A [XXI]), The Covenant, which came into force on 23 March 1976 and to which some 47 countries are now party, provides in its Article 6:

"*1 Every human being has the inherent right to life. This right shall be protected by law. No one shall be arbitrarily deprived of his life.*

*2 In countries which have not abolished the death penalty, sentence of death may be imposed only for the most serious crimes in accordance with the law in force at the time of the commission of the crime and not contrary to the provisions of the present Covenant and to the Convention on the Prevention and Punishment of the Crime of Genocide. This penalty can only be carried out pursuant to a final judgment rendered by a competent court.*

*3 When deprivation of life constitutes the crime of genocide, it is understood that nothing in this article shall authorize any State Party to the present Covenant to derogate in any way from any obligation assumed under the provisions of the Convention on the Prevention and Punishment of the Crime of Genocide.*

*4 Anyone sentenced to death shall have the right to seek pardon or commutation of the sentence. Amnesty, pardon or commutation of the sentence of death may be granted in all cases.*

*5 Sentence of death shall not be imposed for crimes committed by persons below eighteen years of age and shall not be carried out on pregnant women.*

*6 Nothing in this article shall be invoked to delay or to prevent the abolition of capital punishment by any State Party to the present Covenant.*"

This Article raises a number of points of interest. First, all the references to the death penalty are placed in the context of the right to life.[2] Capital punishment is, in effect, maintained as an exception to the rule protecting the right to life of every human being. Secondly, capital punishment is treated as something transitory, pending abolition (paragraph 6). Thirdly, only countries in which the penalty has not been abolished benefit from the exception. It follows that a state party to the Covenant may not re-introduce the penalty, once having abolished it.[3] Presumably the same principle applies with respect to specific crimes. Thus, if a state party retains the penalty for, say, treason, its re-introduction for murder would be unjustified under this Covenant. Fourthly, several substantive criteria and procedural safeguards are required to justify a resort to the penalty. Substantively, it may only be imposed for "the most serious crimes". Unfortunately, there is no guidance on the definition of seriousness at either the international or national level. However, the burden is clearly shifted on to the state to argue the "most serious" nature of the particular offence. Another substantive requirement is for the law offended against to have been in force at the time the offence was committed, in accordance with the most fundamental principle of non-retroactivity of penal law. It is not clear from the words quoted from paragraph 2 whether the death penalty itself has to be the prescribed punishment at the time of the commission of the crime. However, the paragraph does specify that the law must not be contrary to the provisions of the Covenant, and Article 15 of the Covenant restates the principle of non-retroactivity explicitly: "Nor shall a heavier penalty be imposed than the one that was applicable at the time when the criminal offence was committed."

The procedural safeguards which must be respected before execution of the death penalty are: that a final judgment must have been rendered by a competent court; that the offender must have the right to seek pardon or commutation of the sentence; that he or she must have been 18 years of age or more at the time the offence was committed; that the offender must not be a pregnant woman.

No derogation from Article 6 is possible, even in "time of public emergency which threatens the life of the nation" (Article 4). Thus, not only must the safeguards be respected on all occasions, but there can also be no excuse for re-introducing the penalty, whatever internal or external difficulties a government may be facing.

The substance of Article 6 of the Covenant provided the model for the provision on the right to life contained in the American Convention on Human Rights (the Pact of San José signed by 12 states on 22 November 1969). This Convention, which has so far been ratified or adhered to by only six (Colombia, Costa Rica, Ecuador, Haiti, Honduras and Venezuela) of the 11 countries whose adherence is required to bring it into force, provides in its Article 4 for the same protection as that afforded by Article 6 of the Covenant.[4] In some measure it goes beyond the latter. Thus, paragraph 4 of Article 4 provides: "In no case shall capital punishment be inflicted for political offences or related common crimes." This remarkable provision is consistent with the established tradition among Latin American countries of acknowledging the need for co-operation in maintaining some measure of political tolerance. Article 4 not only keeps the minimum age limit of 18 years for offenders to whom the death penalty may apply, but also establishes a maximum age limit of 70 years.

The Convention also deals explicitly with issues implicit in the Covenant, as when it states that the death penalty "shall not be extended to crimes to which it does not presently apply" and "shall not be re-established in states that have abolished it". Moreover, even though Article 27 of the Convention permits derogations from some of the protections of the Convention in "time of war, public danger, or other emergency that threatens the independence or security of a State Party", no such derogation is permitted from Article 4.

By contrast, the pertinent provision of the European Convention for the Protection of Human Rights and Fundamental Freedoms is disconcertingly brief. Article 2, quoted on p. 30, specifically exempts from the protection of the right to life the "execution of a sentence of the court following . . . conviction of a crime for which this penalty is provided by law".

The text of this Article might have been different had the European Convention on Human Rights been adopted later. As it was, the Convention was concluded on 4 November 1950 under the auspices of the Council of Europe. It came into force on 3 September 1953 and is now binding on 18 of the 20 members of the Council of Europe (Portugal and Spain, the two new members of the Council of Europe, have signed the Convention but not yet ratified it). The Council has recently decided to study the possibility of amending the Convention's text to bring it into line with that of the Covenant. This is to be welcomed. The study by the Committee of Experts on Human Rights, referred to in note 3 at the end of the chapter, considers that most of the obligations contained in the Covenant are covered either by other Articles of the Convention or by the national laws or practice of the states at present bound by the European Convention. It is, nevertheless, desirable that all the abolitionist clauses of the Covenant be included in one amended text. The inclusion of the pertinent protections contained in the American Convention would be a further step.

Even the law relating to armed conflict refers to the death penalty. The Geneva Convention of 12 August 1949 relative to the Treatment of Prisoners of War (Third Geneva Convention) addresses itself at some length to the question of penal and disciplinary sanctions which can be imposed on prisoners of war (Section VI, Chapter III). The Convention first of all provides for certain limited penalties for what it calls disciplinary offences (Section VI, Chapter III, Part II) which do not include the death penalty. Article 83 enjoins the competent authorities of the detaining power, when choosing between the application of judicial or disciplinary proceedings, to "exercise the greatest leniency and adopt, wherever possible, disciplinary rather than judicial measures". Moreover, no penalty (other than a disciplinary one) may be prescribed for a prisoner of war that may not be imposed on a member of the forces of the detaining power (Article 82). In respect of all proceedings for judicial offences, elaborate provision is made for a fair trial and the right to appeal and petition for pardon (Chapter III, Part III). Particular safeguards are built in with regard to the death penalty:

***Article 100***

*"Prisoners of war and the Protecting Powers shall be informed, as soon as possible, of the offences which are punishable by the death sentence under the laws of the Detaining Power.*

*"Other offences shall not thereafter be made punishable by the death penalty*

*without the concurrence of the Power upon which the prisoners of war depend.*

*"The death sentence cannot be pronounced on a prisoner of war unless the attention of the court has, in accordance with Article 87, second paragraph*[5] *been particularly called to the fact that since the accused is not a national of the Detaining Power, he is not bound to it by any duty of allegiance, and that he is in its power as the result of circumstances independent of his own will."*

***Article 101***

*"If the death penalty is pronounced on a prisoner of war, the sentence shall not be executed before the expiration of a period of at least six months from the date when the Protecting Power receives, at an indicated address, the detailed communication provided for in Article 107."*[6]

Greater protection is afforded a person protected by the Geneva Convention relative to the Protection of Civilian Persons in Time of War of 12 August 1949 (Fourth Geneva Convention). Article 68 significantly restricts the freedom of an occupying power to impose capital punishment. Its second, third and fourth paragraphs state:

*"The penal provisions promulgated by the Occupying Power in accordance with Articles 64 and 65 may impose the death penalty on a protected person only in cases where the person is guilty of espionage, of serious acts of sabotage against the military installations of the Occupying Power or of international offences which caused the death of one or more persons, provided that such offences were punishable by death under the law of the occupied territory in force before the occupation began.*

*"The death penalty may not be pronounced on a protected person unless the attention of the court has been particularly called to the fact that since the accused is not a national of the Occupying Power, he is not bound to it by any duty of allegiance.*

*"In any case, the death penalty may not be pronounced on a protected person who was under eighteen years of age at the time of the offence."*

Not only is there restriction on the substance of the offences, but the punishment itself may be no heavier than would have been applied before the occupation. Nevertheless, there is cause for concern about the breadth of interpretation given by some jurisdictions to the terms "espionage" and "sabotage". It is not unknown for the former to be stretched to cover any unauthorized acquisition of state information, and the latter to cover the unauthorized divulging of such information.

The procedural requirements which have to be met before the death penalty may be carried out are contained in Article 75 of the Fourth Geneva Convention:

*"In no case shall persons condemned to death be deprived of the right to petition for pardon or reprieve.*

*"No death sentence shall be carried out before the expiration of a period of at least six months from the date of receipt by the Protecting Power of the notification of the final judgment confirming such death sentence, or of an order denying pardon or reprieve.*

*"The six months' period of suspension of the death sentence herein prescribed may be reduced in individual cases in circumstances of grave emergency involving an organized threat to the security of the Occupying Power or its forces, provided always that the Protecting Power is notified of such reduction and is given reasonable time and opportunity to make representations to the competent occupying authorities in respect of such death sentences."*

This Article supplements Article 74, which provides for notification to the Protecting Power of any judgment involving a sentence of death or imprisonment for two years or more, as well as for the period of appeal to run only from the time when such notification is received.

The recently concluded Conference on the Re-affirmation and Development of International Law Applicable in Armed Conflicts has provided in its Protocol to the Geneva Convention of 12 August 1949 relative to the Protection of Victims of International Armed Conflict (Additional Protocol I), an Article bringing the Conventions into line with the International Covenant on Civil and Political Rights. Article 76 states that pregnant women shall not be executed. The Article following it ensures that no one may be executed who was under 18 when the offence was committed.

There is even provision in Article 3, common to the four Geneva Conventions, for regulation of the use of the death penalty in armed conflict which is not international. This Article establishes the minimum international standard below which parties may not fall in their conduct of internal armed hostilities, and in respect of non-combatants, those who have laid down their arms and others placed *hors de combat,* prohibits

"*. . . at any time and in any place whatsoever . . . the passing of sentences and the carrying out of executions without previous judgment pronounced by a regularly constituted court,* affording all the judicial guarantees which are recognized as indispensable by civilized peoples." (Emphasis added.)

In preparation for the humanitarian law Conference mentioned above, the International Committee of the Red Cross had prepared a Draft Protocol Additional to the Geneva Convention of 12 August 1949 relative to the Protection of Victims of Non-International Armed Conflicts (Draft Additional Protocol II). Article 10 of the Draft, which was the working document of the Conference for this area of concern, envisaged a radical extension of the protection contained in common Article 3 of the four Geneva Conventions:

*"The death penalty pronounced on any person found guilty of an offence in relation to the armed conflict shall not be carried out until the hostilities have ceased."*

The provision was amended when adopted in committee (Committee I) by the third session of the Conference in 1976:

*"In cases of prosecutions carried out against a person only by reason of his having taken part in hostilities, the court, when deciding upon the sentence shall take into consideration, to the greatest possible extent, the fact that the accused respected the provisions of the present Protocol. In no such case shall a death penalty be carried out until the end of the armed conflict."*

The first sentence originally constituted a separate paragraph of the Article in question. The combination of the two paragraphs, proposed by Canada, "on the basis of consultations with a number of delegations" was adopted by consensus.

This provision, if adopted, could have led to a significant reduction in the application of the death penalty, especially since paragraph 7 of the same Article would have obliged the authorities in power to endeavour, at the end of hostilities, "to grant amnesty to as many as possible of those who have participated in the armed conflict". The same Article would also preclude pronouncement of the death penalty on persons under 18 years of age, and prevent its being carried out on pregnant women and mothers of young children.

However, when this Article (now Article 6) was put to the vote at the final session of the Conference on 3 June 1977, it was decided to delete the paragraph quoted above. Only 12 countries voted against the deletion, 26 voting in favour. Forty-seven countries – a majority of those present and voting – abstained. While the protection of those under 18, pregnant women and mothers of young children stands, there is no reference to the death penalty in non-international armed conflict. Another opportunity to achieve progress on this issue will not come again soon.

* * *

As suggested elsewhere in this chapter, United Nations activities in relation to the death penalty have not been restricted to the legal confines of the International Covenant on Civil and Political Rights. From 1959 onwards, a number of UN bodies, led by the General Assembly, have regularly considered the question, from the point of view both of social research and of political standard-setting.

Some 18 years ago, the General Assembly first raised the issue of the death penalty in its Resolution 1396 (XIV) of 20 November 1959. By this Resolution, the Assembly invited the Economic and Social Council (ECOSOC) to "initiate a study of the question of capital punishment, of the laws and practices relating thereto, and of the effects of capital punishment, and the abolition thereof, on the rate of criminality". At its very next session, ECOSOC took the matter up and, by Resolution 747 (XXIX) of 6 April 1960, requested the Secretary-General to prepare a factual review of these aspects of the question.

This mandate resulted in the preparation of a report by the noted French jurist, Marc Ancel, who acted as consultant to the UN Secretariat. The report, entitled *Capital Punishment*, was the first major survey of the problem from an international standpoint, having been based on information supplied by member governments, United Nations' national correspondents for social defence, and certain non-governmental organizations, on the deterrent aspects of the death penalty. The report dealt comprehensively with three areas of the matter: (1) legal problems, (2) problems of practical application, and (3) sociological and criminological problems. In this third chapter was the cautious statement "that the deterrent effect of the death penalty is, to say the least, not demonstrated".

This view had been expressed not only by abolitionist countries in their replies to the questionnaires, but also by some retentionist countries.

The Ancel Report was, as suggested by ECOSOC, submitted to the *ad hoc* Advisory Committee of Experts on the Prevention of Crime and the Treatment of Offenders, which examined it in January 1963. The Committee proposed that ECOSOC recommend certain measures to governments. The Committee's report, containing the proposal and the Ancel report, were presented to ECOSOC at its 35th Session, when its Resolution 934 (XXXV) of 9 April 1963 was adopted. By this Resolution, ECOSOC, having expressed its appreciation for "the excellent report of M. Ancel" and for "the cogent observations" of the Committee, urged UN member governments to take the following measures:

(a) to keep under review the efficacy of capital punishment as a deterrent to crime in their countries and to conduct research into the subject wherever necessary, with United Nations assistance;
(b) to remove this punishment from the criminal law concerning any crime to which it is, in fact, not applied or to which there is no intention to apply it (*de facto* abolitionist countries);
(c) to broaden the studies so far carried out to include consideration of the differences between civil and military tribunals, and of the policy of the latter in regard to the death penalty;
(d) to re-examine the facilities available for the medical and social investigation of the case of every offender liable to capital punishment;
(e) to ensure the most careful legal procedures and the greatest possible safeguards for the accused in capital cases;
(f) to study the Ancel report and the Committee's report and to inform the Secretary-General, "after an appropriate interval", of developments in their countries' relevant law and practice;
(g) to provide information about the differences in military and penal jurisdictions mentioned in (c) above.

Finally, the Resolution requested the Secretary-General to prepare a further report based on information received from governments under items (f) and (g) above, and to submit it to the UN Consultative Group on the Prevention of Crime and the Treatment of Offenders (as the *ad hoc* Advisory Committee of Experts was now to be called).

Thus, ECOSOC's reaction to the absence of evidence supporting the supposed deterrent effects of the death penalty was to suggest further research on the topic. Cautious as it might be, such research could be expected to bolster the abolitionist argument, since the deterrence theory is central to the retentionist case. The urging of the *de facto* abolitionist countries to translate the position into *de jure* terms constituted an implicit acceptance of the principle of abolition.

The same year, the General Assembly, by Resolution 1918 (XVIII) of 5 December 1963, endorsed this action of ECOSOC. Furthermore, whereas the death penalty had until then been handled under the UN's social defence program, it requested that ECOSOC invite the Commission on Human Rights to study and make recommendations on the Ancel Report and the comments of the *ad hoc* Advisory Committee of Experts. The Assembly also requested the Secretary-General, after examining the report of the Commission on Human Rights and with the co-operation of the Consultative Group, to present, within four years, a report on new developments, through ECOSOC to the General Assembly. It will be recalled that no schedule had been established by ECOSOC Resolution 934 (XXXV).

At its following (resumed) 36th session in 1964, ECOSOC, complying with the Assembly's request, forwarded the latter's Resolution 1918 (XVIII) to the Commission on Human Rights. The Commission had not considered the substance of the matter by the opening of the 42nd session of ECOSOC in 1967, when the Swedish and Venezuelan delegations introduced a draft resolution. In addition to expressing ECOSOC's regret that neither it nor the Commission had "been able, owing to lack of time, to conduct the said studies or to propose any recommendations on the subject of capital punishment", the draft resolution called on the Council to urge its member states to adopt a number of safeguards applicable before the carrying out of death sentences. The Council itself did not take action on the draft resolution, owing to shortage of time, but decided to remit it to the General Assembly for a decision on the further steps to be taken in the matter (ECOSOC Resolution 1243 [XLII] of 6 June 1967).

This Resolution was before the Assembly at its 22nd session in 1967, but it too, in Resolution 2334 (XXII) of 18 December 1967, expressed regret that its "workload . . . had not permitted [it] to consider the substance of the item". Nevertheless, the same Resolution requested the Secretary-General to provide the Assembly with the information envisaged in Assembly Resolution 1918 (XVIII), and invited ECOSOC to "instruct the Commission on Human Rights to consider the question of capital punishment, including the draft resolution submitted [to the council by Sweden and Venezuela] and to transmit its recommendations on the matter through the Council to the General Assembly at its 23rd session" (i.e., the following year). ECOSOC was also invited to seek the views of the Consultative Group on the Prevention of Crime and the Treatment of Offenders on this draft resolution.

The ECOSOC complied at its resumed 43rd session, and the Commission took up the matter at its 24th session in March 1968. In addition to the Swedish/Venezuelan draft resolution, the Commission had before it the report supplementing the Ancel report, prepared pursuant to Assembly Resolution 1918 (XVIII). The report, prepared by the Secretary-General's consultant Norval Morris, an American professor of criminal law and criminology, and entitled *Capital Punishment: Developments 1961-1965,* summarized its own main points as follows:

"*(a) There is an overall tendency in the world towards fewer executions. This is the result of less frequent use of the death penalty in those States whose statutes provide for that penalty, and of a steady movement towards legislative abolition of capital punishment.*

*(b) There is a slight but perceptible contrary tendency in the world towards legislative provision for and actual application of the death penalty for certain economic and political crimes.*

*(c) Where it is used, capital punishment is increasingly a discretionary rather than a mandatory sanction.*

*(d) Almost all countries have provision for the exclusion of certain offenders from capital punishment because of their mental and physical condition, extenuating circumstances, age and sex: the scope of the categories of offenders thus exempted is broadening.*

*(e) A growing number of offenders who are sentenced to death are spared through judicial processes or by executive clemency.*

(f) *There is a great disparity between the legal provisions for capital punishment and the actual application of those provisions.*

(g) *With increasing frequency, an offender who is sentenced to death is confined, while awaiting execution, in conditions similar to those of other prisoners. Execution, if it takes place, is likely to be accomplished by shooting or hanging and accompanied by a minimum of publicity.*

(h) *The tendency with regard to offenders who are subject to capital punishment but who have been accorded another penalty is to confine them in conditions similar to those of other prisoners and to provide mechanisms for their eventual release.*

(i) *With respect to the influence of the abolition of capital punishment upon the incidence of murder, all of the available data suggest that where the murder rate is increasing, abolition does not appear to hasten the increase; where the rate is decreasing, abolition does not appear to interrupt the decrease; where the rate is stable, the presence or absence of capital punishment does not appear to affect it."*

There is no observation on differences between civilian and military law and practice. While three Annexes to the Report deal with aspects of military practice, no comparative conclusions are drawn. Of particular importance is item (i) regarding the absence of statistical support for the deterrent theory.

As a result, the Austrian, Italian, Swedish and Venezuelan delegations introduced a draft resolution whereby the Commission would recommend to ECOSOC that it submit a draft resolution to the General Assembly. The draft was substantially similar to that introduced by Sweden and Venezuela during ECOSOC's deliberations the previous year. Certain amendments were accepted by the sponsors during the discussion. Thus, a preambular paragraph invoking Article 3 (right to life) of the Universal Declaration of Human Rights was amended to refer to Article 5 (right not to be subjected to torture or cruel, inhuman or degrading treatment or punishment). It was also accepted that the Commission would leave open the question of whether the Assembly would require states to inform the Secretary-General of all executions carried out after 1 January 1969. The Commission then adopted the draft General Assembly Resolution (Commission Resolution 16 [XXIV] of 8 March 1968).

ECOSOC agreed to submit the draft to the General Assembly, having dropped the requirement that states report on the carrying out of death sentences. The UN Consultative Group on the Prevention of Crime and the Treatment of Offenders made the same recommendation to the General Assembly during its meeting in August 1968. It also recommended stringent safeguards concerning the right of the accused to appeal, to seek pardon and commutation of sentences, and to have fully competent and independent legal advice and representation at all stages. In this respect it advocated special provisions for "indigent" accused.

Only this last recommendation was incorporated by the General Assembly when it adopted its Resolution 2393 (XXIII) of 26 November 1968. Otherwise the Resolution followed the text submitted by the Commission, as amended by ECOSOC. By this Resolution, the Assembly invited member governments:

"(a) *To ensure the most careful legal procedures and the greatest possible safeguards for the accused in capital cases in countries where the death penalty obtains,* inter alia, *by providing that:*

*(i) A person condemned to death shall not be deprived of the right to appeal to a higher judicial authority or, as the case may be, to petition for pardon or reprieve;*

*(ii) A death sentence shall not be carried out until the procedures of appeal or, as the case may be, of petition for pardon or reprieve have been terminated;*

*(iii) Special attention be given in the case of indigent persons by the provision of adequate legal assistance at all stages of the proceedings;*

*(b) To consider whether the careful legal procedures and safeguards referred to in sub-paragraph* (a) *above may not be further strengthened by the fixing of a certain time limit or time limits before the expiry of which no death sentence shall be carried out, as has already been recognized in certain international conventions dealing with specific situations;*

*(c) To inform the Secretary-General not later than 10 December 1970 of actions which may have been taken in accordance with sub-paragraph* (a) *above, and of the results to which their consideration in accordance with sub-paragraph* (b) *above may have led."*

The Resolution went on to request the Secretary-General to invite member governments "to inform him of their present attitude to possible further restricting the use of the death penalty or to its total abolition", and of changes that have taken place since 1965. He was also requested to submit a report on the items about which governments were to supply information to ECOSOC in 1971.

The introduction of a time limit was a new development. It had been a requirement of the original Swedish/Venezuelan draft submitted during the ECOSOC session in 1967. Its model was, presumably, the Geneva Conventions. Now governments were being asked to consider the feasibility of a norm which would govern the period of time which must elapse before a death sentence should be carried out.

Most governments had not replied when the Secretary-General submitted his report to ECOSOC at its 50th session in 1971. The report found little support for a fixed time limit. It did find that "most countries are gradually restricting the number of offences for which the death penalty is to be applied, and a few have totally abolished capital offences even in wartime." ECOSOC's discussion led to its adoption of Resolution 1574 (L) of 20 May 1971 which was re-affirmed by General Assembly Resolution 2857 (XXVI) of 20 December 1971. This latter Resolution represents the strongest statement of the UN on the question. According to it, the General Assembly

"Affirms *that, in order fully to guarantee the right to life, provided for in Article 3 of the Universal Declaration of Human Rights, the main objective to be pursued is that of progressively restricting the number of offences for which capital punishment may be imposed,* with a view to the desirability of abolishing this punishment in all countries." (Emphasis added.)

The Resolution clearly constitutes the present limit of developments at normative level. Indeed, subsequent ECOSOC resolutions re-affirming this principle dropped the phrase "in all countries". This development does not, of course, change the meaning and, in any event, the position of the General Assembly remains authoritative. Nevertheless, it is a sobering reminder of how difficult it is to progress beyond the Assembly's 1971 position.

Since the passage of this Resolution, there have been a number of other General Assembly and ECOSOC resolutions envisaging continuation of the studies prepared by the UN Secretariat. The next such study is due in 1980 – in time, it is hoped, for the sixth session of the UN Committee on Crime Prevention and Control (the successor to the Consultative Group on the Prevention of Crime and the Treatment of Offenders) and for the Sixth UN Congress on the Prevention of Crime and the Treatment of Offenders.

A hopeful sign was the adoption by the General Assembly at its 32nd session of Resolution 32/61 of 8 December 1977 (see Appendix B). This Resolution reaffirmed "the desirability of abolishing this punishment" (with reference this time to "all countries") and called upon the Sixth UN Congress "to discuss the various aspects of the use of capital punishment and the possible restriction thereof". The General Assembly also decided to reconsider the question of capital punishment, "with high priority", at its 35th session–that is to say, in the autumn of 1980, on the heels of the Sixth UN Congress. Perhaps the Congress,[7] which has already been the forum for the drafting of the Standard Minimum Rules for the Treatment of Prisoners and the Declaration on the Protection of All Persons from Torture and Other Cruel, Inhuman or Degrading Treatment or Punishment, might provide the occasion for drawing up another major human rights instrument.

It is to be noted that no regional inter-governmental organization has acted on the death penalty issue, although there have been moves in the Council of Europe. In the Consultative Assembly, 11 members issued a motion for a resolution on the abolition of capital punishment on 16 May 1973 (Doc. 3297). The motion would have required the Assembly to call upon "those members of the Council of Europe that retain capital punishment for certain crimes to abolish it as a legal sanction" and to urge "all parliamentarians represented in the Consultative Assembly to take initiatives to seek such abolition in their own countries". This initiative was transmitted to the Assembly's Legal Affairs Committee. On 23 January 1975, after discussing the matter, the Legal Affairs Committee proposed deletion of the item from its agenda. This proposal was overwhelmingly rejected by the Assembly at its 27th session on 23 April 1975. The matter, having thus returned to the Legal Committee, has yet to re-appear on the agenda of the Parliamentary Assembly (as it is now called). It is understood that Bertil Lidgard (Sweden), the Legal Affairs Committee's former rapporteur on the question of capital punishment, has resigned because of the Committee's inaction.

### *The death penalty without process of law*

The bulk of this chapter has dealt with the death penalty as a punishment executed according to law. However, a final word needs to be said about murders committed or acquiesced in by governments (see Chapter IV). For, while parallels may be drawn between such murders and capital punishment properly so called (they both result in death for which the authorities are responsible), they clearly must be seen in different legal perspectives.

The first is that in those national legal systems which employ the death penalty, it exists as a formal and legally authorized sanction, whereas murder, by whomsoever committed, is, by definition, a violation of law. Further, in those cases where the murder is committed or acquiesced in by the authorities, it represents an abdication of the formal procedure of government. The second difference is that international law treats the two types of killings differently.

Thus, the International Covenant on Civil and Political Rights (Article 6, see p. 19) and the American Convention on Human Rights (Article 4, see note 4) both provide that "no one shall be arbitrarily deprived of his life." The European Convention on Human Rights provides similar protection by its Article 2:

> "1 *Everyone's right to life shall be protected by law. No one shall be deprived of his life intentionally save in the execution of a sentence of the court following his conviction of a crime for which this penalty is provided by law.*
>
> 2 *Deprivation of life shall not be regarded as inflicted in contravention of this article when it results from the use of force which is no more than absolutely necessary:*
>
> *(a) in defence of any person from unlawful violence;*
>
> *(b) in order to effect a lawful arrest or to prevent the escape of a person lawfully detained;*
>
> *(c) in action lawfully taken for the purpose of quelling a riot or insurrection."*

However, the provisions of paragraph 2 give cause for concern, for it is in the area of the summary use of force that the practices described in Chapter IV may often occur. This paragraph very properly abides by the principle of proportionality in restricting the permitted use of force to that "which is no more than absolutely necessary" to achieve the authorized objective. The grounds for concern are the breadth of the authorized object, for which deprivation of life appears to be sanctioned. To take these objects in turn:

(a) *Defence from unlawful violence:* It is clearly a proper function of the authorities to protect citizens from unlawful violence. But it is easy to imagine situations in which this violence could be less than might be used to suppress it. For instance, industrial disputes sometimes lead to strike action and picketing which involve the unauthorized use of violence, but to use all degrees of force up to and including killing to suppress such violence would generally be out of all proportion.

(b) *To effect arrest or prevent escape:* These are normal law-enforcement tasks; however, considering the number of offences for which people can be arrested and how little evidence against a suspect is needed to justify an arrest, it is disturbing that the Convention seems to legitimate the use of lethal force in order to arrest or detain a suspected offender—even someone suspected of perjury. For the necessary force may be used regardless of the gravity of the offence for which detention is prescribed. Unfortunately, the principle is not new. In Spanish-speaking countries, for example, it is known as the *Ley de Fuga* (Law of Escape) – a term considered in many parts of Latin America as a synonym for arbitrary killings by the police, the military or prison officials.

(c) *To quell a riot or insurrection.* The remarks made under (a) are also applicable here. In addition, it is disquieting that the terms "riot" and "insurrection" are given the same weight. Riots are not necessarily directed against people: indeed, they are often against property. To suggest that the use of lethal force, if it is necessary to quell the latter kind of riot, is legitimate, raises serious questions of social priority. The bloodshed in Soweto, near Johannesburg in June 1976, is an appropriate reminder of the implications of this principle.

The type of incident dealt with in Chapter IV is an unusual phenomenon in most of Western Europe; this is not the case in some states of Latin America and Africa, despite the (largely unratified) American Convention. However, the increasing incidence of politically motivated killing in, for example, Italy and Turkey, suggests the need for vigilance. An amended Article 2 could, perhaps, borrow from the Draft Code of Conduct for Law Enforcement Officials prepared by the UN Committee on Crime Prevention and Control, in June 1976.[8] The draft code which will be placed before the 32nd session of the General Assembly in 1978 provides, by its Article 3 that "Law enforcement officials may never use more force than necessary in the performance of their duty." It is stated in the commentary[9] to this Article that: "In no case . . . should this provision be interpreted to authorize the use of force which is disproportionate to the legitimate objective to be achieved." Such a provision could be a constructive answer to the criticism made here of Article 2, paragraph 2, of the European Convention.[10]

It must also be noted that not only do all these conventions provide protection against arbitrary killings, they also prohibit any derogation from this protection even in time of war or other public emergency threatening the life of the nation.[11]

In addition, the Geneva Conventions of 12 August 1949 on the Protection of Victims of War clearly prohibit murder and other acts of violence against protected persons.[12] Indeed, they explicitly provide that "wilful killing" is to be considered a "grave breach" of the Conventions: that is to say, war crimes.[13] Similarly, Article 75 of the recently concluded Additional Protocol I to the Geneva Convention (see p. 23) prohibits "violence to . . . life . . . in particular . . . murder" in respect of all persons who are in the power of a party to an international armed conflict.

The Geneva Convention (common Article 3) further prohibit "at any time and in any place whatsoever . . . violence to life and person, in particular murder of all kinds", in respect of non-international armed conflict. Violence to life is also "prohibited at any time and in any place whatsoever" by Additional Protocol II to the Geneva Convention (see p. 23) in respect of persons who are not taking a direct part or have ceased to take part in hostilities during an armed conflict not of an international character (Article 4).

It follows that since murder committed or acquiesced in by governments (including, in the case of an armed conflict, other parties to the conflict) is condemned both by "general principles of law recognized by civilized nations"[14] and by all pertinent international treaties, it may properly be considered incompatible with general international law.

## *Notes*

1 This chapter is a revised version of the paper prepared by Nigel Rodley, Legal Adviser, Amnesty International, for the International Conference on the Abolition of the Death Penalty, Stockholm, 1977. It takes account of developments up to the end of March 1978.

2 On the background to the adoption of the right to life Articles of the *Universal Declaration of Human Rights* and of the *International Covenant on Civil and Political Rights,* see Lilly E. Landerer, "Capital Punishment as a Human Rights Issue before the United Nations", 4, *Human Rights Journal* 511, 1971. See also James Avery Joyce, *The Right to Life: A World View of Capital Punishment,* Chap.6, Gollancz, London, 1966.

3 The Committee of Ministers' Committee of Experts on Human Rights of the Council of Europe concluded that the terms of paragraph 2 were "not clear" in this respect and "did not consider that this was the intention". The study in which this unsupported view was stated did not offer an alternative meaning to a form of words which seems to be unambiguous. See Council of Europe, "Human Rights Problems arising from the co-existence of the United Nations Covenants on Human Rights and the European Convention on Human Rights-Differences as regards the Rights Guaranteed-Report of the Committee of Experts on Human Rights to the Committee of Ministers", Strasbourg 1970, Doc. H (70)7, p.25.

4 *Right to Life*

Article 4

1 Every person has the right to have his life respected. This right shall be protected by law, and, in general, from the moment of conception. No one shall be arbitrarily deprived of his life.

2 In countries that have not abolished the death penalty, it may be imposed only for the most serious crimes and pursuant to a final judgment rendered by a competent court and in accordance with a law establishing such punishment, enacted prior to the commission of the crime. The application of such punishment shall not be extended to crimes to which it does not presently apply.

3 The death penalty shall not be re-established in states that have abolished it.

4 In no case shall capital punishment be inflicted for political offences or related common crimes.

5 Capital punishment shall not be imposed upon persons who, at the time the crime was committed, were under 18 years of age or over 70 years of age; nor shall it be applied to pregnant women.

6 Every person condemned to death shall have the right to apply for amnesty, pardon, or commutation of sentence, which may be granted in all cases. Capital punishment shall not be imposed while such a petition is pending decision by the competent authority.

5 Article 87, paragraph 2 provides: "When fixing the penalty, the courts or authorities of the Detaining Power shall take into consideration, to the widest extent possible, the fact that the accused, not being a national of the Detaining Power, is not bound to it by any duty of allegiance, and that he is in its power as the result of circumstances independent of his own will. The said courts or authorities shall be at liberty to reduce the penalty provided for the violation of which the prisoner of war is accused, and shall therefore not be bound to apply the minimum penalty prescribed."

6 Article 107 provides: "Any judgment and sentence pronounced upon a prisoner of war shall be immediately reported to the Protecting Power in the form of a summary communication, which shall also indicate whether he has the right of appeal with a view to the quashing of the sentence or the re-opening of the trial. This communication shall likewise be sent to the prisoner's representative concerned. It shall also be sent to the accused prisoner of war in a language he understands, if the sentence was not pronounced in his presence. The Detaining Power shall also immediately communicate to the Protecting Power the decision of the prisoner of war to use or waive his right of appeal.

"Furthermore, if a prisoner of war is finally convicted or if a sentence pronounced against a prisoner of war in the first instance is a death sentence, the Detaining Power shall as soon as possible address to the Protecting Power a detailed communication containing:

(i) the precise wording of the finding and sentence:

(ii) a summarized report of any preliminary investigation and of the trial, emphasizing in particular the elements of the prosecution and the defence;
(iii) notification, where applicable, of the establishment where the sentence will be served.

The communications provided for in the foregoing sub-paragraphs shall be sent to the Protecting Power at the address previously made known to the Detaining Power."

7 Twenty-six non-governmental organizations submitted a statement to the Fifth UN Congress on the Prevention of Crime and the Treatment of Offenders, held in Toronto, 1-15 September 1975, calling on the Congress to adopt the suggestion that the General Assembly promulgate a declaration urging total, worldwide abolition of the death penalty (see Appendix C). Two NGOs, Amnesty International and the Howard League for Penal Reform, made oral interventions on the subject. Unfortunately, the death penalty was not a specific item on the agenda, and the Congress did not act on the NGO proposals.

8 United Nations Report of the Committee on Crime Prevention and Control on its Fourth Session, UN Doc. E/CN.5/536, 15 October 1976, Annexe V.

9 The commentary was considered by the committee as "an integral part of the code". UN Doc. E/CN.5/536, p.29.

10 An example of the practical application of this principle would be the instruction to law enforcement officials that lethal force may be used only when such force is the minimum necessary to prevent loss of life.

11 Covenant, Article 4; American Convention, Article 27; European Convention, Article 15.

12 Geneva Convention for the Amelioration of the Condition of the Wounded and Sick in Armed Forces in the Field (ConventionI), Article 12; Geneva Convention for the Amelioration of the Condition of Wounded, Sick and Shipwrecked Members of Armed Forces at Sea (Convention II), Article 12; Geneva Convention relative to the Treatment of Prisoners of War (Convention III), Article 13; Geneva Convention relative to the Protection of Civilian Persons in time of War (Convention IV), Article 32.

13 Convention I, Article 50; Convention II, Article 51; Convention III, Article 130; Convention IV, Article 147.

14 Statute of the International Court of Justice, Article 38, paragraph 1(c).

CHAPTER III

# THE DEATH PENALTY: A SURVEY BY COUNTRY

In compiling the following survey, Amnesty International has found that existing information on the imposition and carrying out of the death penalty is both sporadic and incomplete. Censorship of news media, secret executions, government reticence on the subject of the death penalty (especially when it is inflicted on political offenders) – all these factors combine to make the task of monitoring the world-wide use of the death penalty difficult. This is especially so in relation to closed societies where Amnesty International has no sources to provide the material by which the accuracy of government statements on the death penalty may be checked, and to governments which fail to respond even to UN questionnaires on the subject.

The same problem surrounded any attempt to compile a survey of the legal situation in each country. For some countries, the penal codes and their amendments were readily available, but for others they were not. In the process of preparing this whole *Report*, Amnesty International wrote to all the embassies in London, asking for information on the legislation governing the death penalty and the practice relating to it. The answers which were received were not uniform and only in some cases were they comprehensive.

The following survey, therefore, does not and cannot claim to provide a complete information on the use of the death penalty throughout the world. It describes only those situations about which Amnesty International has been able to obtain adequate information and deals with legislation which is in the organization's files. It describes, where data is available, the practice with regard to the death penalty in each country during the period 1974–1976 and any significant changes in trend which occurred in 1977. Where necessary, the historical background to certain legal developments has been explained.

Where murder committed or acquiesced in by governments is a significant occurrence, it receives brief mention. The focus of Chapter III, however, is on the use of the judicial death penalty; four case-studies of murder by governments are in Chapter IV.

**Most of the information below covers the period 1973-76. Also included are important changes in 1977 and early 1978.**

## AFRICA

Most African countries provide for the use of the death penalty, although the frequency with which it is imposed and inflicted varies considerably from country to country. In Mozambique, for example, the FRELIMO Government, which took power in mid 1975, has followed Portuguese practice and adopted an abolitionist position. In other countries, however, death sentences are normally commuted to a term of imprisonment, either on appeal to the Head of State or on the occasion of a national anniversary. In the Malagasy Republic (Madagascar), for example, executive clemency has been granted in respect of all death sentences imposed since the country became independent from France in 1960, and death sentences passed for subversion in Ghana have, in recent years, invariably been commuted.

In Africa the death penalty is used to punish a wide variety of offences. It is commonly imposed for violent criminal offences such as murder or rape, but may also, according to the social and political circumstances prevailing in a particular country, be applied for a whole range of other offences which might be regarded as relatively minor in other situations. In Ethiopia and Uganda, for example – two countries that have experienced severe economic difficulties in recent years – the death penalty has been introduced for certain "economic crimes", such as hoarding grain or consumer goods, embezzlement and fraud, and illegal currency dealings.

Faced with a rapid increase in the incidence of armed robbery, the Governments of Zambia and Kenya introduced a mandatory death sentence for this offence, in 1974 and 1975 respectively. In Rhodesia, Prime Minister Ian Smith's White minority régime attempted to use the death penalty to intimidate the country's African civilian population into betraying the whereabouts and activities of nationalist guerillas. Successive amendments to the Law and Order (Maintenance) Act have made it a capital offence to provide them with food, shelter or any other form of assistance, or to fail to report their presence to Rhodesian security forces within a specified time.

For some years, South Africa has had one of the highest rates of judicial executions in the world. Moreover, statistics for 1973–76 show that most of the 217 people executed during the period were African.

In Nigeria, public executions were introduced in 1970 and since then, many people convicted of armed robbery have been publicly executed by firing squad. Public executions take place in Uganda, Ethiopia and Equatorial Guinea.

One of the most disturbing features of the use of the death penalty in Africa is the frequency with which people charged with political offences are tried and executed after the most summary of judicial hearings. In a number of African countries, particularly those under military régimes, summary executions have followed periods of national crisis. In Nigeria, 37 people were executed in March and May 1976, after the assassination of Brigadier Murtala Mohamed, the country's Head of State. Ninety-eight people were executed in Sudan during August 1976, after an abortive *coup* the previous month against the Government of President Jaafar Numeiri. In Ethiopia, successive waves of executions have been carried out on the orders of the military Government (the *Derg*) since it replaced the government of Emperor Haile Selassie in 1974. No doubt such killings as these are intended both to punish political dissidents and to deter those who might in the future attempt to bring about political change by violent or non-violent means. They also indicate, perhaps, political instability and the need for a clearer sense of the importance of individual human rights. This is, of course, especially necessary in countries such as Uganda, Equatorial Guinea and Ethiopia, where murder pure and simple, directed against people who oppose the government and against certain population groups, and carried out in some instances on a massive scale, has been organized and brought about by government authorities.

There are, of course, countries such as Zambia that have well-established and courageously independent appeal courts which, on occasion, have acquitted prisoners condemned to death by lower courts and roundly rebuked the authorities for bringing an unjustified prosecution. Too often, however, the existence of fair and humane conditions is overshadowed by reports of repression and widespread killing elsewhere.

Detailed information on death penalty legislation in some African states has proved difficult to obtain, and it has not been possible to get hold of full details of the procedures involved in sentencing, granting clemency and carrying out executions in several jurisdictions – particularly the French-speaking countries of West Africa.

Most of the countries in Africa south of the Sahara which were colonized by France inherited penal codes and judicial systems based on the French model. Several of them subsequently broke with the French tradition and many amended the laws governing state security and introduced special State Security Courts. The most radical break occurred in those states that set up various types of "revolutionary" court. This has often meant an end to the independence of the judiciary and the introduction of a more summary form of justice. It has also frequently led to the right of a condemned person to appeal against sentence being curtailed.

In the following survey of legislation on the death penalty in Africa and the use to which it has been put in recent years, based on data from Amnesty International files, only those countries about which the organization has adequate information are included.

### ***Algeria** (the People's Democratic Republic of)*

The death penalty exists in Algeria for a number of offences, including crimes against state security, economic espionage and, since February 1975, drug smuggling.

In March 1976, a State Security Court sentenced to death three people described as being part of an "international anti-Algerian subversive network", and in May 1976 a defendant found guilty *in absentia* of economic espionage received the same sentence.

There is no appeal against sentences passed by the State Security Court, but the President has the right to pardon or commute death sentences, and commutations were granted in the case of the four defendants referred to above.

### ***Angola** (the People's Republic of)*

On 10 July 1976, four foreign mercenaries – three Britons and one American – were executed by firing squad in Luanda. Two weeks earlier, they had been sentenced to death by a People's Revolutionary Court, established in accordance with Law 7/76 of Angola's Revolutionary Penal Legislation. They had been convicted of, among other things, being "mercenaries" during the war which came in the wake of Portugal's withdrawal from its former colony. They were executed by firing squad after unsuccessful applications for clemency to the President of Angola.

A number of other executions are believed to have taken place in Angola during the second half of 1976. Those executed – by firing squad – included members of the FAPLA (the military wing of the MPLA) convicted of serious breaches of military discipline. In January 1977, three FAPLA soldiers were executed in Luanda after being convicted by a military court of having murdered a Portuguese technician.

Several hundred people are believed to have been arrested after an abortive attempt to overthrow the Government of President Agostinho Neto on 27 May 1977. The unsuccessful *coup*, led by the former Minister of the Interior, Nito Alves and an ex-MPLA Central Committee member, José Van Dunem, resulted in a number of deaths: one Government minister and several officials were killed by the rebels.

No open political trials took place of those accused of complicity in the *coup* but a number of prisoners are believed to have been executed by firing squad in the following months.

### *Benin (the People's Republic of)*

From independence until 1972, Dahomey (as Benin was known until 1975) retained a judicial and legal system based on that of France, the former colonial power. In October 1972, the civilian Government was overthrown in a military *coup* led by Lieutenant-Colonel Matthieu Kérékou. Several changes to the legal system followed. In May 1974, a special criminal court was established in the capital, Cotonou, with jurisdiction over crimes of violence. There is no right of appeal from this Court, although the President retains the authority to pardon offenders or commute death sentences. The Special Criminal Court imposed the death penalty for the first time in June 1974, when six men were sentenced to death for murder. They were executed by firing squad.

In November 1974 an ordinance was published (Number 74-68 of 8 November 1974) enabling the ruling military Government to transform itself into a court – the National Revolutionary Tribunal – in order to try major political cases. Following an attempted *coup d'état* in January 1975, this special court tried the cases of those accused of complicity in the conspiracy to overthrow the Government. At the conclusion of the proceedings, in March 1975, it imposed seven death sentences. At the time of writing, these sentences have not been carried out, nor have they yet been commuted.

The National Revolutionary Tribunal was again used in February 1976, following a new and equally unsuccessful attempt in October 1975 to overthrow the Government. Eleven people, mainly officials under a previous civilian government, were sentenced to death. It is not known if the sentences have been carried out.

### *Cameroon (the United Republic of)*

The United Republic of Cameroon became independent in 1961. Its legal and judicial system reflects the country's colonial past and contains elements of both the English and French systems. However, during the long period of internal political instability between 1961 and 1973, normal legal procedures were suspended. Throughout this time, while the banned opposition party, the *UPC* (*Union des populations du Cameroun*) was in armed revolt against the central Government of President Ahidjo, military tribunals were used not only for political cases but also to try people accused of criminal offences. In 1970, after being captured by Government forces, a number of *UPC* leaders were brought to trial before a military tribunal in Yaoundé. At least six of them were convicted, condemned to death and executed in January 1971. Ernest Ouandié, the leader of the *UPC*, was among those executed. The Roman Catholic Bishop of N'Kongsamba, Mgr. Albert Ndongmo, was also sentenced to death at this time, but President Ahidjo subsequently commuted his sentence to life imprisonment. Mgr. Ndongmo was given a Presidential pardon and released in an amnesty for political prisoners in May 1975.

Cameroon adopted a new Penal Code in 1968, also largely based on an amalgam of the English and French colonial systems. In recent years, various amendments have been introduced to provide severer sentences for theft. The death penalty may now be, and frequently is, imposed for armed robbery and for any form of theft which involves the use of a weapon or an implement which can be used for picking locks. Although the wide terms of this provision suggest that the death penalty may often be imposed in Cameroon, Amnesty International has no information about the number of death sentences and executions carried out between 1973 and 1977.

### *Central African Empire (the)*

Although the Central African Empire has a legal system based on that of France, and has both a Supreme Court and Appeal Courts, applicable procedures and practices offer defendants only nominal protection from arbitrary treatment.

Emperor Bokassa I is said to have been involved personally in assaulting and sometimes killing convicted criminals and suspected political opponents. In August 1972, following a burglary at his palace, he went to the central prison in Bangui (the capital) and took part in kicking, beating and clubbing some forty prisoners, three of whom are known to have died as a result of these assaults.

Murder is punishable by death. In 1973 the death penalty was introduced for embezzlement of public funds and offences involving damage to state property. Trial is before a Permanent Military Tribunal.

Most of Emperor Bokassa's suspected political opponents have disappeared and are believed dead. In February 1976, following an attempt on the life of the President (as the Emperor then was) a military tribunal sentenced eight men to death. They were executed within hours of the trial. Among them were several members of the army and two foreigners.

Since Central Africa was declared an Empire in December 1976, it has had a Constitution in which every defendant is assured representation. Article 48 of the Constitution provides that a defendant should be presumed innocent until proven guilty. It is, however, clear that these rights are frequently violated.

### *Chad (the Republic of)*

Under the Government of President N'garta Tombalbaye (overthrown in April 1975), large numbers of political opponents disappeared and are believed to have been murdered by Government authorities. Between January 1974 and April

1975, at least 72 people are believed to have been murdered while in detention in N'Djamena (the capital), and in September and October 1974 between 50 and 100 Protestant pastors are reported to have been killed in southern Chad for refusing to take part in an initiation ritual which had been re-introduced by President Tombalbaye.

In April 1975, President Tombalbaye was killed in a military *coup* which claimed the lives of several hundred people. Following the *coup*, the Supreme Court was abolished.

A year later, in April 1976, members of *FROLINAT*, the National Liberation Front fighting for the autonomy of northern Chad, tried to assassinate the Head of State, General Felix Malloum. After the attempt, the ruling Supreme Military Council established, in October 1976, a State Security Court to handle cases of conspiracy, espionage, treason, subversion and armed rebellion. This Court consists of eight military or civilian members. The first cases tried before it were those of the *FROLINAT* members accused of trying to assassinate General Malloum. Four of them were found guilty and sentenced to death at the beginning of April 1977. They were executed almost immediately. A few days later, another attempt was made to kill General Malloum and overthrow the Government. This time the authorities acted swiftly, establishing a special military tribunal which sentenced seven soldiers and four civilians to death for complicity in the attempted *coup d'état*. They were not permitted to petition the Head of State for clemency, and are believed to have been executed soon after being sentenced.

In June 1977, another member of *FROLINAT* appearing before the State Security Court, charged with armed rebellion against the Government, was sentenced to death. At the time of writing it is not known whether the sentence was carried out.

***Congo** (the People's Republic of)*

Although the Congo adopted a French-based penal code and judicial system when it became independent from France in 1960, a number of changes were made to the legal system in 1963. A Revolutionary Court of Justice was established in January 1969 with jurisdiction over prosecutions including matters of state security. The Revolutionary Court is presided over by nine judges selected from a list compiled by the Central Committee of the Congo's only political party, the Congolese Labour Party (*Parti congolais du travail*). The Supreme Court has jurisdiction over ordinary civil and criminal cases.

In 1972 there were two unsuccessful attempts to overthrow the Government of the then President, Marien Ngouabi. Both were directed by a former member of the Government, Lieutenant Ange Diawara. He was sentenced to death *in absentia* in 1972, while leading a band of guerillas in armed opposition to the Government. In February 1973 the Government announced that it had uncovered a major conspiracy directed by Lieutenant Diawara. Those accused of complicity in it were tried by the Revolutionary Court of Justice, which sentenced four of them to death in April 1973.

In March 1973, one of Diawara's guerilla fighters was captured and immediately executed. In April, Diawara himself and his deputy were shot dead while trying to escape capture by the Congolese army.

It is believed that no executions for criminal offences have taken place in the

Congo between 1960 and 1974. However, in November 1974, a man who had been convicted and sentenced to death by Brazzaville Criminal Court for several murders, rapes and armed robberies was executed by firing squad. Several months later, in March 1975, the Criminal Court imposed the death penalty on 11 members of a religious sect which practised sorcery, magic and ritual murder. It is not known whether those sentences were carried out.

On 18 March 1977, President Ngouabi was assassinated by a small group of soldiers. A military tribunal was immediately set up to try those allegedly responsible. More than 20 people are known to have appeared before this tribunal, out of a total of at least 50 detained for complicity in the assassination. The first person to be brought before the Tribunal was the ex-President of Congo, Alphonse Massamba-Debat. He was found guilty and immediately executed. Several others were also tried summarily and executed.

In the days following the assassination of President Ngouabi, the issue was complicated by another murder, that of the Roman Catholic Archbishop of Brazzaville, Cardinal Emile Biayenda. Several people accused of complicity in this murder were also brought before the military tribunal and two of them were sentenced to death. Detainees brought before the tribunal were not given any opportunity to defend themselves, nor were they allowed to appeal against their sentences. Ten people in all are known to have been condemned to death; three of these sentences were imposed *in absentia.*

In January 1978, a public trial took place of more than 40 people suspected of complicity in the assassination of President Ngouabi. Although the defendants had state-appointed lawyers to defend them, the latter did not have adequate opportunity to address the court. After a month-long trial, eleven men were condemned to death (one *in absentia*), four were sentenced to life imprisonment and 17 others were given shorter prison sentences. The ten condemned to death were given no opportunity to appeal and were executed on 7 February 1978, the morning after sentence was passed.

### ***Equatorial Guinea*** *(the Republic of)*

Since Equatorial Guinea became independent in 1968, the Government of President Macías Nguema has been responsible for thousands of deaths. Political opposition has been systematically eliminated, by the destruction of entire villages and their populations, and by the arrest and execution of opponents in Equatorial Guinea's two main towns, Bata (on the mainland) and Malabo – formerly Santa Isabel (on the Island of Fernando Po). More than two-thirds of the country's original (1968) National Assembly have been assassinated on President Macías' orders, and thousands of others have been shot, beaten or burned to death.

Equatorial Guinea lacks any organized judicial system. The National Guard is reported to be responsible for most deaths; people are known to die under torture, which includes beating, burning and crucifixion. Public executions have become commonplace since their introduction in Bata and Santa Isabel in 1969. At least 27 out of 114 prisoners condemned to death in June 1974 were executed in public. The President himself is alleged to have taken part in several killings, including one in which a prisoner was drenched in petrol and burnt alive.

Exact figures for the number of killings and executions in Equatorial Guinea are unavailable. At the end of 1976, however, a list was published outside the country of 490 people – of whom a large number were civil servants – who were believed to have been killed during President Macías' rule. If correct, the list suggests that he has ruthlessly attempted to wipe out a substantial proportion of the country's educated élite.

***Ethiopia***

Since the assumption of power by the military between February and September 1974, use of the judicial death penalty has increased. So, too, has the incidence of summary executions by security forces.

For the period up to November 1974, the 1957 Penal Code was in force. This provided the death penalty for a range of offences: attempts on the life of the Emperor, his wife or his children; changing the constitution or government by violence; armed insurrection or civil war, undermining the unity of the people or detaching part of the territory or people (i.e., secession); provoking foreign intervention; sabotage, mutiny, desertion, high treason, diplomatic treason (betrayal of state secrets); collaboration with the enemy in time of war and espionage.

The death penalty was mandatory for offences against the Constitution, the security of the state, its territorial integrity or its armed forces, and for conspiracy to commit the above if internal peace were threatened, or if a danger of civil war or an emergency existed, and if arms or explosives were used. The death penalty was also mandatory for war crimes – genocide, pillage, wounding an enemy who had surrendered, mutilating a corpse, violence against a wounded person with intent to rob, desertion, causing lowering of morale, cowardice, or capitulation to the enemy.

The death penalty was mandatory also for armed robbery by professional gangs, and was the maximum penalty for premediated murder (mandatory if the offender were already serving a life sentence), other forms of armed robbery, looting and piracy.

The Special Penal Code Proclamation No. 8 of 16 November 1974, introduced by decree of the Provisional Military Administrative Council (*Derg*), supplemented and, where applicable, replaced the 1957 Code with another range of capital offences. The death sentence became the maximum penalty for anyone who "destroys or endangers the independence of the state, or who provokes foreign intervention calculated to endanger the state's independence, or who involves the state in a blockade or an occupation" (Article 1); who "... commits an act designed to destroy the unity of the people or to detach part of the state's territory" (Article 2); who "... stages or who prepares to stage an armed revolt, mutiny or rebellion against the government", or who "... foments civil war by arming citizens or inciting them to take up arms against one another" (Article 3); who "... intentionally impairs the defensive power of the state" (Article 5); who "... intentionally causes famine, an epidemic or distress (if this leads to loss of life)" (Article 27); or who "... procures or aids the escape of an arrested person awaiting trial by special court martial or a person who has been convicted by such a court (if the escape succeeds or where death occurs during the attempt)" (Article 33).

The death sentence is mandatory if the offences listed under Article 1, 2, 3 and 5 are committed during or under the threat of internal disturbance, civil or foreign war, and during States of Emergency or martial law; where offences involve a conspiracy; where the offender has used arms supplied from abroad; or where he has used explosives or other terrorist means (Article 6). This applies also to "... anyone whose attack on a member of the Provisional Military Administrative Council, his spouse or children, or a court martial official, results in death" (Article 7); who "... attempts to destroy the Provisional Military Administrative Council by violence or other unlawful means – if this results in death" (Article 9); who "... abducts by force or trickery another person abroad or secludes him within Ethiopia; or who orders such abduction – if the abducted person is murdered or disappears" (Article 26).

This decree was accompanied by the establishment, also by proclamation, of special courts to hear cases brought under its provisions. These tribunals were empowered to try civilians, and there was no provision for appeal, except in the case of the death penalty being imposed. In such cases appeal for clemency might be made to the Chairman of the Provisional Military Administrative Council, who is Head of State. Most death sentences appear to have been confirmed. The military tribunals have a wider jurisdiction than civil courts, whose authority has become very limited.

The Code, retroactive to February 1974, was severely criticized in December 1974 by the International Commission of Jurists, which expressed "grave concern" about the likelihood of defendants securing fair trial. Amnesty International also commented to the Ethiopian Government on aspects of the Code and on the proceedings of military tribunals observed by an Amnesty International mission in February 1975. Objections to the Code include the lack of definition of those circumstances in which the death penalty is mandatory, such as "threat of internal disturbance".

In 1974 and early 1975 the proceedings of military tribunals were, on occasion, held in open court, with legal representation of defendants, but this was not always the case. During 1975 and later, such trials were increasingly held *in camera*, without legal representation for the defence. Trials appear to have become summary and findings and sentences took on a harsh and arbitrary nature.

New amendments to the 1974 Penal Code relevant to the death penalty were introduced on 5 July 1976. They replace the previous clauses in the following way:

(1) Special Criminal Code Section 17(a) – causing grave damage to the economy: the death penalty becomes the maximum punishment for such offences as hoarding grain or consumer commodities; manufacturing, making or using false currency; overcharging; preventing grain and other commodities from reaching the public; destroying public transport vehicles and damaging government property.

(2) Section 17(b) – anti-revolutionary activities: the death penalty becomes the maximum punishment for anyone who "prevents or discourages, directly or indirectly, farmers or other workers from following the various decrees to organize themselves and puts obstacles in the way of revolutionary progress; ... establishes contact with anti-revolution and anti-people organizations, within and outside the country, and sympathizes with them or assists them; ... leaves the country illegally or attempts to leave, by betraying the people and the country".

(3) Under Section 19, the death penalty becomes the maximum punishment for taking bribes or enriching oneself illegally. This offence includes "... any government employee who takes bribes or solicits a bribe in order to assist people illegally; ... any official or any other person who demands to be given documents, agreements or other official files from the office in which he or she is employed, or promises to transfer them to other people".

It is likely that many trials under this legislation lacked proper formality and safeguards. Death penalties were often imposed and carried out speedily.

It is not known exactly how many people have been sentenced to death and executed according to judicial procedure under the military régime. For the period from September 1974 to the end of 1977, the number is probably several hundred. Announcements of executions, if made at all, are often confined to the minimum details – describing the offence in general terms (e.g.: "banditry", "opposing Ethiopia's popular movement", "acts of terrorism", "counter-revolutionary crimes"). One example is that of 50 people executed in November 1976 for a variety of "counter-revolutionary" offences, including alleged murder and political crimes; most were said to be members of the illegal left-wing Ethiopian People's Revolutionary Party.

During 1977 the rule of law virtually broke down, as "revolutionary measures" – that is, murder committed by Government security forces or other officials – intensified and replaced any system of judicial procedure. Political killing was officially encouraged by the military Government and approved as "revolutionary justice". (This is described more fully in Chapter IV). In some cases there were official announcements of "executions" after trial by military tribunal, but it is thought that the system of military tribunals was, in fact, defunct in 1977.

Death penalties were also reportedly imposed by *kebelle* (urban association) tribunals. Such trials were both summary and arbitrary in their procedures and no right of appeal existed. An official *kebelle* Chairman, Girma Kebede, was reported to have been sentenced to death by military tribunal for torture and murders. He was publicly executed with two colleagues on 2 April 1977. However, such practices by Government officials are common and are usually condoned.

### *Gabon (the Gabonese Republic)*

Like other former French colonies in West Africa, Gabon has a penal code and system of justice inherited from France. However, the system has been modified by the introduction of a Court of State Security, whose 12 members are under the chairmanship of the President. This Court has jurisdiction over political cases.

No executions are reported to have taken place in Gabon from the time of independence in 1960 until 1974. A number of people were sentenced to death for criminal offences during this period, but all of them had their sentences commuted to 25 years' imprisonment in March 1973, when President Omar Bongo granted a general amnesty. In June 1974, a man who had been convicted of two murders was executed.

### *Gambia, The (the Republic of)*

Available information indicates that the 1933 (pre-independence) Penal Code is still in force, with amendments made in 1961, 1964 and 1965.

Treason and murder are punishable by death, as is the offence of inciting a foreign power to invade The Gambia. By Section 186 of the Criminal Code, the death penalty is not available for homicide committed as a sudden result of provocation, infanticide or where the court finds the offender is suffering from insanity. Pregnant women and people under 16 may not be sentenced to death. Those condemned may appeal to a higher court. Execution is by hanging. It is not known whether any death sentences were imposed or executions carried out in the period 1973–77.

***Ghana** (the Republic of)*

The Ghanaian Criminal Code of 1960 provided for the death penalty in Sections 46, 49, 180 and 194. Section 46 lays down the death penalty for murder, but extenuating circumstances may be taken into consideration. Section 49 provides the death sentence for prisoners who attempt to commit murder while imprisoned for three years or more. Section 180 prescribes the death sentence for treason, when committed by any Ghanaian citizen whether inside or outside Ghana, and Section 194 provides the same penalty for people convicted of piracy. In 1962, an amendment to the Criminal Code introduced the death penalty for the crime of possession of armaments. A decree in 1966 – by which time the civilian Government had been overthrown and the country was under military rule – provided for a discretionary death penalty for subversion. Trial was by military tribunal and there was no possibility of appeal.

Civilian rule was restored in Ghana between 1969 and 1972, but shortly after coming to power in a bloodless *coup* in January 1972, the military Government, led by the then Lieutenant-Colonel I.K. Acheampong, ruling by decree, made the death sentence mandatory on conviction for robbery, where death resulted (Suppression of Robbery Decree, 1972). In July 1972, the ruling National Redemption Council issued a Subversion Decree making certain offences, including any attempt to overthrow the Government, punishable by execution by firing squad. Other offences constituting "subversion" according to the Decree were robbery, smuggling, theft and wilful damage to property. Under the Decree, trial is by military tribunal, with no appeal.

Eight people allegedly involved in a plot in support of Dr K.A. Busia, whose elected civilian Government had been overthrown by the January 1972 *coup*, were arrested in July of that year, and in November sentenced to death under the provisions of the Subversion Decree. The sentences were later commuted to life imprisonment. In October 1973, five people, including Kojo Botsio, a former Foreign Minister, were also tried under the Decree on charges of plotting to overthrow the Government. The trial resulted in the imposition of the death penalty on Kojo Botsio and two others in December 1973. The following month, a trade unionist, Alex Hammah, was tried separately on similar charges, and likewise sentenced to death. Once again, the sentences were commuted to life imprisonment.

Arrests in the armed forces in November 1975 were followed by a major subversion trial, beginning in Accra in May 1976. Eight people, five of them soldiers, faced charges of subversion, stemming from an alleged plot late in the previous year. The trial ended in August 1976 with death sentences on five of the accused, all members of the Ewe minority ethnic group. Hardly was this trial over when a second began, of four military personnel charged with similar offences. This trial was before a military tribunal, and resulted, in mid November 1976, in two death sentences, one prison sentence, and an acquittal. These sentences were not carried out: the prisoners were released during 1978.

In September 1976, agitation on the part of Ghanaian secessionists based in neighbouring Togo led to the issuing of a decree to amend the Subversion Decree of 1972, so that it would provide for people who organize or promote the secession or breaking away of any part of Ghana to be held guilty of the offence of subversion, with its mandatory sentence of death by firing squad. There is no report of anyone having been charged or tried under the amended Decree.

In January 1977, to mark its fifth anniversary in power, the military Government commuted to life imprisonment all death sentences imposed on prisoners other than those convicted of subversion. A similar measure had been decreed in January 1976, when the Government commuted to life imprisonment the death sentences on all prisoners awaiting execution. It is not known how many death sentences, if any, were passed in Ghana for non-political offences in the period 1973–1976. However, in one notable case, in May 1977, 11 people were sentenced to death by a Sekondi High Court for the murder of a traditional leader, Nana Atta Agyeman IV, in April 1976.

***Guinea** (the Republic of)*

Little information is available concerning the use of the death penalty in Guinea. All that is known is that offences such as treason, smuggling, theft and drug-taking may incur a capital sentence, apparently on a discretionary basis. It is likely that other offences also, such as murder, may be punished by death.

During the period under review (1973–77), no executions were officially reported by the Guinean authorities. However, it was widely believed that a number of political prisoners were executed in secret, or died as a result of starvation or physical ill-treatment, at the detention camps in which they were held. In fact, this form of treatment appears to have replaced the more formal imposition of death sentences since January 1971, when a series of summary executions aroused international protest. They followed an attack on Guinea's capital, Conakry, in November 1970, by a combined force of Portuguese soldiers and people opposed to the Guinean régime. In all, a total of 91 death sentences were passed, including 33 *in absentia.* Eight were carried out immediately. Reports stated that the other condemned prisoners were executed soon afterwards.

***Ivory Coast** (the) (the Republic of)*

In 1964 Ivory Coast modified the legal code which it had inherited at independence in 1960 from the former colonial power, France. The modifications concerned state security, and included several new articles in the Penal Code, as well as the introduction of a State Security Court. Articles 67 and 91 of the 1964 Penal Code allow for the death penalty for crimes against the security of the state. Article 91 provides the death penalty for incitement to war, devastation, massacre and pillage.

The State Security Court introduced in 1964 consists of a president and six judges, all appointed for five-year periods. The Court tries all offences against the security of the state, and its introduction was the direct result of attempts made in the early 1960s to overthrow the existing civilian Government of President Houphouët-Boigny.

In 1973, 12 army officers were arrested and accused of planning a military *coup.* They were tried by court martial and seven of them were sentenced to death. However, no executions were carried out. In October 1975, President Houphouët-Boigny announced that the sentences on all prisoners awaiting execution had been commuted to terms of 20 years' imprisonment. All 12 army officers convicted in 1973 were later pardoned by the President and released. President Houphouët-Boigny is believed to oppose the use of the death penalty, even though Ivory Coast is officially retentionist.

***Kenya** (the Republic of)*

The death penalty is mandatory for treason; attempting to overthrow the Government or to change laws or policies by unlawful means or by force; incitement to invade or attack the country with armed force; rendering assistance to the enemy in time of war; murder.

In late 1975, the death penalty was made mandatory for robbery with violence or attempted robbery with violence by the so-called "Hanging Bill". On 6 October 1976, the Attorney General announced a mandatory death penalty for "encompassing, imagining, devising or intending the death or deposition of the President of Kenya". There have been no charges to date under this provision. In 1976, President Jomo Kenyatta was given affirmative support by acclamation for his public announcement that "all persons convicted of stealing [not merely for violent robbery] would be publicly executed." This measure was not, however, brought into effect.

The death penalty may only be imposed by the High Court, after preliminary inquiries before a subordinate court. The person charged with an offence carrying the death penalty may receive legal aid, and if convicted, has automatic right of appeal to the Court of Appeal of East Africa. No death penalty can be carried out until this Court has heard the case and made its decision. The condemned person then has the constitutional right to petition for the exercise of the Prerogative of Mercy, under Section 27 of the Constitution. The President may commute the death penalty to a defined prison term, on the advice of an Advisory Committee on the Prerogative of Mercy. The President may also grant a stay of execution for an indefinite or finite period. The death penalty may not be carried out until all avenues of appeal have been exhausted. In the case of the "Hanging Bill", appeals to the East African Court of Appeal must be lodged within 14 days. The death penalty is commuted to life imprisonment for pregnant women and young people.

In Kenya no death penalty has been imposed for a political offence since independence. A substantial number of death penalties have been imposed, and many probably carried out, in homicide cases. The majority of death penalties during 1975–76 were imposed under the "Hanging Bill". For example, two men were executed in November 1975 for attacking a man with a machete, stealing his wrist watch, shoes and the equivalent of the UK £16. In March 1976, two men were hanged, one for robbery at knife point, and the other for murdering his uncle and stealing money. It is not known how many others have been condemned to death for robbery with violence in this period but the number of sentences commuted by Presidential mercy is probably relatively small. Some judicial appeals have succeeded. Execution is carried out in Kamiti Maximum Security Prison in Nairobi, by hanging. Public reports of executions are not made.

A prominent radical Member of Parliament, J.M. Kariuki, "disappeared" on 2 March 1975. According to a Parliamentary commission, he was murdered for political reasons by senior Government and security officials. No judicial action has been taken to investigate this allegation.
**N.B.** Following the disintegration of the East African Community at the end of 1977, provision was being made in Kenya for the establishment of a national Court of Appeal.

***Lesotho** (the Kingdom of)*

Lesotho's Criminal Procedure and Evidence Proclamation 1938 provides that the death penalty be the only available punishment for murder unless the Court finds that "extenuating circumstances" are present. The death penalty also exists on a discretionary basis for rape and treason. People under 18 at the time the offence is committed may not be sentenced to death.

Anyone sentenced to death may appeal to the Court of Appeal, which has the jurisdiction to change a verdict or reduce the punishment imposed by the High Court. Those under sentence of death may also petition for clemency to the King who takes decisions about whether to intervene with the help of the Pardons Committee.

In practice, few executions have been carried out and these only for murder. At the time of writing no rape or treason cases have resulted in the death penalty although there were two major treason trials involving a total of more than 40 prisoners during 1974–75.

***Liberia** (the Republic of)*

The statutory penalty for murder in Liberia is death by hanging (Penal Law S.232). However, between 1954 and his death in 1971, President William Tubman refused to sign any death warrants. Since then, an increase in the number of crimes of violence has been voiced as reason for the re-introduction of the use of the death penalty. Amnesty International has no information concerning the rate and frequency with which the death penalty is imposed and carried out in Liberia. It is known, however, that three convicted murderers were hanged in August 1974 after their appeals for clemency had been rejected. In June 1974 President William Tolbert commuted the death sentences imposed on two people convicted of plotting his assassination.

***Madagascar** (the Democratic Republic of) [Malagasy]*

The death penalty has stayed in the Penal Code, but there have been no executions since 1958, when Madagascar was under French colonial rule. Although the death sentence has been pronounced on several occasions since independence in 1960, the Head of State has always used his right to grant clemency. There has been no case since independence of the death penalty being imposed for political offences.

Under the 1962 Penal Code, the death penalty is available for certain offences against State security: bearing arms against the Republic; passing State secrets; provoking civil war; sabotage of State property; incitement to looting; leading armed gangs; rebellion; striking a judge, Government official, or policeman with intent to kill. It is also imposed for premeditated murder; torture; castration which results in death; certain forms of arson; grievous bodily harm with specified aggravating circumstances, and certain thefts with aggravating circumstances.

Defendants charged with offences carrying the death penalty are granted legal aid if they have no other resources with which to obtain legal representation. If convicted, they may appeal to the Supreme Court and, when avenues for appeal through the courts are exhausted, may petition the President to exercise his prerogative of mercy. No death sentence may be carried out until clemency has been refused. The death penalty may be commuted to a fixed prison term. A pregnant woman may not be executed until after her confinement, and nobody under 18 may be sentenced to death.

***Malawi** (the Republic of)*

The death penalty is mandatory for treason and murder, and discretionary for rape. It may not be imposed on anyone who was under 18 at the time of the commission of the offence, nor may it be inflicted on pregnant women.

In 1969, Malawi's local magistrates' courts were re-named Traditional Courts and given authority to impose capital sentences in murder and rape cases. In 1976, shortly before the beginning of a major treason trial (see below), this authority was extended to include treason cases. Before 1969, only the High Court had authority to impose the death penalty.

Anyone condemned to death by a Traditional Court is allowed 30 days in which to appeal to the Traditional Court of Appeal. Appeals may also be made beyond the jurisdiction of the Traditional Court of Appeal to the High Court and, ultimately, to the Supreme Court of Appeal, although access to these higher courts may be blocked by the Minister of Justice. The President, as Head of State, has final authority to grant clemency or commute death sentences to terms of imprisonment.

Executions – by hanging – are carried out in Zomba Prison, usually a number at a time. No official figures are available for the numbers of people sentenced to death and executed, but well-informed sources indicate that at least 27 people were hanged between May 1972 and August 1973. A further 25 people are reported to have been executed between December 1973 and September 1975. More than 100 prisoners under sentence of death were said to be held in the condemned cell section of Zomba Prison in late 1975.

Almost without exception, those executed are criminal offenders. Political opponents of the Malawi Government are rarely charged and brought to trial in open court: instead, they are normally subjected to long-term detention without trial under the provisions of the Public Safety Regulations. However, a major political trial involving the use of the death penalty occurred in early 1977, following the dismissal in April 1976 of a Cabinet Minister, Albert Muwalo Nqumayo.

In January 1977, Albert Muwalo Nqumayo, former Minister of State in the President's Office, and Focus Martin Gwede, Head of the Malawi Security Police until his arrest in October 1976, appeared before a Traditional Court in Blantyre on charges of treason. Both men were alleged to have been involved in a plot to assassinate Life President Dr Hastings Kamuzu Banda while he was on a visit to the town of Karonga, and to overthrow his ruling Malawi Congress Party Government. Muwalo and Gwede denied all charges, but were convicted and sentenced to death on 14 February 1977. They were allowed 30 days in which to appeal against conviction and sentence to the Traditional Court of Appeal. In April 1977, the Court rejected their appeal and confirmed the death penalty in both cases. Muwalo Nqumayo is reported to have been hanged at Zomba Prison on 3 September 1977. Gwede also is believed to have been executed.

***Mali*** *(the Republic of)*

Mali has kept a legal system based on that of France. A Supreme Court was established in 1969. In 1976, a Special Court of State Security was set up, consisting of two magistrates and eight army officers. Since 1976, offences such as causing damage to state property and embezzlement have come before this court instead of before the civil and criminal courts.

After taking power in November 1968, the present military Government of Lieutenant-Colonel Moussa Traouré promised to bring to trial members of the previous civilian régime but the former President, Modibo Keita and some twenty of his associates were held in prolonged detention without trial at prison camps in the Sahara, where conditions were particularly harsh. Several of the detainees died in the early 1970s, probably because of the severe prison conditions. In May 1977, Modibo Keita also died, reportedly as a result of a lung infection. He had been detained continuously since November 1968.

In June 1977, 12 people were condemned to death for political offences by the Special Court of State Security. They included seven non-commissioned officers and soldiers convicted of taking part in an attempt to overthrow the Government in 1976. The five other prisoners sentenced to death were Tuareg nomads who had taken part in an insurrection against the central Government of President Modibo Keita in 1963. It is not known whether executions have been carried out.

In July 1977, five people were executed by firing squad after being convicted of murder and "trafficking in human heads". They were said to have murdered people in Mali and to have sold their heads in neighbouring countries for use as fetishes.

***Morocco*** *(the Kingdom of)*

Crimes of "exceptional gravity" may incur the death penalty, according to the Penal Code which came into force on 26 November 1962. Such crimes include an attempt on the life of the King (which carries the mandatory death penalty), the heir to the throne or members of the royal family. Treason may also be punished with death, irrespective of whether the offence is committed in time of peace or war. Similarly, Articles 201 and 202 of the Penal Code make provision for the death penalty for serious offences against the internal security of the State, such as promoting civil war, or seizing command of an army unit or military installations. The ordinary offences which may incur the death penalty are murder and arson of an inhabited building or vehicle.

People sentenced to death have the right to appeal to the Supreme Court. The King, as Head of State, may exercise clemency. Executions take place on the instructions of the Minister of Justice and are carried out by military firing squad. They take place in private unless the Minister of Justice expressly orders a public execution. However, all executions are witnessed by a number of people designated to attend them, including judicial officers, defence counsel, and medical and religious personnel. Bodies of executed prisoners are returned to their relatives for burial.

In January 1973, 11 people were executed, and in November of the same year, 15 others. In January 1974, 22 people were sentenced to death, 16 of them *in absentia.* The crime in these cases was "plotting against the King", and executions were carried out shortly after the trials.

### *Namibia*

Namibia continued to be administered by South Africa during the period 1973–77, although the Mandate over the territory granted to South Africa by the League of Nations in 1920 was unilaterally revoked by resolution of the United Nations General Assembly in October 1966.

As in South Africa, the death penalty may be imposed for a variety of criminal offences. It is imposed for murder, except where extenuating circumstances prevail, and is available for rape, kidnapping and armed robbery with violence.

Together with treason, certain political offences may also incur the death penalty. In 1976, the law was amended. The Internal Security Act (previously the Suppression of Communism Act) makes it a capital offence for any person to undergo, or encourage others to undergo, any form of "training" in order to achieve any of the objectives of communism, as this is defined in the Act. The Act further provides for a possible death penalty in cases where a past or present resident of South Africa or Namibia is convicted of having advocated, while abroad, foreign intervention to effect change in Namibia or the achievement of the objectives of communism.

The Sabotage Act of 1962 and the Terrorism Act of 1967 (which was made retroactive to 1962 when introduced and applied to Namibia) also makes provision for the use of the death penalty against persons convicted of sabotage and terrorism, as these offences are defined in the two Acts.

People charged with offences which may incur the death penalty are normally tried summarily, i.e., without a previous determination as to whether there is a *prima facie* case, by the Supreme Court before a judge sitting with assessors. There is no provision for trial by jury. The Supreme Court in Namibia is a division of the Supreme Court of South Africa, and appeals are therefore directed to the Appellate Division of the South African Supreme Court. The judiciary is exclusively White. Court proceedings are conducted in either English or Afrikaans. Interpreters are employed in cases involving people who only understand Namibia's indigenous languages.

In cases where a death sentence is passed and upheld upon appeal, a report is sent to the State President of South Africa, who may then make a recommendation for clemency. At the same time, a report on the case is also passed to the South African Department of Justice, for scrutiny and for a decision on whether an execution should take place. Executions are authorized by the South African Minister of Justice and are carried out by hanging, either at Windhoek Prison in Namibia or at Pretoria Prison in South Africa.

Each year the South African Government issues statistics relating to the number of people sentenced to death and executed. However, since no distinction is made between Namibia and South Africa for this purpose, it is difficult to state with certainty how many of the death sentences imposed within Namibia in a particular year are subsequently carried out.

Only two Namibians are known to have been sentenced to death for explicitly political offences. Hendrik Shikongo and Aaron Muchimba, two supporters of the South West Africa People's Organization (SWAPO), Namibia's main African nationalist organization, were sentenced to death in May 1976. They were convicted under the Terrorism Act on the grounds that they had been involved, albeit indirectly, in the murder of Chief Filemon Elifas, Chief Minister of the Ovamboland "bantustan", who was killed by unknown assassins in August 1975. However, in March 1977, both convictions were reversed by the South African Appeal Court and both men were released. The Court held that interference by security police with the conduct of the case for the defence constituted a gross violation of the rights of the defendants.

A further death sentence with political connotations was passed in September 1976, when Filemon Nangolo, alleged to be a member of SWAPO's guerilla forces, was convicted on four counts of murder. In October 1976, Nangola was refused leave to appeal. He was executed in May 1977, despite international appeals for clemency.

### ***Niger*** *(the) (the Republic of )*

Niger retains the death penalty but it is not known how often, if at all, the death penalty has been applied for criminal cases. In March and April 1976, following an unsuccessful *coup* attempt in the March, nine alleged leaders of the plot were sentenced to death. On 21 April, seven of the nine, including Major Moussa Bayere, Captain Sidi Mohamed and Ahmed Moudour (the Secretary General of the Niger National Union of Workers, who was alleged to have organized the *coup* attempt) were executed.

In April 1974, the Government of President Hamani Diori was overthrown in a military *coup* led by Lieutenant-Colonel Seyni Kountché, who then became President. More than 100 people were killed during the course of the *coup*. The new military Government did not greatly amend the existing legal system which had been inherited from France, but the Supreme Court was suspended. Already, before President Kountché came to power, the previous Government had made use of a Court of State Security to try political opponents. Further use was made of this Court in 1976. Nine people convicted in March 1976 of conspiring to overthrow President Kountché's Government were sentenced to death. Seven of them were executed the following month. It is not known whether the other two were executed.

### ***Nigeria*** *(the Federal Republic of)*

The death sentence is mandatorily imposed for treason, armed robbery, plotting to overthrow the Government, sabotaging the production or distribution of petroleum products and premeditated murder. Murder is tried by the civilian High Court, but all other capital offences are tried by special military tribunals. The death penalty was further extended in 1974–75 to cover kidnapping or lynching resulting in death, but the decreed provision of the death penalty for counterfeiting local currency, possession of equipment or materials for forging Nigerian bank notes or coins and trafficking in forged local currency was repealed in late 1975 by Decree No. 37.

Defendants in capital cases are allowed their own lawyers, or those appointed and paid for by the state; trials are conducted in open court. There is right of appeal from the High Court to the Supreme Court. Petitions for clemency may be made to the Head of State. From special tribunals, consisting of two military or police officers and presided over by a High Court judge, the only further avenue of appeal is to petition the Head of State for executive clemency. Death sentences are not carried out on pregnant women and young people.

An Armed Robbery Decree, providing the death penalty for that offence, was promulgated in 1970, soon after the end of the Nigerian Civil War. By April 1973, 214 people had been executed under this Decree, and by October 1974 the number was 251. They were publicly executed by firing squad in various towns in Nigeria, including the capital, Lagos. Large crowds attended the executions, and in all cases firing went on for several minutes. The number of people executed under this Decree between 1975 and 1977 is not known.

In March 1976, 30 people – 29 of them military personnel – were executed after being sentenced to death by special court martial for involvement in the assassination the previous month of Brigadier Murtala Mohamed, the then Head of State. The sentences were rapidly confirmed by the Head of State and carried out without any delay. Seven other people were sentenced to death in similar courts martial two months later. Their execution was delayed because there was an intention to confront them with a former Head of State, General Gowon, the alleged mastermind of the *coup* attempt, who was living in Britain: they were executed as soon as a message was received from the British Government that the General would not be handed over to Nigeria. It is not clear whether, in all, 37 or 39 people were executed. The courts martial appear to have been lacking in safeguards and proper legal formality.

During 1977, the use of the death penalty was extended. In May, a new decree laid down the death penalty as the maximum punishment for armed smugglers convicted of causing injury to customs officers. In June, a special tribunal was established to hear cases under the 1974 decree involving counterfeit currency offences and was empowered to impose a mandatory death penalty for counterfeiting Nigerian currency. These changes were made as a result of a wave of armed robberies and similar crimes at about that time. More public executions for armed robbery took place in several parts of Nigeria during the year (1977).

In August, the Commissioner for Internal Affairs stated that 608 people awaited execution after being condemned to death. The delay, he said, could be up to two years. Presumably this referred to the time during which review would take place by the Head of State. The incidence of commutation is not known.

### *Rhodesia [Zimbabwe]*

Capital punishment has become an essential part of the Rhodesian Government's machinery of repression. Since the Unilateral Declaration of Independence (UDI) by the Government of Mr Ian Smith in 1965, approximately 420 people have been sentenced to death by Rhodesia's courts; more than 200 are believed to have been executed. They include people convicted of ordinary crimes such as murder or rape, and others convicted of certain political offences under the far-reaching Law and Order (Maintenance) Act 1960. By far the majority of executions have been carried out since 1972, when guerilla warfare began in earnest, and most of those executed are believed to have been sentenced to death because of their involvement in the nationalist armed struggle.

Not only is the death penalty extensively used, frequently on a mandatory basis, but it is also sometimes imposed at the end of trials conducted wholly or partly *in camera.* Executions are carried out without public notification. Moreover, the lawful authority of the Smith Government to carry out executions has been denied by both the British Government and the United Nations.

Since UDI, the Rhodesian Front Government has been regarded as an illegal régime, lacking all constitutional and legal validity both by Britain, the colonial power responsible for Rhodesia, and by the United Nations. As an illegal régime, the Rhodesian Front Government has no lawful authority to impose or carry out executions.

In January 1968, the Appellate Division of the High Court of Rhodesia ruled that the régime could lawfully do anything its predecessors could have done. These powers included the right to impose and inflict death penalties, the final warrant for which should be signed by the Officer Administering the Government – the régime's presidential figurehead – if the Governor (the British Queen's representative) should refuse to cooperate.

The Rhodesian judges, in accepting that the Constitution was still in force, did not challenge the authority of the Judicial Committee of the Privy Council in London as the highest court of appeal for Rhodesian cases. In February 1968, however, Rhodesia's Chief Justice, Sir Hugh Beadle, sitting in the Appeal Court, refused permission for an appeal to be made to the Judicial Committee of the Privy Council in London by counsel representing the first three men due to be executed. This decision was reached on the basis that such an appeal, whatever its outcome, would have no effect in Rhodesia, as the régime refused to recognize the authority of the Judicial Committee.

For its part, the British Government reasserted the authority of the Privy Council, and warned that those responsible for the infliction of executions in Rhodesia "would bear the gravest personal responsibility" if they denied the right of appeal to the Judicial Committee. Acting on the advice of her ministers, Queen Elizabeth II then used her authority as constitutional Head of State to exercise the Royal Prerogative of Mercy and reprieve the first three men due to be executed. Under the terms of their reprieve, their death sentences were commuted to life imprisonment.

Once again, the Rhodesian régime and the Rhodesian Appeal Court both denied the Queen's authority, and ratified the sentence of death on the three condemned prisoners, James Dhlamini, Victor Mlambo and Duly Shadreck. They were hanged at Salisbury Central Prison on the morning of 6 March 1968.

In March 1968, shortly before the first executions took place, a total of 85 people were reported to be under sentence of death in Rhodesia. Five of them were executed in March, but by December 1968 the number of people under sentence of death had risen to 118. The storm of international protest provoked by the March executions caused a cessation of hanging in Rhodesia until 1973, when the outbreak of guerilla warfare led the régime to resume executions. More than 190 people are believed to have been executed between 1973 and 1977. However, in contrast to the position adopted in 1968, it is not now British Government policy to advise Queen Elizabeth II to exercise clemency as a matter of course in all cases where the death sentence is imposed in Rhodesia. Indeed, it seems clear that the British Government does not intend to hold the members of the illegal Rhodesian Front administration personally accountable for the continued use of the death penalty in Rhodesia.

The Law and Order (Maintenance) Act, introduced in 1960, has since been amended and strengthened many times. It created a wide range of political offences and thereby imposed strict limitations on all forms of African political activity and organization. Moreover, it reversed the onus of proof so that it is now for the defendant to demonstrate innocence, rather than for the State to prove guilt.

In 1963, Section 37 of the Act was amended so as to provide the mandatory death penalty for crimes involving arson or the use of explosives. In 1967, Section 48A of the Act was also amended so as to introduce the mandatory death penalty for acts of terrorism. Both these amendments were repealed the following year on the grounds that the existence of the death penalty on a mandatory basis made so-called terrorists more liable to resist arrest. In December 1974, the Law and Order (Maintenance) Act was again amended when a *mandatory* death penalty was introduced under Section 23A of the Act, covering unlawful military training and the recruitment of guerillas.

Various sections of the Law and Order (Maintenance) Act also provide for the use of capital punishment on a discretionary basis. Therefore, at the end of 1977, the death penalty could be imposed under any of the following sections of the Act:

Section 23A, subsection 1: for recruiting or encouraging any person to undergo terrorist training within or outside Rhodesia. Section 23A, subsection 2: for persons who undergo terrorist training. Section 36: for the possession of arms of war. Section 37: for arson and the use of explosives. Section 48A, subsection 8: for the commission of any act of terrorism or sabotage with intent to endanger the maintenance of law and order. This includes, *inter alia*, an act which causes, or is likely to cause, substantial financial loss in Rhodesia to any person or to the Government, as well as crimes of violence. Section 48B:

(a) harbouring, concealing or assisting a person whom the offender knows, or has reason to believe to be, a terrorist; or

(b) refusing to disclose information relating to a terrorist he has harboured, concealed or assisted.

On 8 September 1976, an amendment to the Law and Order (Maintenance) Act was introduced in the Rhodesian Parliament. Under the terms of the amendment, the death penalty would have been made *mandatory* for a wide range of offences under the Law and Order (Maintenance) Act. However, the amendment was not proceeded with, as it was decided that more time was required to study the full implications of the legislation.

Pregnant women and people under 16 may not be executed under Rhodesian law. People aged between 16 and 18 may either be executed or sentenced to life imprisonment.

Many of the 200 people believed to have been executed since UDI have been either captured guerilla fighters or people convicted of offences connected in some way with the guerilla war. In the view of African nationalists, captured guerillas should be regarded as prisoners of war and treated in accordance with the Geneva Convention. The Rhodesian régime refutes this view, however, and continues to prosecute captured guerillas either for murder or under the provisions of the Law and Order (Maintenance) Act. More death penalties were imposed and carried out in Rhodesia during 1976 than in any other year since UDI.

On 22 April 1975, the Rhodesian Ministry of Justice announced that information concerning executions would no longer be made available to the public. The Government had decided upon this course of action, according to a spokesman for the Ministry, because the issue of the death penalty in Rhodesia had become "an emotive one". He said that in future the public should assume that a prisoner who had been sentenced to death, and whose appeal had been rejected, would be executed in the normal way. In effect, therefore, all executions in Rhodesia are now carried out without formal public notification.

It is also clear that relatives of prisoners under sentence of death are not informed of the date of execution. In January 1977, relatives of eight young African National Council supporters, sentenced to death for a series of bomb offences, only discovered that the executions had been carried out when they went to visit the prisoners several hours after the hangings had taken place. Bodies of executed prisoners are not returned to their families for burial.

By the end of 1976, more than 100 political prisoners had been tried before so-called Special Courts. These courts, which were established in May 1976, had imposed 29 death sentences by the end of the same year. The Special Courts were introduced so as to minimize the delay between charging individuals and bringing them to trial. In addition, the Special Court, which often sits *in camera,* was made mobile – that is, it moves round the country and holds its sessions in areas which have experienced guerilla incursions – in order that the Smith Government might clearly demonstrate to its White electorate its determination to act with ruthlessness against everyone charged in connection with the guerilla war.

Those who appear for trial before the Special Court no longer have the right to remain silent. Any defendant who declines to give evidence when questioned by the prosecution or the Court is presumed to be guilty. In the past, many political prisoners have refused to recognize the legal validity of Rhodesian courts.

In July 1977, the régime proceeded with the execution of Robert Mangaliso Bhebe, a long-time member of the Zimbabwe African People's Union and a former Amnesty International adopted prisoner of conscience, despite concerted international appeals. He had been convicted of encouraging several young Blacks to leave Rhodesia to join African nationalist guerillas in Zambia. Two other prisoners whose identities were not revealed were hanged with him.

Throughout 1977 the régime continued to execute captured guerilla fighters and African civilians convicted of providing them with support. This occurred even after the presentation of the Anglo-American plan for a settlement in Rhodesia which contained provisions for a total indemnity for all actions carried out by the régime since UDI. In other words, the Rhodesian régime was able to continue to execute its opponents in the knowledge that, in the event of a constitutional settlement, there was little likelihood that it would be held responsible for what had earlier been described by the British Government as acts of judicial murder.

### *Rwanda (the Rwandese Republic)*

Rwanda is a retentionist jurisdiction, but Amnesty International has no information on offences which carry the death penalty. It is known, however, that defendants have right of appeal from a sentence of death. When judicial procedures are exhausted, those convicted may petition for Presidential clemency. A commission advises the President on commutations of death penalties and amnesties for prisoners.

The death penalty was imposed in 1973 on former President Gregoire Kayibanda and seven advisers. However, all these sentences were commuted by the new Head of State, Major-General Juvenal Habyalimena, in July 1974, on the first anniversary of the *coup* which brought him to power. The death sentences had been imposed by court martial.

It seems that only 13 out of 120 death sentences imposed for criminal offences during the period 1969–1974 were carried out. Those whose sentences were commuted included five women.

The Rwanda Government has stated that it was considering new criminal legislation that would serve to increase the offences for which the death penalty was mandatory. The Government has also stated that the number of death sentences actually carried out has fallen.

***Seychelles** (the Republic of)*

Under Seychelles law, the death penalty may only be imposed for the crime of treason. The death penalty for murder has been suspended for a three-year period, due to expire in 1979. According to Amnesty International's information, no death sentences have been passed in the Seychelles since the Second World War.

***Sierra Leone** (the Republic of)*

The death penalty is available in law for treason and murder. Trial by jury exists in the civilian courts, and the verdict must be unanimous for conviction. The procedural rules of the military courts make no requirement for a jury.

The legal system of Sierra Leone is based on an English model, but trials are conducted by either magistrates' courts, the High Court or the Supreme Court. Offences which carry the death penalty include murder, robbery with violence, treason, mutiny and cannibalism. However, Amnesty International has little information about the frequency with which the death penalty is imposed and carried out in Sierra Leone, particularly in criminal cases. Until 1973 all executions were carried out by hanging, but an amendment to the Criminal Procedure Act in November 1973 provided for the use of a firing squad in some cases. One of the first people executed in this way was Alimamy Khazali, a former Minister of Information and Broadcasting, who was executed with three others after being convicted of murder.

Two major political trials took place in 1974–75 after a bomb explosion in April 1974 at the home of Christian Kamera-Taylor, then Minister of Finance. Fifteen civilians, including two former Government ministers, and nine soldiers were arrested after this incident and charged with treason. They were alleged to have conspired between 1 June 1973 and 30 July 1974 to overthrow the Government.

The trial of the civilians took place in the High Court. All 15 accused were found guilty and sentenced to death. Subsequently, the Court of Appeal confirmed the sentences in 14 of the cases, one appeal being allowed.

The nine soldiers were tried by a court martial consisting of five military officers. Seven of the accused were convicted and sentenced to death, but the court recommended clemency in one of these cases.

The cases of all those under sentence of death, both civilians and soldiers, were reviewed by a Committee on the Prerogative of Mercy, which recommended that the death sentences on eight civilians and three soldiers should be commuted to life imprisonment. Subsequently, President Siaka Stevens granted clemency to two other civilians and one soldier under sentence of death. He ordered that the remaining prisoners, six civilians and two soldiers, should be hanged. They were executed at Pademba Road Prison, Freetown, on 19 July 1975.

***Somalia** (the Somali Democratic Republic)*

Under the Penal Code 1960 the death penalty was reserved for "the most serious crimes against human life or the personality of the state". The death penalty is carried out by shooting within the confines of a prison.

A mandatory death penalty was introduced for the following offences: bearing arms against the State; espionage; passing State or industrial secrets to unauthorized persons; sabotage of military installations; armed insurrection; committing an act designed to cause devastation, pillage, slaughter or civil war; acts endangering public safety resulting in death; pollution of water or food resulting in death; premeditated murder; assisting in or inciting the suicide of a person who is under 18 or insane.

After the overthrow of the civilian government of Somalia in October 1969, a National Security Law was issued in September 1970 by the ruling Supreme Revolutionary Council headed by Major-General Mohamed Syad Barre. Seventeen of the Law's 18 articles provide for the death penalty, for such crimes as, for example, "committing offences adverse or damaging to the independence, unity and security of the Somali State" (Article 1); using arms against the State when it is at war (Article 2); forming organizations "whose purpose and work is hostile to the security of the Somali State" (Article 3); conspiring with a foreign power (Article 4); engaging in armed banditry (Article 8); "using religion for the purpose of breaking up the unity of the Somali people or weakening or damaging the authority of the Somali State" (Article 12); trading with a country hostile to the Somali Democratic Republic (Article 16); and displaying or distributing information "aimed at damaging the sovereignty of the revolution of the Somali nation".

A National Security Court and a system of Regional Security Courts was set up to hear cases under the National Security Law. In January 1975, the death penalty was imposed for opposing a law giving equality to the sexes in property and inheritance. In March 1975, the death penalty was made mandatory for misappropriation of Government funds over 100,000 shillings ($16,000 [US]).

The legal procedures which apply for political and ordinary offences are different. The Security Courts have jurisdiction over "political offences", which range from "tribalism" to treason.

A Security Court comprises a president and vice-president (from the armed forces) and two judges (from the armed forces or judiciary). Both the National and Regional Security Courts may impose death sentences, which require confirmation by the President. It appears that Security Courts may also try cases of murder, which were formerly tried by the civilian judiciary.

It is not known how many cases of murder have led to the death penalty, but there have probably been several each year. Amnesty International knows of four persons sentenced to death for murder by a Security Court in July 1976.

The most notorious case of the death penalty imposed for "political offences" was the public execution, by firing squad, on 23 January 1975, of 10 Muslim sheikhs. According to official Somali Government report, they were executed one week after being sentenced to death for "exploiting religion, creating national disunity, subverting state authority and making propaganda at religious ceremonies in mosques against the decision of the Somali Supreme Revolutionary Council to give equal rights to women".

All death penalty cases are reviewed by the Supreme Revolutionary Council, under its chairman, the President. Commutation does not appear to be common but occurred in some cases in October 1975.

Pregnant women or people suffering from mental disability are not executed.

### *South Africa (the Republic of)*

South Africa has one of the highest rates of judicial execution in the world. In 1974, for example, 86 people were sentenced to death and 40 were executed. The following year, 103 sentences were passed by the courts, and 68 executions carried out. Sixty-seven people were executed in 1976. The death penalty may be imposed for a wide range of serious crimes such as murder, rape or robbery with aggravating circumstances, and for certain political offences covered by the Terrorism Act and related security legislation. People convicted of treason may also be sentenced to death, although there have been no prosecutions for this offence in recent years.

Three main security laws make provision for the imposition of the death penalty on a discretionary basis – the Internal Security Act, the Terrorism Act and the so-called "Sabotage Act" (Section 21 of the General Law Amendment Act, No.76 of 1962).

The Internal Security Act which, in 1976, superseded the earlier Suppression of Communism Act, makes it a capital offence for any person to undergo, or encourage others to undergo, any form of "training" in order to achieve any of the objectives of communism, as these are widely defined under the terms of the Act. The Internal Security Act further provides for a possible death penalty where a past or present resident of South Africa or Namibia is convicted of having advocated, while abroad, foreign intervention to effect change in the South African system or the achievement of the objectives of communism.

The Terrorism Act, which was introduced in 1967 but made retroactive to 1962, is widely regarded as the cornerstone of South African security legislation. It created the new offence of "terrorism", which is defined in very broad terms as any activity likely "to endanger the maintenance of law and order". Activities which may have any of 12 listed "results" fall within this category. They include activities which may result in the promotion of "general dislocation, disturbance or disorder"; "prejudice" to "any industry or undertaking"; "the achievement of any political aim, including the bringing about of any social or economic change, by violent or forcible means"; cause "financial loss to any person or the State"; increase "hostility between the White and other inhabitants of the Republic"; "obstruction" to the "free movement of any traffic on land, at sea or in the air"; or "embarrassment" to "the administration of the affairs of the State". The law covers activities which take place in South Africa, Namibia, or even abroad.

Those engaging in activities which may have any of the afore-mentioned consequences may be judged under the Act to have committed the offence of participation in terrorist activities. In so doing, they are presumed to have acted with intent unless they can demonstrate beyond "reasonable doubt" that they did not intend their actions to have any of the listed results. In other words, the onus of proof is placed upon the accused to show the innocence of their intentions rather than on the State to prove their guilt.

The "Sabotage Act", as Section 21 of the General Law Amendment Act of 1962 is commonly known, has many similarities with the later and more far-reaching Terrorism Act. It defines as "sabotage" any "wrongful and wilful act which injures, destroys, renders useless, puts out of action, obstructs, tampers with, pollutes or endangers the health of the public; law and order; public services and means of transport and communication; and property". The maximum penalty is death. As with the Terrorism Act, the onus of proof is upon the accused person to show that there was no intent to commit the offence of "sabotage".

The Terrorism, "Sabotage" and Internal Security Acts are all applicable not only in South Africa but in Namibia also, while that country remains under South African occupation. They are not applicable in the Transkei, where they have been replaced by a new Public Security Act. This not only duplicates the main provisions of the South African security laws but adds a clause to the effect that any person convicted of repudiating the sovereignty and independence of the Transkei, or claiming that the Transkei is a part of South Africa, is guilty of treason and liable to the death penalty. Introduced in early 1977, several months after South Africa declared the Transkei "independent", the Public Security Act was made retroactive to 1975. It is clearly designed to effect wider recognition of the independent status claimed for the Transkei by Chief Matanzima's administration and thus help to legitimize the South African Government's "bantustan" programme.

Political trials in South Africa are conducted summarily, i.e., without previous judicial determination of whether there is a *prima facie* case. They are heard either in the Supreme Court or before a regional magistrate. The absence of the necessity for the State to show a *prima facie* case is generally considered to be disadvantageous to defendants, since defence counsel may be kept in ignorance of the precise nature of a State case until the actual start of a trial. Cases on appeal from the Supreme Court are referred to the Appellate Division of the Supreme Court of South Africa, which sits in Bloemfontein.

Despite the spate of political trials involving offences under the Terrorism and "Sabotage" Acts which occurred in the period 1973–77, no death sentences were imposed for political offences.

Convicted murderers comprise the majority of prisoners sentenced to death and executed in South Africa. Murder is punished with death unless extenuating circumstances are held to apply. The death penalty may not, however, be imposed upon pregnant women or people under 18. When a death penalty is passed and upheld upon appeal, a report is sent to the State President who may then make a recommendation for clemency. At the same time, a report is also passed to the Department of Justice for scrutiny and for a decision as to whether an execution should take place. Executions are authorized by the Minister of Justice and are normally carried out at Pretoria Central Prison. It is not unusual for multiple executions to take place.

Most of the prisoners sentenced to death and executed are Africans. This is partly a result of the fact that Africans comprise not only the overwhelming majority of the population but also constitute the group which, under the apartheid system, suffer the greatest social deprivation. However, it is also widely believed that the courts tend to discriminate against Africans and impose on them heavier penalties for specific offences than they would normally impose on members of other racial groups, in particular the White group. No comprehensive study of this subject has been undertaken, but individual cases do lend support to the general supposition. In cases involving cross-racial rape, for example, White men are not executed for the rape of Black women but in the case of rape of a White woman by a Black man, the assailant's race is regarded as an "aggravating factor", and quite frequently the death penalty is imposed.

Murder trials involving White people certainly arouse much more publicity and public comment than those involving Blacks. Moreover, White people accused of murder or other serious crimes tend to have the benefits of eminent and experienced defence counsel, who try to ensure, where it is necessary, that psychiatric evidence is available. In most instances where the defendant is Black, this is not the case. The following official figures for the years 1973 to 1975 provide a clear indication of the extent to which Africans predominate as victims of the death penalty in South Africa.

| Executions carried out (by year) | Africans | Asians | Coloureds | Whites |
|---|---|---|---|---|
| 1973 | 29 | – | 12 | 1 |
| 1974 | 30 | 2 | 7 | 1 |
| 1975 | 50 | – | 18 | – |

A succession of deaths of detainees in security police custody in the period 1976–77 focused international attention on this issue. After the outbreak of the Soweto disturbances in June 1976, the deaths of political detainees occurred with unprecedented frequency. At least 20 are known to have died in security police custody between August 1976 and September 1977 (when the Black Consciousness movement leader, Steve Biko, died in detention in Pretoria). Even this figure may be an underestimate, because of uncertainty in some cases as to whether particular detainees were arrested for political reasons, as their families claim, or for non-political offences, as the authorities state.

In fact, the death rate for people detained by the South African police is even more alarming than the above figure for political detainees suggests. In 1976, for example, of 130 untried prisoners who died in police custody, only 13 were officially recognized as having been held under security laws.

### **Sudan** *(Sudan Democratic Republic)*

Little information on the death penalty in the Sudan is available to Amnesty International but treason, mutiny, attempting to overthrow the State and premeditated murder are capital offences, carrying a mandatory death sentence.

It appears, however, that the majority of executions since 1974 have been of people (mostly military) convicted of mutiny or killing soldiers, or of attempting to overthrow the Government by means of a *coup*. They have been tried by military courts, and the only available avenue of appeal is to petition the President for clemency.

In July 1975, 10 soldiers were executed by firing squad for a mutiny which had taken place in March of the same year, and which resulted in the death of the commanding officer and seven soldiers. Two other death penalties were commuted and 48 other accused were jailed in the same case. After another mutiny in February 1976, two soldiers were executed in October 1976.

In January and February 1976, 19 people were executed following their conviction for taking part in an abortive *coup* attempt in September 1975. One sentence was commuted, but all the rest were carried out on the day they were confirmed by the President. In all, 105 people were tried for the same offence, the others receiving prison terms. In August 1976, 98 people were executed over a period of two days for their alleged part in an unsuccessful *coup* attempt in July 1976. Two other death sentences were imposed on people convicted *in absentia* of being leaders of the *coup* attempt. Allegations that a further 200 or more people were secretly executed in custody have been denied by the Sudan Government.

All death sentences were by firing squad, and were carried out in prison.

On 5 July 1977, six people were sentenced to death for their involvement in the July 1976 attempted *coup*, in which they had all been injured. They were executed shortly afterwards. However, on 18 July, President Nimeiri announced a national reconciliation with opposition groups, including an amnesty for all political prisoners and those convicted of involvement in the unsuccessful *coup*.

***Tanzania** (the Union Republic of)*

Although the mainland (formerly Tanganyika) and Zanzibar are united within the Union Republic of Tanzania, they have different legal systems, legal codes and procedures for appeal.

The Tanzania Government informed the UN in January 1972: "With regard to the problem of capital punishment, the Tanzania Government is currently studying it with a view to its possible further restriction or total abolition in Tanzania." On Zanzibar, there is no official abolitionist policy, although the Attorney General in his summing up at the conclusion of the appeal in a major treason trial in December 1976, stated that he personally was an abolitionist.

Throughout Tanzania, the death penalty is the mandatory punishment for treason and premeditated murder. The definition of treason includes: murder or attempted murder of the President: conspiracy to overthrow the Government; intimidation of the executive or judiciary; assisting enemies of the Republic; armed insurrection; committing an act designed to impede the maintenance of public order or the operations of the defence forces. The death penalty is carried out by hanging within a prison, although in Zanzibar the Afro-Shirazi Party proposed in 1972 that the death penalty for treason (in respect of those accused of plotting to overthrow the State in connection with the assassination of the President of Zanzibar, Abeid Karume, in April 1972) should be carried out by firing squad in public.

In Zanzibar, a mandatory death penalty has been decreed by the Zanzibar Revolutionary Council for the smuggling of cloves. It is also a capital offence to "enter the island with the intention of organizing counter-revolutionary activities against the Government or inciting others to do the same".

On the mainland the death penalty may be imposed by the High Court, with a right of judicial appeal to the East African Court of Appeal. Defendants are allowed their own legal representation, or counsel provided by the State, and trial is in open court. There is also right of petition to the President to exercise his prerogative of mercy. Pregnant women and young people are not executed.

In Zanzibar, the death penalty may be imposed by the People's Court, after which there is right of appeal to the High Court, and to the Supreme Council of the Afro-Shirazi Party, and a possibility to petition for clemency to the President of the Zanzibar Revolutionary Council.

On the mainland there have been no executions for political offences, but several people have been convicted and given death sentences for premeditated murder. In nearly all cases, these have been commuted by the President. Tanzania reported to the UN in 1974 that of 232 death penalties imposed between 1969 and 1974, only four had been carried out: presumably the others were commuted to prison terms. In February 1977, five executions took place in Dodoma Prison; a further 60 or more prisoners were under sentence of death.

In Zanzibar, it is not known how many death sentences have been imposed or carried out during 1973–77. Death sentences for murder appear to be commuted in practice, and many of those sentenced to death for clove smuggling (19 in the period 1974–75) were pardoned. In the Zanzibar Treason Trial of 1973–74, 42 death penalties had been imposed by the People's Court. Thirteen of these sentences were imposed *in absentia* on people detained on the mainland but not handed over to the Zanzibar authorities because the Tanzanian authorities considered that defendants would not receive a fair trial. Eighteen of the 42 death sentences were commuted on appeal to the High Court of Zanzibar in 1975.

On 9 February 1977, the Supreme Council of the Afro-Shirazi Party announced the result of the final judicial appeal in the Zanzibar Treason Trial. Seven death sentences were confirmed (four of them *in absentia* on mainland detainees), and 17 were commuted to 30- or 35-year prison terms (six of them *in absentia*). The remaining death sentences awaited review by the Chairman of the Zanzibar Revolutionary Council, Aboud Jumbe. No result had been announced by the end of 1977.

**N.B.** After the disintegration of the East African Community at the end of 1977, provision was being made in Tanzania for the establishment of a national Court of Appeal.

### *Togo (the Togolese Republic)*

The Togolese Government stated in 1969 that the question of the abolition of the death penalty would be examined by a plenary commission. No details of the results of this examination are available to Amnesty International.

### ***Tunisia*** *(the Republic of)*

Under the 1956 Penal Code, the death penalty may be imposed for a variety of offences, including premeditated murder and arson of an inhabited building. Attempts against the life of the President and certain activities which threaten the external security of the country may also be punished with death. The President has the right of pardon.

Executions are carried out by hanging. However, insufficient data is available concerning the extent to which the death penalty is used in practice. A Libyan national was sentenced to death in May 1975 after being convicted of planning to kidnap members of the Tunisian Cabinet. It is not known whether the sentence was carried out.

*Uganda (the Republic of)*

The death penalty in Uganda cannot be seen merely in terms of executions being carried out after the completion of judicial trials. Murder committed or acquiesced in by government is a common phenomenon. Such murders are dealt with in Chapter IV; this survey contains reference to judicial executions alone.

Until the 1971 military *coup* which brought President Idi Amin to power, the death penalty, which was and is within the jurisdiction of the High Court, was reserved for treason, murder, also kidnapping with intent to murder, and both robbery and attempted robbery using deadly weapons. After 1971, rule by Presidential decree replaced other forms of legislation. Security forces officers were given immunity from prosecution and licence to shoot on sight those they suspected of armed robbery (which already carried the death penalty). In January 1973, the military tribunal was empowered to try citizens for capital offences of treason, sedition and subversion. Its members were appointed by the Defence Council. In June 1973, the President decreed that "acts calculated to intimidate or alarm members of the public or bring the military under contempt or into disrepute" would be tried by military tribunal. The death penalty could be imposed by the tribunal for this offence. In March 1975, the death penalty was decreed for various "economic" crimes – overcharging, hoarding, smuggling, corruption, fraud, embezzlement, illegal currency sales.

In January 1977 a new capital offence was decreed – "diverting certain commodities to unscheduled destinations, even within Uganda". This covered a wide range of basic commodities and was an attempt to stop widespread smuggling. Offenders were to be brought before the Economic Crimes Military Tribunal. It is not known how many have been condemned and executed under this decree.

Accepted judicial and legal safeguards do not exist in the system of military tribunals. Members of the tribunals have no judicial training and many, like Major Juma Ali, the Chairman of the Central Military Tribunal in 1975–76, have very little education.

Defendants are denied any choice of counsel; the legally qualified "court adviser" has no power to intervene where rules of evidence or procedure are not followed; trials are often closed to the public and transcripts are not available. There is no appeal from these tribunals to a non-military legal authority, the only recourse available to the defendant being to petition the President for clemency.

The largest category of formal executions carried out from 1973 to 1976 comprises persons convicted of carrying out guerilla warfare. In February 1973, 12 persons were executed in public by firing squad for alleged guerilla activities, after conviction by special military tribunal. Facilities for defence were not available. Public executions have taken place in various districts of Uganda since then, but how many is not known.

Four soldiers were hanged in Luzira Prison in March 1974 for atrocities against civilians; three civilians and one policeman were hanged for robbery and murder at the same time.

It is not known how many people have been sentenced to death by military tribunals, but it appears that most of those sentenced have not yet been executed.

Twenty people sentenced to death by Major Juma Ali in 1976 were pardoned when he was transferred – reportedly on the grounds of corruption. Others who have received the death penalty have subsequently been granted clemency – for example, the British lecturer, Dennis Hills, who was sentenced to death in 1975.

On 25 March 1977, President Amin announced that 37 convicted murderers, whose appeals had been rejected by the East African Court of Appeal (see last paragraph), would be executed. Fifteen others had their sentences commuted, while one man was pardoned and freed. It is thought that the executions took place immediately after this announcement. It is not known how long elapsed between the commission of the offence and execution – probably several years in some cases.

On 23 July 1977 the National Theatre Director, Dan Kintu, the playwright, John Male, and an Under-Secretary at the Ministry of Culture, John Sebuliba, were executed secretly after trial by military tribunal, also secret. They were alleged to have insulted the President in a play performed at the Uganda National Theatre.

On 9 September 1977, 15 men were publicly executed after trial by military tribunal, despite widespread appeals for clemency. Twelve of them had been arrested in February in connection with the "plot" allegedly organized by Anglican Archbishop Janani Luwum (who was murdered in February 1977 – see Chapter IV). They included Abdalla Anyuru, the former Public Service Commission Chairman, John Olobo, the Assistant Labour Commissioner, Y.Y. Okot, the Chief Inspector of Schools, senior police and prison officials, and others. Their trial was in secret, and they were denied legal representation. Three other men sentenced to death on other charges were executed at the same time.

**N.B.** After the East African Community disintegrated at the end of 1977, provision was being made in Uganda for the establishment of a national Court of Appeal.

### *Upper Volta (the) (the Republic of)*

The death penalty is reserved for "rare and exceptional cases". A right of appeal to a higher court and the possibility of petitioning the President for mercy exist in the civilian courts; the latter alone applies in the military court system.

### *Zaire (the Republic of)*

Embezzlement of public funds of 10,000 *zaires* or more became punishable by death in a Presidential decree dated 1973; according to information which Amnesty International has, no sentence has been passed under this decree.

In September 1975, seven army officers were sentenced to death after trial *in camera* by military tribunal, for plotting an abortive *coup* against the Government of President Mobutu Sese Seko some months earlier. Available information indicates that no execution has yet been carried out, but there has also been no report of clemency or commutation of the sentences.

In the wake of the Shaba War in March–May 1977, when a force described as ex-Katangan Gendarmes invaded southern Zaire, several leading military officers and political figures were accused of high treason and, upon conviction, sentenced to death. They included Colonel Mampa Ngankwe Salamayi, former commander of military operations in Shaba Province, who was found guilty of high treason, endangering state security and misappropriation of public funds, and sentenced to death in August 1977. It is not known whether he was executed. At the same time, Monguya Mbenge, a former Governor of Shaba Province, was sentenced to death *in absentia* on treason charges. This occurred after he published a book in support of General Mbumba, leader of the "Katangan Gendarmes", in Belgium, where he had been living for five years.

In August 1977, the Foreign Minister, Karl I. Bond, was abruptly dismissed from power and accused of treason. Widely regarded as President Mobutu's most influential adviser, he was accused of failing to give the President information about Mbumba's plans to invade Zaire the previous March. He was convicted by a State Security Court and sentenced to death in September 1977, but, perhaps as a result of international pressure, President Mobutu commuted his sentence two days later to life imprisonment.

***Zambia** (the Republic of)*

Since independence in 1964, the death penalty has been retained under the Zambian Penal Code on a mandatory basis for treason and murder. In 1974, the mandatory death penalty was also introduced for "aggravated robbery", this being defined as theft involving the actual or threatened use of violence. However, under Section 25 of the Penal Code, people under the age of 18 and pregnant women are not executed.

People charged with capital offences are tried in the High Court, normally by a judge sitting alone, and after a preliminary examination in a lower court. Cases in which the death penalty is imposed are referred automatically to the Zambian Appeal Court. No execution may be carried out until the Appeal Court has made its pronouncement on the case. If conviction and sentence are upheld by the Appeal Court, the condemned person may then petition the President for clemency. Section 54 of the Zambian Independence Order, 1964, authorized the President, as Head of State, to grant pardons to those convicted and to suspend or commute sentences. Prisoners who have been condemned to death and denied clemency are hanged at Kabwe Maximum Security Prison.

Three major political trials resulted in the imposition of the death penalty in the period under review. Two of these trials involved people charged with high treason and resulted from political developments within Zambia. The third trial, that of Tyupo Shumba Chigowe, was the result of a political dispute in the Zimbabwe African Nationalist Union (ZANU), a banned Rhodesian African nationalist organization then based in Zambia (see below).

After their arrest at the beginning of 1973, Timothy Kalimbwe, Bothwell Kabila and Joseph Muvangwa were brought to trial in mid 1974 on charges of high treason. They were alleged to have undergone illegal military training in Namibia, to have recruited other Zambians for training, and to have intended to return to Zambia in order to bring about the violent overthrow of President Kenneth Kaunda's United National Independence Party (UNIP) Government. They were convicted and sentenced to death in July 1974. The Appeal Court subsequently set aside the sentences imposed on Muvangwa and Bothwell Kabila, but confirmed the imposition of the death penalty in Timothy Kalimbwe's case.

During 1975, the four alleged ringleaders of the same plot were brought to trial in the Lusaka High Court. They included William Chipango, a former Mayor of Livingstone, and Sefulo Kakoma, a former Member of Parliament for the Sesheke area. Allegations of ill-treatment during detention were made by the defendants during the course of the trial. Judgment was delivered in June 1976. The four defendants were all convicted and sentenced to death. They were acquitted on appeal and freed in 1978.

The third political trial to result in the imposition of a death penalty was that involving Tyupo Shumba Chigowe. He was charged with the murder of another ZANU member, Edgar Madekurozwa, convicted and sentenced to death in the Lusaka High Court in April 1976. During his trial, part of which was conducted *in camera,* Chigowe alleged that he had been physically assaulted while detained by Zambian security police. He was acquitted of all charges by the Appeal Court and released early in 1977.

## ASIA AND AUSTRALASIA

Legal provision for the death penalty exists in every Asian country: Hong Kong is the one partial exception, where treason and murder are punishable by death, but where all death sentences since 1966 have been commuted to life imprisonment in accordance with British Government policy.

Except in the countries of South Asia, the death penalty tends apparently to be used as a way of maintaining law and order. This seems to be the case particularly in The People's Republic of China, where recently at least 100 people have been reported to have been sentenced to death, and some of them summarily executed, for a wide range of political and criminal offences. Examples include the case of a man said to have been sentenced to death in November 1976 for defacing wall posters announcing the appointment of Hua Kuo-feng as Party Chairman. In February 1977, a person was reported to have been executed for the crimes of buggery and sadism; further cases reported have involved such offences as the distribution of leaflets, murder, robbery and rape.

The severe use of the death penalty is also to be observed in attempts to suppress drug trafficking. Several Asian countries, including Singapore, Malaysia, Indonesia, Burma, Taiwan and the Philippines, have passed laws making the death penalty mandatory for a variety of drug offences. In Singapore, for example, under legislation recently amended, the mere possession of more than three grammes of morphine or two grammes of diamorphine (heroin) for the purposes of trafficking carries a mandatory death sentence; at least four people have been sentenced to death under the amended law. In Thailand, a man accused of possession of 14 kilogrammes of heroin was executed without trial in April 1977.

It is in matters relating to trial and in appeal procedures affecting capital offences that provisions and practices vary most widely in Asian countries. As one extreme example, the Prime Minister of Thailand has sweeping constitutional powers to order executions without trial in cases allegedly affecting national security: it was acting under such powers, derived from Article 21 of the Constitution, that the Prime Minister, Thanin Kraivichien, was able to order the execution without trial of the accused heroin trafficker mentioned above. Six days after that execution, the Prime Minister ordered another execution without trial of a Thai general accused of involvement in an abortive *coup* attempt. In Indonesia, appeals against death sentences imposed by extraordinary military tribunals on people accused of subversion were similarly refused, until, in recent years, subversion cases were increasingly heard before the ordinary courts with the normal appellate process up to the Supreme Court.

The large-scale killings reported in Democratic Kampuchea (Cambodia) since the change of Government in March 1975 appear to reflect the total abrogation of the judicial process; according to refugee accounts, large numbers of people have been summarily killed.

In a different context, there have been mass trials in the People's Republic of China; after sentence, the defendants were immediately executed. It would appear that appeal against death sentences imposed in mass trials is not possible, although appeal to the higher courts has been affected by a resolution adopted in 1957 by the National People's Congress, requiring all death sentences to be submitted for approval to the Supreme Court.

In the law of the Philippines, a provision requires a unanimous judgment of the Supreme Court to confirm the death penalty in every case on appeal. Elsewhere, especially in Indonesia, the long period necessary for the appeal process up to the Supreme Court in many cases provides a substantial delay – sometimes one of many years – before the death sentence is carried out. Moreover, although, in many countries, there is provision for acts of presidential clemency, nowhere in Asia has the ready availability of such clemency been marked.

The practice of imposing and carrying out sentences of death varies in Asia between those countries partly following traditional practices, and those tending to follow the inherited practices of the former colonial power. Thus, it is noticeable that the countries of East Asia tend to follow the indigenous, historical approach of harsh punishment for those considered to have committed serious crimes. The extensive use of the death penalty in the People's Republic of China, and to a lesser degree in South Korea, Japan and Taiwan, reflects this tendency. Elsewhere, particularly in those countries that have become independent from former British imperial rule, the colonial provisions for the death penalty have been retained. Indonesia has retained the provisions of the former Dutch colonial Penal Code, which does not allow for the death penalty for murder. Historical inheritance is indicated also in the methods of execution. Electrocution is used in the Philippines, while hanging is common in South Asian countries and those formerly under British colonial rule. In Thailand and the People's Republic of China, execution is by shooting.

The region as a whole tends to be noteworthy in the emphasis given to the death penalty for certain categories of capital offences other than treason and murder. In many Asian countries, the death penalty is available for the offences of rape or drug trafficking. A few countries impose it for economic offences; these include the People's Republic of China and Indonesia.

Throughout Asia – with the notable exception of Sri Lanka – there is not strongly expressed public opinion in favour of abolition of the death penalty. The suspension of the death penalty in Sri Lanka in 1956, however, was a move towards abolition. A majority of the Commission on Capital Punishment, set up by the then Prime Minister, S.W.R.D. Bandaranaike, recommended that the death penalty remain suspended, and came to the conclusion that the death penalty had no deterrent effect in cases of homicide. Although the death penalty was reintroduced in 1959, following the assassination of Mr Bandaranaike, demand for its abolition has continued to be firm and clearly expressed.

In India, there has been considerable public debate on the question of abolition. The execution of two suspected "Naxalites" in December 1975, apparently carried out to create an example, provoked strong protest from Indian lawyers and supporters of civil liberties. The Report of the Law Commission in 1967 had put forward remarkably weak arguments for retaining the death penalty.

In Japan, in July 1975, the Prime Minister's Office announced that it had conducted a poll purporting to show that 57 per cent of those people questioned were in opposition to the abolition of the death penalty.

On the South Asian sub-continent, the death penalty has been retained for those offences for which it was introduced during British colonial government. Similar provisions apply in the various penal codes of India, Pakistan and Bangladesh, but in Pakistan, the death penalty was additionally introduced under the Explosive Substances (Amendment) Act of 1975 for the offence of keeping or using explosives. Under martial law in Bangladesh the death penalty was introduced for a number of offences in addition to those already punishable by death under the penal code.

The position of Nepal is exceptional, in that it is the only country in South Asia known to Amnesty International to have abolished the death penalty for ordinary crimes (in 1931). However, in 1975, two people were sentenced to death – one for an attempt on the life of the king, the other for treason.

Except in the case of Sri Lanka, very little statistical information is available to Amnesty International on the number of people in Asia sentenced to death by the courts each year, or on what percentage of them is executed. But it is known that in India and Pakistan, dozens of people are executed every year by hanging for crimes punishable under the Criminal Code.

The detailed reports that follow are restricted to those countries on which information is available to Amnesty International. Information on the application of the death penalty is not available from the Democratic People's Republic of Korea (North Korea) or from Mongolia.

### *Afghanistan (the Republic of, later the Democratic Republic of)*

Since 1973, when Sardar Mohammed Daud, the President of Afghanistan, came to power in a military *coup d'état*, there has been a series of cases involving people sentenced to death for alleged complicity in attempts to overthrow his Government.

These alleged counter-*coup* attempts, together with other forms of alleged anti-Government activity, particularly in the provinces of Afghanistan, have given rise to a number of military trials of those allegedly involved.

The first counter-*coup* attempt announced by the Daud Government was an alleged plot by ex-air force chief General Abdul Razzaq, General Khan Mohammed Khan of the army, ex-Prime Minister Hashim Maiwandwal and others to overthrow the Daud administration with the complicity of Pakistan. The military trial of the accused ended in December 1973 with death sentences being passed on the two generals and sentences of between four and 15 years' imprisonment passed on 20 others. Hashim Maiwandwal, also sentenced to death, was said to have committed suicide in prison during the trial.

A second alleged plot came to light in June 1974 with the reported arrest of 200 army officers and students said to be working for the restoration of a conservative Muslim state. The plot was alleged to be led by Habibur Rahman with 11 others, mostly army officers. As the result of a trial by military tribunal in August 1974, Habibur Rahman was sentenced to death and was later reported to have been executed. Prison terms ranging from three years to life were passed on the other defendants.

All the defendants in these trials were tried by military tribunal, in accordance with the ruling in September 1973 of the Central Committee of the Afghan Republic (a body that has since ceased to function) that "the trials of individuals, whether military or civilian, accused of causing disorder in the internal and external security of the Government of the Republic of Afghanistan will be by military tribunal."

On 7 August 1977, the official daily newspaper *Gham'hurie jat* reported the execution of three alleged anti-Government agitators.

Referring to the official announcement in August 1975 of the arrest of "agitators carrying weapons" allegedly responsible for attempting to create unrest by means of robbery and other disturbances in various provinces of Afghanistan, including Parwan, Laghman and Paktia, the article in the paper named three men who, it said, had since been executed by firing squad on an unspecified date. The three men were Habib Rahman, alias Seif Ollah, a lecturer at Kabul University, described as the "leader of the agitators"; Khodja Mahfus, alias Mansur, also a lecturer at Kabul University, described as the leader of another group of agitators: and Mohammad Omar, a medical assistant, alleged to belong to a third group accused of conspiring to overthrow the Government. The article in *Gham'hurie jat* also gave the names of 21 others originally sentenced to death in connection with the alleged acts of agitation whose sentences were later commuted to life imprisonment.

The same article referred to the constitutional provision by which all death sentences must be confirmed by the President.

***Australia** (the Commonwealth of)*

In Australia, there exists Commonwealth (Federal) legislation, and the legislation of the individual States and Territories. In 1968, the Australian Commonwealth Government abolished the death penalty, except for the offences of treason and murder; this is presumed to apply only in the territories under its direct jurisdiction: these include the Australian Capital Territory (the area around Canberra) and the Northern Territory.

The position in the six Australian States is as follows: Queensland abolished the death penalty in 1921, Tasmania in 1968, Victoria in 1975. Western Australia retains the death penalty for piracy with violence as well as for treason and wilful murder (Section 282, Criminal Code 1913). South Australia retains the death penalty for piracy with violence as well as for treason and wilful murder. However, the South Australia Criminal Law Consolidation Act 1935 specifies that the death penalty is mandatory only for murder. "For treason and other felonies punishable by death, the court may abstain from pronouncing the death penalty." Section 301 of the Act states that the Governor, acting on the advice of the Executive Council, may grant pardon to a person sentenced to death, or may commute the sentence to life imprisonment. In New South Wales, the death penalty was abolished for all offences except treason and piracy with violence, by an amendment of the Crimes Act 1955. Treason includes the putting to death or the imprisonment of the monarch or his or her heirs and successors. Deposing the soverign is punishable by life imprisonment (Sections 11 and 12, Crimes Act 1955).

Appeals from the Supreme Courts of the States and the Territories are to the High Court of Australia. In cases within non-Federal jurisdictions, appeal may go from the Supreme Courts of the States direct to the Judicial Committee of the Privy Council in London.

Throughout Australia death sentences are carried out by hanging. The last instance of hanging in Australia was in February 1967, when a man was executed for the murder of a warder during an escape from a prison in the State of Victoria.

***Bangladesh** (the People's Republic of)*

The establishment of the State of Bangladesh after nine months of intensive fighting in East Bengal was notable for the absence of large-scale executions of those who had backed the Pakistan army's intervention and opposed the establishment of an independent state (i.e., those called "collaborators"). The Bangladesh Collaborators Order, introduced by the new Government, made criminal law offences such as the "waging of war against the State", murder, and *dacoity* (robbery by five or more persons) punishable by death under the Penal Code, subject to the jurisdiction of special tribunals. Amnesty International does not know of any cases in which "collaborators" were sentenced to death, by special tribunals set up under the order, solely on being convicted of "waging war against the State" or "collaboration with the occupation forces". A few cases are known of people having been sentenced to death for kidnapping, murder and *dacoity* committed during the war. It is not known whether these executions were carried out.

The death penalty could be applied on a wider scale after the introduction of the Emergency Powers Act of 25 January 1975, in which the death penalty was made applicable for any act "contravening or attempting to contravene any emergency provisions". The Act was introduced during the last period of Government under President Sheikh Mujibur Rahman, the first Bangladesh Head of State, during which there had been a marked deterioration in the maintenance of law and order in the country.

According to a report in *Le Monde* of 11 July 1974, the then Home Minister, Mansoor Ali, stated in Parliament that 264 political leaders and militants had been killed between 1 January 1972 and 31 May 1974, including four members of the Constituent Assembly and three Members of Parliament. In the first five months of 1974, 69 political assassinations had taken place. Victims of such killings were members of the then ruling Awami League, and leaders and members of various underground left-wing groups.

Martial law was declared on 15 August 1975, following the assassination of Sheikh Mujibur Rahman. Four of his closest associates, who had been arrested after the military *coup,* were killed in jail on the night of 2/3 November, on the eve of a second military *coup.* They included two former Prime Ministers, Tajuddin Ahmed and Mansoor Ali. The circumstances in which these killings were allowed to take place have never been clear, since, according to a report in *Le Monde*, dated 13 November 1975, those who came to power after the third military *coup* disbanded a commission of inquiry set up to investigate the incident.

The new authorities immediately introduced legislation providing for the application of the death penalty for offences including corruption, the illegal possession of arms, sedition, treason and "misuse of influence".

Trials on such charges take place before martial law courts, whose jurisdiction is extended to cover acts committed before martial law was declared. Appeal against sentence of death can be made only to the Government. Provisions for the application of the death penalty were widened on 27 October 1975, when martial law was amended so that the death penalty could be imposed for the crimes of corruption or "activity detrimental to the security or economic interest of the State". Under the Martial Law (Fourth Amendment) Regulation, certain activities prejudicial to the defence, security or interests of the State, such as inciting mutiny, or any other anti-State activity, carry the death penalty. (This Amendment came into effect on 2 November 1975.) Furthermore, the Martial Law (20th Amendment) Regulation 1976 introduced the death penalty for former military or police personnel who attempted to undermine the allegiance to the Government of serving colleagues. This would include political activities which could be categorized as inimical to defence or police interests. It also covers the general concept of anti-State activity.

The 20th Martial Law Amendment was promulgated only 10 days after Colonel Abu Taher, a hero of the Bangladesh freedom movement and commander of the People's Revolutionary Army (the armed section of the left-wing JSD or National Socialist Party), had been sentenced to death on charges of plotting to overthrow the Government and subvert the armed forces. Colonel Taher was hanged in Dacca Central Jail on 21 July 1976, only four days after a swift and secret trial had taken place inside the jail. A petition for clemency had been rejected by the President of Bangladesh. News of the Colonel's execution was not confirmed until weeks after it had taken place. Until 1976, so far as Amnesty International is aware, this was the only execution following a trial of a political prisoner to have taken place in Bangladesh since independence.

Large-scale executions took place in October 1977 following two attempted military *coups* in Bogra, an army base north of Dacca on 30 September, and in Dacca on 2 October, in which, according to unofficial reports, at least 230 people died. Official reports stated that by 20 October, 37 people had already been executed following trial by specially constituted military tribunals for their alleged involvement in the Dacca incident. By 28 October, 55 others were awaiting execution after being sentenced by similar tribunals in connection with the Bogra incident. Amnesty International publicly opposed these executions on humanitarian grounds; it also opposed them because of the unsatisfactory nature of military trial procedures under which trials are held *in camera,* without the right of appeal to any court of law, thus falling short of internationally accepted standards.

The Government has not published the names of any of those executed and, as of December 1977, Amnesty International had strong reason to believe that executions were still continuing (in December 1977, 15 military men were reliably reported to have been executed in Comilla Jail). Amnesty International received a list, dated December 1977, of 129 military personnel executed after the *coup* attempts, as well as the names of 27 others still awaiting execution. In spite of assurances given to the organization's Secretary General by the President in Dacca on 29 December 1977 that executions had stopped, there was reason to believe that they still continued and that at least 130 and perhaps several hundred military men had been executed in the months after September 1977, following trials of an unsatisfactory nature.

Against a background of conflict on the Indo-Bangladesh border between the

Bangladesh army and guerilla supporters of the former régime of Sheikh Mujibur Rahman, the Government again amended the Martial Law on 13 November 1976: the death penalty became applicable also for anyone convicted of "armed insurrection or sabotage". According to a Government statement, this meant people "waging war, making insurrection, or ... illegally entering Bangladesh with intent to do any such thing".

***Burma** (the Socialist Republic of the Union of)*

Amnesty International has no information on the number of death sentences imposed in the Socialist Republic of Burma, or on the number of executions which have taken place in the period 1973–77. The Burmese Government permits the publication of verdicts in cases of high treason but Amnesty International is not in a position to list the other offences which carry the death penalty. The following information is limited, therefore, to cases of alleged high treason. This offence may be punished by death or life imprisonment.

In March 1974 U Soe, a former leader of the Red Flag Communist Party, was sentenced to death by a Special Criminal Court under Section 122 (1) of the Penal Code. His appeal was rejected by the Special Criminal Court. U Soe was found guilty of high treason.

In April 1976, Tin Maung U, a former Burmese student leader, was found guilty by a Special Crimes Tribunal of plotting to assassinate Burmese Government leaders and rebelling against the State. He was sentenced to death.

In November 1976, Lo Nsing-han, the so-called "opium king" of South-east Asia, was sentenced to death on charges of high treason. His trial had taken over three years to complete.

In January 1977, Captain Ohn Kyaw Myint was sentenced to death for high treason for his involvement in a plot to assassinate the President and to overthrow the Government of Burma. He was given one week to appeal against the death sentence.

***Cambodia***

See Kampuchea (Democratic Kampuchea) [Cambodia]

***China** (the People's Republic of)*

Under the Act of the People's Republic of China for Punishment of Counter-revolution (1951), the death penalty may be imposed for, among other things, collaborating with "imperialists to betray the motherland" (Article 3), insurrection (Article 4), the commission of "major evil crimes" in a mass armed uprising (Article 5), espionage or aiding the enemy (Article 6), participation in organizations of counter-revolutionary secret agents or spies (Article 7), making use of feudal societies to conduct counter-revolutionary activity (Article 8), planning or indulging in certain major acts of provocation or incitement, with a counter-revolutionary purpose (this would include, for example, provoking dissension, conducting counter-revolutionary propaganda and agitation, or spreading rumours). The death penalty also exists for the offences of secretly crossing the border of the State with a counter-revolutionary purpose (Article 11), organizing mass prison raids or violent prison breaks (Article 12) or harbouring major counter-revolutionary criminals (Article 13).

For offences under Articles 3 and 4, the minimum sentence is life imprisonment; Article 5 specifies no minimum and the other minimum sentences range from three years to 10 years.

Article 14 provides for exemption from punishment or a reduced punishment for those defendants who have, for example, "atoned", who were originally coerced into committing the offence or who voluntarily surrendered to the authorities.

Under the Act of the People's Republic of China for Punishment of Corruption (1952), the death penalty may be imposed for corruption where the amount involved is 100,000,000 *yuan* or more and the circumstances of the case are especially serious, or for purchasing economic intelligence for private interest or obtaining the same by force.

Under the Provisional Statute for the Punishment of Crimes that Endanger the State Currency (1951), the death penalty may be imposed for very serious cases of counterfeiting state banknotes for counter-revolutionary purposes or for private gain.

The *Lectures on the general principles of criminal law of the People's Republic of China* published in 1957 by the Central Political-Legal Cadres School in Peking, make it clear that the death sentence should not be passed on pregnant women or minors. However, in the case of the former, the *Lectures* refer to a text approved by the Ministry of Justice, the relevant part of which reads as follows:

> *"For the protection of the life and normal development of a child in the womb a criminal who is pregnant generally shall not be sentenced to death. If death alone can pacify the people's anger, it* [the death penalty] *shall be pronounced one year after the birth of the child. . . ."* (Jerome A. Cohen, *The Criminal Process in the People's Republic of China, 1949–1963,* Harvard University Press, 1968, p.538)

Chinese law provides for one appeal to a superior court. If the defendant does not accept the sentence, an application for review can be made to a People's Court at the next higher level (Organic Law of the People's Court 1954, Article 3). In death penalty cases, there is an automatic review by a High People's Court, even if the defendant does not appeal.

In July 1957, the Standing Committee of the National People's Congress adopted a resolution requiring that all death sentences be approved by the Supreme People's Court, after the sentence had been imposed, or reviewed by a High People's Court. (*Jen-min Jih-pao* (*People's Daily*), in Shao-chuan Leng, *Justice in Communist China*, Oceana Publications, New York, 1967, p. 167)

It has been the practice since quite early in the history of the People's Republic of China (PRC) that, in cases considered appropriate, execution is suspended for a period of two years. During such a period the condemned prisoner's behaviour determines whether execution actually takes place. If the prisoner repents and shows a willingness to reform, the death sentence may be commuted. Both suspension for two years and execution without this suspension have always coexisted and are now applied as two distinct and separate sanctions.

As with other sentences in the PRC, the imposition of the death penalty depends on the circumstances of the case and the background of the accused. According to Chinese legal officials, the criteria for determining whether or not a prisoner sentenced to death should be executed are the "seriousness" of the case and whether it provokes the "great indignation of the masses".

"Consultation with the masses" – generally neighbours and colleagues of the accused – does not necessarily influence the judges' decision. During a meeting in October 1974 with two American lawyers, members of the Law Faculty of Peking University said: "Usually before making a decision we will ask the masses who know the criminal to come and give their opinions. This does not mean that we would listen and follow what they say. The judges have to make an analysis of the opinion of the masses, and the final decision is made by the People's Court." (Richard P. Brown, "Present Day Law in the People's Republic of China", *American Bar Association Journal,* Vol. 61, April 1975, p. 477)

During the interview with American lawyers mentioned above, the representatives from the Law Faculty of Peking University stated: "Capital punishment is very rarely used. It is applied only to very serious cases, such as counter-revolutionary cases, assassination, and serious cases of murder, depending upon the intent and the result...It is subject to the approval of the Central Government... It is not a good way to carry out our proletariat dictatorship by killing people."

Comments on the death penalty made in the 1950s by Chinese leaders and legal cadres indicated that the principle of its gradual abolition was then being considered. However, the discussions on formalization of law which were taking place in the early years of the PRC have not continued. Since the Cultural Revolution in particular, political considerations have taken on increased importance in the treatment of offenders. Although, on several occasions, instructions were issued to restrict the use of the death penalty, there is no evidence that its partial or total abolition is being considered.

Official accounts of executions in China are rare and details of the cases and numbers of people executed in the past few years are generally lacking. However, since 1973, a few foreigners have been granted interviews with Chinese legal cadres, and travellers to China occasionally report seeing public notices in various Chinese cities announcing executions. A few examples are quoted below.

During an interview in August 1975 with Reuters' Correspondent, Peter Griffiths, the Deputy-Director of Tientsin People's High Court, Mr Hao, cited the case of a double murderer who had been executed. He explained that the man was permitted to appeal to an intermediate court, but his sentence was ratified and, after a mass rally to "criticize and repudiate" him, he was shot by a policeman on one of the city's several execution sites. Mr Hao said that the murderer had had "vicious motivation" and had aroused "great indignation among the masses". According to him, only a "small handful" of criminals face execution; rapists and murderers are liable to be shot, but the punishment depends far more on the circumstances of the case and the character of the accused (Reuters, 7 August 1975).

The matter may not have been put to Mr Hao, but this account made no reference to the approval of the death sentence by the Supreme People's Court. The information available on recent death penalty cases generally gives no indication as to whether the National People's Congress 1957 resolution requiring approval of death penalties by the Supreme Court is still applied. It is reported that, after the Cultural Revolution, the power to order execution had been passed down to the level of the basic People's Court (existing at county and city district level) but this has not been confirmed by official statements. In 1977, a judge from Shanghai High Court interviewed by a Swedish journalist mentioned that Supreme Court authorization was necessary for the carrying out of each death sentence.*

In the past ten years, it seems that the cases of people arrested went through a normal legal process mainly when there was political stability in the country, and that harsh measures were applied in periods of political tension. Reports referring to times of internal struggle and disorder, such as the Cultural Revolution, give some information on executions carried out immediately after mass public trials.† It also seems that some of the political campaigns which marked the end of the Cultural Revolution were followed by drastic measures to restore order in the country, including "exemplary" public executions.

During one such campaign, said to have been partly initiated by the former Vice-Chairman, Lin Piao, it is reported that a group of about 40 people in Canton were executed immediately after a mass public trial in the spring of 1970. The trial was of more than 60 people, several of whom had committed murders during the Cultural Revolution. A summary of the verdicts appeared later in official notices posted in the streets of the city.

It is also alleged that public executions are carried out in China's most important cities after mass public trials before the annual festivals–National Day (1 October), Labour Day (1 May) and the Chinese New Year; this is seen as a deterrent to possible disorders on those occasions.

From what is known of public executions, they generally take place immediately after the sentence has been pronounced during a mass meeting involving several hundred or, sometimes, several thousand people.

In such cases, the prisoner's hands are tied behind his or her back and, depending on local practice, the feet or some other part of the body may also be bound. A placard is fixed on the prisoner's back, on which name, crime and sometimes "death", circled in red, are inscribed. The prisoner kneels with his or her back to the executioner. The execution is then carried out by shooting by one or several officers of the Public Security or by soldiers.

In executions which are not carried out in public, it seems that the length of time between the sentencing and the execution varies from several days to several weeks or months, at the discretion of the local authorities. However, information on such executions is too sparse to give any account of how such a decision is reached. Equally, it is impossible to say whether a condemned person may receive visitors, although it is reported that when the execution follows closely after sentencing, permission for a visit is not granted.

No statistics are available for the number of death sentences and executions in 1973–77. The cases below, taken from press reports, are given here as examples, and are not a comprehensive account for the period.

*Le Monde* reported on 17 April 1975 that a young man, who, in March of

* "Justice in China" by Sven-Erik Larsson in the Swedish paper *Dagens Nyheter* of 6 November 1977.

† "Les Grands Procès Publics en Chine Populaire", *Bulletin de la Commission Internationale des Juristes,* September 1968. According to this article, about 70 people were sentenced to death and executed from August 1967 to May 1968, and at least 70 other death sentences were pronounced during the same period with suspension of execution for two years.

the same year, had attacked and wounded the wife of a French Embassy staff member, was sentenced to death on 11 April and executed immediately.

According to the Hong Kong newspaper *South China Morning Post* of 7 October 1976, quoting an unnamed immigrant from Sining (in Tsinghai Province), executions of common criminals convicted of capital offences had become "rather frequent" in this provincial city. The immigrant, reported to have lived in Sining for over 20 years, said that this was a recent phenomenon and that those executed were not political offenders but murderers, robbers and rapists.

However, in November 1976, various press agencies in Peking reported that travellers arriving from Changsha, the capital of the central Province of Hunan, had seen official notices in the city reporting that a man had been sentenced to death after defacing Hua Kuo-feng's name on wall posters announcing his appointment as Party Chairman.

During the first few months of 1977, the international press reported that public notices announcing death sentences had appeared in various cities in China, and noted that this followed widespread political unrest after the death of Chairman Mao Tse-tung and the purge of the four "radical" party leaders. It was reported that in Wuhan (the capital of Hupei Province) eight death sentences were announced in this way at the beginning of February 1977. One person among the eight, who had committed crimes of "buggery and sadism", was executed immediately after being sentenced.

A large number of death sentences and executions were reported in March and April 1977 by travellers who had seen official public notices announcing the sentences. Although, according to the notices, some of the offenders had been executed for crimes such as murder or rape, others were apparently sentenced for political reasons. Some of the notices, however, gave little or no indication of the reasons for sentencing.

Among such reports is one of the execution of eight young people, including two women, in Hangchow (Chekiang Province) in February 1977. Several of these eight people were apparently sentenced for "printing" or "preparing to distribute" leaflets said to urge resistance to China's new administration. Another report, in March, indicated that 18 party activists, including the secretary of a commune party committee, were executed in Fukien Province. Eight of the number were cadres from Putien county and the others were from Chin-chiang County. The report did not give the reason for the execution.

In the middle of March 1977, a public notice from the High People's Court of Shanghai announced death sentences passed on 53 convicted criminals. Among them, 27 benefited from a two-year suspension of execution and 26 were ordered to be executed immediately. They included 24 ordinary criminals and two people charged with "political crimes". One of the two was said to have hampered the criticism of the purged "gang of four" and the other had reportedly opposed the official policy of sending "educated youth" to work in the countryside after graduation in an urban middle school.

Commenting on the purge of the "gang of four" leaders, accused of having instigated factional violence in several provinces in 1976, the Vice-Premier, Li Hsien-nien, was reported (in the British newspaper, the *Sunday Times*, 27 March 1977) as saying, during an interview with Sir Denis Hamilton, that the Chinese people were demanding severe punishment, "possibly of the type that is being given to those who are being executed in the provinces". Observers generally noted that the large number of executions reported during that period were evidence of the serious problem faced by the authorities in restoring "law and order", as well as the severity shown in dealing with it.

*Le Monde* of 14 April 1977 published reports by travellers to Canton who had seen an official notice announcing the death sentence for five men charged with ordinary crimes. The sentences had been passed on 3 April.

In May 1977, it was reported that eight people, most of them in their twenties, were sentenced to death in Shenyang, one of them with suspension of execution for two years. A ninth offender was sentenced to life imprisonment. Among them was a twenty-four-year-old man accused of having formed his own political party, having listened to "enemy radio" and having attempted to cross the Soviet border. Another of the condemned men, aged 39, was alleged to have kept a "revisionist diary" since 1958, to have painted "counter-revolutionary" pictures and slogans and to have been a supporter of the "gang of four". Two others were accused of having disrupted rail traffic for three days by tearing up a fifty-metre stretch of railway track.

Reuters reported on 4 August 1977 that one man had been executed and two others given suspended death sentences in Canton in July. A court notice stated that the three men belonged to a group of seven who had carried out a series of violent but unsuccessful robberies in Canton. The four other members of the gang received sentences of hard labour of varying length.

According to people travelling to the city of Anyang (Honan Province), 12 alleged supporters of the "gang of four" were executed there on 2 August 1977. Among them were the former Chairman of the Anyang County Revolutionary Committee, his deputy and two of their lieutenants. These executions reportedly followed a bitter power struggle in the city over the previous 18 months between supporters of the "gang of four" and their opponents. On 2 August the 12 men, wearing placards round their necks, were reportedly driven in procession through crowded streets to their execution.

Also in August, an execution notice appeared in Canton concerning a twenty-two-year-old Hong Kong student, accused of disturbing public order and waving the Taiwan flag (*Agence France Presse,* 14 August 1977). On 26 September, a native of Shensi was executed in Peking for having a week earlier attacked an American businessman on a short visit to China.

At least 23 people were executed in Kunming (Yunnan Province) in September 1977, according to travellers who reported seeing several lists of condemned people in the city. They were able to read only one list, which included 47 names, 23 of them of people listed for immediate execution. Some were accused of counter-revolutionary activities, including distributing leaflets and forming their own groups; others were executed for "revenge killing". An official notice announcing 10 executions was seen in Peking also, in late October. The 10 people executed had been sentenced to death for ordinary (i.e., non-political) crimes, including murder, theft and rape. The notice was signed by Peking People's Court and dated 11 October.

A court notice posted publicly in Nanking in spring 1977 announced sentences passed on several offenders. According to the translation published in the German magazine, *Der Spiegel*, dated 22 August 1977, the notice gave the following information about a man who was executed:

*The "counter-revolutionary Liu Jung-ta, male, 32 years old, from Kiangsu Province, was in Prison No. 1 of Kiangsu where he had been sent for labour-reform", prior to the last review of his sentence.*

*Liu had first been given the "cap" (label) of "bad element" in 1966 for "misbehaving with a young girl" and "spreading reactionary talk" and consequently had to work under supervision. "In 1969 he wrote reactionary slogans" and was sentenced to five years "to be served under the supervision of the masses".*

*"In 1971 he again wrote reactionary slogans and his sentence was increased by five years. But during the time of reform through labour the criminal Liu again wrote reactionary slogans and announced reactionary solutions", for which he was sentenced to death with suspension of execution for two years.*

*"The criminal Liu, however, was obstinate in his counter-revolutionary attitude; on 19 September 1976 he again pronounced counter-revolutionary slogans and his attacks were aimed directly at our great leader, Chairman Mao." ... "His counter-revolutionary arrogance was truly extreme and facts show that the crime was considerable. The court in accordance with the law imposed the death sentence on the counter-revolutionary Liu, which is to be carried out on the spot."*

*"On 1 April 1977 the court had the criminal Liu taken bound to the place of execution, where he was shot."*

On 28 November 1977 the official Chinese newspaper *People's Daily* called for moderation in the use of the death penalty. The article was contributed by a theoretical study group of the Ministry of Public Security. The authors recognized that "serious" crimes called for the death penalty but added that it is preferable to stay the execution for a period of two years to give the condemned a chance to "repent". They stressed at the same time that a "hard blow" had to be struck against "those who break everything, smash everything and grab everybody" and those who pose a "serious threat to social discipline through subversion and sabotage".

***China, Republic of***

See Taiwan (the Republic of China)

***Democratic Kampuchea** (Cambodia)*

See Kampuchea (Democratic Kampuchea) [Cambodia]

***Fiji***

The death penalty is mandatory for murder, under Section 229 of the Penal Code (Re-enactment of Provisions) Act No. 28 of 1972. This brought to an end a moratorium on the death penalty which had lasted from 1966 to 1972. A judge may, however, certify that the case is "a proper [one] for not sentencing the accused to death", in which case the sentence will be reduced to life imprisonment. Two types of murder, known as "capital murder" do not qualify for such a reduction of sentence.

Section 228(1) of the 1972 Act defines murder as the causing of the death of another person, with "malice aforethought", by an unlawful act of omission.

(Suicide pacts are exempted from this definition, however.) Section 229(1) of the Act goes on to state that two types of murder shall be "capital murder":

(1) the murder of a police officer acting in the execution of his duty (or of any person assisting a police officer so acting); and
(2) any murder committed by a person who was a prisoner at the time of its commission.

Amnesty International has no information on the frequency with which the death penalty is imposed in Fiji.

***Hong Kong***

In the British Crown Colony, treason and murder are punishable by death, but no executions have been carried out since November 1966. Britain, having suspended the death penalty in 1965, does not allow it to be carried out in Hong Kong. All death sentences since 1966 have been commuted to life imprisonment by the Governor of the Colony, acting on behalf of Queen Elizabeth II. A total of 21 death sentences were commuted to life sentences in 1977, and at the time of writing a further 12 convicted criminals are awaiting commutation of their sentences.

***India** (the Republic of)*

"The death penalty is being retained but its imposition will be restricted to extreme cases." R.N. Mirdha, Minister of State for Home Affairs, made this statement in the *Rajya Sabha* (Upper House) when introducing the Criminal Code (Amendment) Bill in December 1972 (quoted in *The Statesman*, 16 December 1972). On 23 November 1975, the *Hindustan Times* quoted the Union Shipping and Transport Minister, Uma Shankar Dikshit, as saying that " 'extra-liberal reforms including the proposed abandonment of the death penalty', while well meant and philosophically supportable, have proved to be 'premature' in the existing conditions of society in many countries. Mr Dikshit firmly believed that deterrence was an essential part of human life, both individual and social."

The Indian Penal Code provides for the imposition of the death penalty in Section 121 (waging war against the Government), in Section 132 (abetting mutiny by a member of the armed forces), in Section 194 (fabricating false evidence with intent to procure conviction of another for a capital offence), in Sections 302–303 (murder), Section 305 (abetting the suicide of a child or insane person), Section 307 (attempted murder "if hurt is caused" when committed by a person serving life imprisonment) and in Section 396 (*dacoity* and murder). In most cases the death penalty is the maximum punishment in a full range of types of punishment; however, in the case of waging war and murder, life imprisonment or the death penalty only may be imposed.

The sentence of death may be imposed by a Court of Sessions or by the High Court when exercising original jurisdiction. If the death penalty has been imposed by a Court of Sessions, it requires confirmation by the High Court. There is an appeal to the Supreme Court under Articles 132, 134 and 136 of the Constitution. Also, if an acquittal has been reversed by the High Court, and sentence of death has been imposed, the accused has the right of appeal to the Supreme Court (Article 134 of the Constitution).

Both the President and the governor of a State have the power to grant clemency (Articles 72 and 161 of the Constitution). On the occasion of the 25th

Anniversary of Independence (on 14 August 1972), the Indian Government declared that death sentences passed on or before 15 August 1972 would be commuted. On 25 July 1975, the Government was reported to have accepted the recommendation of the Uttar Pradesh Mahavir Nirvan Samiti to commute the death sentence to life imprisonment for convicts sentenced to death since 13 November 1974 (*Statesman*, 26 July 1975). However, executions were carried out on two political prisoners, in spite of the Government's declaration, on the eve of the 25th Anniversary of Independence (see below). According to official sources, the number of executions in the period 1971–75 was 200.

There have been several moves for the abolition of the death penalty in India by legislative means. Bills for the abolition of the death penalty were introduced in the Legislative Assembly in 1931 and 1950, but both were defeated after Government opposition. In the *Rajya Sabha* resolutions calling for abolition were presented in 1958 and 1961; a similar resolution presented in the *Rajya Sabha* in 1962 led to the matter being referred to the Law Commission. The result was a Law Commission Report on Capital Punishment, presented to the Government in September 1967 (Law Commission Vols I–III (Capital Punishment) 35th Report, September 1967). The Law Commission considered that there was a need to retain the death penalty, while recommending the retention of powers of mercy, but felt it would not be desirable to lay down any rigid or exhaustive principle on which the sentence of death might be commuted (page 317 of the Report). It included among situations where clemency might be appropriate cases of homicide without premeditation – for example, under provocation – or those where the offender was mentally abnormal although not insane (a successful plea of insanity precludes conviction).

The Law Commission did not consider it necessary to exempt women from execution, but Article 382 of the Code of Criminal Procedure provides that if a woman is sentenced to death and found to be pregnant, the execution of the sentence should be postponed and, if appropriate, commuted to imprisonment for life.

The only recommendation made for changing the law was that an article be inserted in the Indian Penal Code (Article 55B) to the effect that, for the imposition of the death penalty, the offender must be at least 18 at the time of the offence. However, this amendment has not appeared in the Indian Penal Code, amended up to 1973, nor was a relevant Act passed by July 1977.

The 1967 Report was tabled in the *Lok Sabha* (the Lower House) on 16 November 1971 and marked the end of the hopes of abolitionists in India that the death penalty might be brought to an end by legislative action. Several attempts were subsequently made in the Supreme Court of India to declare the death penalty unconstitutional, but were dismissed in October 1972 in the case of Jagmohan Singh.

The death penalty exists on a discretionary basis in India and the various considerations which might – or should – weigh with the court in exercising discretion are not codified. The criteria usually applied by the courts in exercising their discretion were listed, for example, in a case in 1974 (Ediga Anamma), as follows:

*"Where the murderer is too young or too old, the clemency of penal justice helps him. Where the offender suffers from socio-economic, psychic or penal*

*compulsions insufficient to attract a legal exception or to downgrade the crime into a lesser one, judicial commutation is permissible. Other general social pressures, warranting judicial notice, with an extenuating impact, may, in special cases, induce the lesser penalty. Extraordinary features in the judicial process, such as that the death sentence has hung over the head of the culprit excrutiatingly long, may persuade the Court to be compassionate. Likewise, if others involved in the crime and similarly situated have received the benefit of life imprisonment or if the offence is only constructive (i.e., combining the 'murder' provision with the 'unlawful assembly' provision) . . . or again* [if] *the accused has acted suddenly under another's instigation, without premeditation, perhaps the Court may humanely opt for life, even as where a just cause or real suspicion of wifely infidelity pushed the criminal into the crime."*

The Supreme Court judgment in this case has been seen to be significant on the ground that it reveals a tendency, at least in this context, towards "cautious, partial abolition". The observations of the Supreme Court relate to changes in the Code of Criminal Procedure enacted between 1955 and 1973 regarding the obligations of the court to state its reasoning when convicting a person of an offence punishable by death. Before 1955, the rule – as laid down in Section 367(5) of the Code of Criminal Procedure – was that the court in its judgment should state the reason why in such cases the death sentence had not been imposed. But under the amended Section 354(3) (which became law on 1 April 1974), the court is obliged to state its special reasons for imposing the death penalty. From this legislative change, the court inferred that "life imprisonment for murder is the rule and capital sentence the exception to be resorted to for reasons to be stated". Unfortunately, however, this judgment has not led to a marked increase in judicial commutations of the death penalty, as might have been expected after the significant Ediga Anamma judgment.

According to the instructions issued in the former State of Bombay, the period in that State between confirmation of sentence by the High Court and execution is from 21 to 28 days. However, the Law Commission points out that in practice the periods may be much longer because of appeal or petition for mercy. In a number of cases known to Amnesty International, the period between sentence and execution has been disturbingly protracted. Examples include the case of Amrit Bhushan Gupta who was convicted on charges of murder in 1968. The death penalty was confirmed by the High Court on 25 September 1969 and the Supreme Court upheld the sentence on 29 November 1976.

Amnesty International has been informed that, since the execution of V.N. Godse, who assassinated Mahatma Gandhi in January 1948, no prisoners have been executed for politically motivated killings. In 1973, Nagabhusan Patnaik, a forty-year-old lawyer and leading member of the Communist Party of India (Marxist-Leninist), (commonly known as the "Naxalites") was granted commutation of a death sentence for murder, the order being given by the President after a Cabinet decision. In 1976, the Andhra Pradesh High Court commuted the death sentence imposed on two "Naxalites" to life imprisonment. But Kista Gowd, a forty-five-year-old farmer, and R. Bhoomaiah, a village tailor, were executed by hanging on 1 December 1975, after being sentenced to death on a similar charge of murder. These cases aroused much protest from supporters of civil liberties and lawyers in India.

In these cases, the superior courts recognized the political element in the killing, and put on record their strong reservations about the advisability of imposing the death penalty in such circumstances. After the petition by the accused for mercy had been turned down by the President and the State Governor, the Supreme Court was forced to dismiss the special petition for leave to appeal, but not without stating clear reservations about the application of the death penalty. When the attention of the court was drawn by the defence to political executions in Spain and the "revulsion" which these executions had created in the world, Mr Justice Krishna Iyer observed: "We share the revulsion with the world, but the jurisdiction of this court is limited" (PTI Report, 1 October 1975).

Kista Gowd and R. Bhoomaiah were executed three years and seven months after they had been sentenced to death.

Some members of political parties have been sentenced to death following convictions for murder. The death penalty imposed by the Srinagar High Court on Mohammad Maqbool Butt, a member of the Jammu and Kashmir National Liberation Front, convicted of murdering an Indian Head Constable in 1968, was confirmed by the Supreme Court, and at the time of writing, a petition for clemency is before the President. In the State of West Bengal, Kalipada Sarkar, Netai Biswas, Sudeb Biswas, Shantimoy Akhurey and Molina Dhak, all "Naxalites", have been sentenced to death on murder charges, but appeals have not yet been confirmed in the higher courts. During its mission to India in January 1978, Amnesty International was assured by the Chief Minister of West Bengal that the West Bengal Government opposes the death penalty.

***Indonesia** (the Republic of)*

No change was made in the Penal Code when Indonesia became independent from Dutch colonial rule in 1949. Up to the present it makes no provision for the death penalty. However, a number of extraordinary legislative instruments, passed since independence, have introduced the death penalty as the maximum punishment for a wide range of political, economic and criminal offences. The maximum penalty for murder remains life imprisonment.

The Economic Law, enacted in the 1950s, made the death penalty the maximum penalty for a variety of offences related to hoarding and market-fixing with the aim of raising prices to extraordinary levels and thereby making unreasonable profits. In 1963, the late President Sukarno promulgated a Presidential Decree, referred to as the Subversion Act, which specified the death penalty on a discretionary basis for a number of offences relating to subversion, espionage and sabotage. Sabotage includes disruption of production and trade in commodities, and thereby also covers economic as well as political offences. The 1963 Decree did not have the force of law, and was only passed by due legislative process in 1969; that is when it became known as the Subversion Act.

Another legislative instrument – the Narcotics Act – was passed in 1975–76. This Act imposes a discretionary death penalty for dealing in certain drugs. As far as is known at the time of writing, the death penalty has not yet been passed under this law. Indonesian Military Law, with jurisdiction over armed forces personnel, does not specify the death penalty for any offence. In cases since 1965 in which military personnel have been tried and sentenced to death, the 1963 Presidential Decree on Subversion has been invoked.

Most cases in which the death penalty has been imposed have been in connection with charges under this 1963 Subversion Decree. In October 1965, there was an "attempted *coup*" in which a group of army officers of middle rank plotted to destroy the army high command. When the plot was crushed, the army captured a number of officers held responsible for it, and kept hundreds of thousands of civilians under arrest as suspects. It was the view of army leaders that the Indonesian Communist Party was involved in the plot, and several of the leaders of the Party who were captured were placed on trial and sentenced to death. In addition, the death penalty was also passed on several senior military officers and a leading Cabinet Minister. All were tried under the 1963 Presidential Decree, which did not then have the force of law.

Immediately after 1965, when cases were tried under the 1963 Presidential Subversion Decree, the hearings came before extraordinary military tribunals, beyond which no formal judicial appeal existed; the only recourse was a petition for clemency to the President. From about 1969, the subversion trials tended to be heard in civilian courts rather than before military tribunals and, coincidentally, the death penalty began to be less frequently imposed, although it continues to be imposed in subversion cases.

Since 1972, with the exception of Brigadier-General Sopardjo, a senior police and intelligence officer executed in 1973, it appears that those sentenced to death on subversion charges have, in fact, not been executed. One reason for believing that fewer executions have taken place is that appeal is possible from the civilian courts to the Supreme Court of Indonesia; and process before the latter is known to take four or five years before the death penalty is upheld in any given case. Appeal is not automatic, but in all known cases defendants have lodged appeals.

The death sentence is known to have been passed under the Economic Law in at least one case, in a trial which began in 1964. Although the defendant, charged with profiteering, was sentenced to death in 1965, his appeal to the Supreme Court has yet to be decided upon and he is waiting for that decision in prison.

The case of Dr Subandrio, Deputy Prime Minister and Foreign Minister until 11 March 1966, is of interest. He was arrested five months after the attempted *coup* of 1965, and his trial began in October 1966. Two sets of charges were brought against him. The first was that he attempted to assist others in preparing a conspiracy to overthrow the legal Government. This related to, among other things, his actions in office and the advice he gave then. This included advocating the policy of purchasing arms from China and of halting repayment of debts to the USSR, and advising the withdrawal of Indonesia from the United Nations. The first set of charges related to numerous other matters, such as allegedly spreading rumours to incite left-wing feelings against the Indonesian army, thereby helping to encourage the preparation of a *coup*.

The second set of charges related to events after the attempted *coup*. Dr Subandrio was accused of undermining the authority of the State in the form of General Suharto's developing New Order. He was accused of supporting the attempted *coup*, of attempting to minimise its significance, and of actively encouraging demonstrations countering those in support of General Suharto. The charges were made under the Presidential Decree on Subversion, which, it should be noted, did not have the force of law at the time of Dr Subandrio's trial.

The case, clearly intended by the military Government to be a publicity exercise, was tried before an extraordinary military tribunal. No judicial appeal was allowed against the death sentence. Dr Subandrio petitioned for clemency directly to the President. Although there have been reports in the Indonesian and foreign press from time to time that President Suharto had considered the plea for clemency, no decision has been publicly announced. Dr Subandrio was a well-known international figure, and it was possibly in order to avoid external criticism that the death sentence was not carried out.

Under the Subversion Law defendants in most cases have not been sentenced to death, but to long periods of imprisonment.

At the time of writing, it is estimated that there are about 50 people under sentence of death. In total, about 15 people have been executed for alleged involvement in the attempted *coup* of 1965. The executions were by firing squad.

***Japan***

While Japanese law provides the death penalty for 13 crimes, including murder and arson, it is only mandatory for the incitement of foreign aggression against Japan. Two capital offences cover the unlawful seizure of an aircraft resulting in death.

The Legislative Council stated on 29 May 1974 in its consideration of the overall revision of the Japanese Penal Code that, while it did not support the abolition of the death penalty, it did support the reduction of the number of crimes for which it is available and also the introduction of safeguards to promote the utmost care and certainty in the exercise of the court's discretion in deciding on the death penalty.

Between 1969 and 1973, 71 people – 69 men and two women – were executed: 52 for homicide related to robbery, 13 for homicide, five for homicide related to rape, and one for arson.

A report from Reuters, quoting official sources, said that a man who had raped and murdered eight young women in 1971 was hanged in a Tokyo jail on 22 January 1976. The man, aged 41, had been sentenced to death on 22 February 1973, after pleading guilty to the charges.

In another case, a forty-eight-year-old carpenter, Matsuzo Ohama, was sentenced to death by a Yokohama court in October 1975, for murdering a woman and her two daughters. In December 1976 the defendant asked to be executed, but his lawyer appealed against the death sentence, claiming that Ohama was insane at the time of the murder. In the same month, Ohama withdrew the appeal without consulting his lawyer. Despite a ruling from the High Court that Ohama was entitled to take such a course of action, Ohama's lawyer himself applied to the court for his client's withdrawal to be declared void. This was rejected. However, in January 1977, a High Court judge issued a stay of execution, pending a new ruling on the validity of the lawyer's application (Reuters, 18 January 1977).

An earlier death sentence case, pending since 1958, has generated much debate in the Japanese press. It involves Masao Akahori, arrested in May 1954 for the murder of a six-year-old girl, found dead two months earlier. Akahori was sentenced to death in May 1958 by Shizuoka District Court. According to report, he had previously had periods of mental instability, and had found it difficult to get proper employment. Little evidence was produced against him when he was indicted in June 1954, apart from a confession, which he later claimed had been made under duress during police interrogation.

During his trial in 1958, Masao Akahori maintained his innocence, and appealed against conviction and sentence to the Tokyo High Court. The High Court rejected the appeal in February 1960, and a further appeal to the Supreme Court was rejected in December 1960. Since then, lawyers for Akahori have unsuccessfully undertaken several actions to obtain a review of the judgment. The case is still unresolved after *19* years. Akahori has been detained since 1954 (24 years), and is reported to be held in Miyagi Prison.

Executions in Japan are reported to be carried out in seven prisons, each, it is said, with its own hangman. Hanging has been the method of execution since 1896.

A Reuters report of 18 April 1977 stated that the Japanese Ministry of Justice declines to give information either on the numbers of people executed in recent years, or on the numbers sentenced to death. According to the same report, the only way to find out whether or not a death sentence has been carried out, is to check the family register in the condemned person's home town. When the name of the condemned is struck out, the execution has apparently taken place.

Reuters correspondent wrote that, according to unconfirmed reports, 336 people were hanged in Japan between 1954 and 1974.

***Kampuchea** (Democratic Kampuchea) [Cambodia]*

According to refugee accounts, the situation in Democratic Kampuchea since the change of Government in April 1975 has been characterized by executions and killings on a wide scale. The accounts have been so numerous and so constant that it is a matter of grave concern that the Kampuchean Government has not even troubled to deny reports of atrocities or the alleged scale of killings, beyond the widely reported statements by a Kampuchean Government leader, Ieng Sary, in May 1977, denying reports that hundreds of thousands of people had been executed, saying: "We only condemned the worst criminals."

The information provided by refugees has tended to refer mainly to the provinces close to Thailand, namely Battambang, Pursat, Oddor Meanchey and Siem Reap (reports about other provinces are more fragmentary). It was also reported that internal armed resistance to the new authorities was continuing in some parts of those provinces.

From 1975, there has been a flow of refugees to Thailand. In 1975 and early 1976, reports came from refugees that many officers of the defeated Republican Army had been executed during the months after the Khmer Rouge accession to power. Their accounts showed similarities, although details varied. According to them, groups of officers of the former army had been gathered by Khmer Rouge soldiers in various places to go to Phnom Penh and were then executed while in transit. Details were generally not available as to the individuals involved and the circumstances. Most of the accounts were not based on first-hand observation; the refugees generally reported what they had heard about atrocities from acquaintances or, in some cases, from Khmer Rouge soldiers, while others claimed that they had seen mass graves or corpses with army clothing.

In the cases of members of the former Government and administration, Khmer Rouge soldiers or local authorities were reported to have conducted investigations into their past history, so as to identify particularly those who had formerly held positions of authority. According to refugees, many former officials were "taken away" and never heard of again, and were subsequently thought to have been killed. Among them were said to be people with professional qualifications, such as doctors and teachers. However, at the same time there were indications that some of those with medical knowledge were taken to work in distant clinics or in pharmaceutical factories. It is possible that some people were forcibly transferred to work in outlying places; until late 1977, there were reports of constant forced migration of people to various work sites, although this appears to have lessened later.

Various outside observers have tried to estimate the number of deaths in Democratic Kampuchea since March 1975; the largest estimate is about two million. It should be pointed out that such figures include deaths from causes such as starvation and disease, which were themselves attributed to Government policy. Further, there were indications of severe dislocation of internal services in the country as a consequence of the war, which had built up markedly in its closing stages. Large numbers had died as a result of malnutrition and disease, which were made worse by the Government's drastic policy of large-scale enforced migration of people. Some observers have estimated that as many as 200,000 deaths can be attributed to killings carried out by the local authorities and Khmer Rouge soldiers.

All independent organizations concerned with events in Democratic Kampuchea have been deeply troubled by the fact that independent observers have been denied any access by the Government to investigate atrocities reported in the refugee accounts. Although outside observers have not been able to verify the reports of atrocities or their scale, nevertheless, the frequency and similarity of allegations about them have reinforced the view that they must be taken most seriously.

Of the judicial system and laws of Democratic Kampuchea, only the Constitution is known to Amnesty International. Article 9 states that: "The judiciary organ is formed of the people's courts of justice which represent and defend the people's justice, defend the people's democratic liberties and punish any act directed against the people's State or transgressing the laws of the people's State."

Article 10 describes the acts transgressing the laws of the people's State as follows:

– any systematic, hostile or destructive activity that endangers the people's State receives the most severe punishment;

– any case besides the above-mentioned activities is treated by means of re-education within the State's organs or people's organizations.

***Korea** (the Republic of) [South Korea]*

The Criminal Code of 1953 specifies the death penalty for a wide range of offences. The death sentence is mandatory only for the offence of taking up arms against the Republic of Korea by joining the forces of an enemy country (Article 93).

The death sentence on a discretionary basis is available for a number of other crimes against the State. These include, among other things, subversion of the constitution; leading a plot to create disorder for the purpose of seizing national territory; conspiring with a foreign country to wage war against the Republic of Korea and certain military offences. The minimum penalty for these offences is life imprisonment. A person who acts as a spy or who aids a spy for an enemy country, or who divulges military secrets to an enemy country, is liable to receive the maximum penalty of death, with a specified minimum penalty of seven years' penal servitude (Article 98 of National Security Law).

The death sentence may also be imposed for the offences of using explosives and thereby causing injury, damaging property or disturbing the public peace (Article 119); causing death by arson (Article 164) or damaging means of transport (Article 188). Murder; using force or fraudulent means to induce another person to commit suicide (Article 253); murder whilst committing robbery or piracy (Articles 338 and 340); rape whilst committing piracy; these are all offences which carry the death penalty.

The Code of Criminal Procedure, 1954, as amended in 1961 and 1963, specifies that appeals against sentences may be lodged by a public prosecutor or by the accused, first in the High Court, and then in the Supreme Court. If a pregnant woman or a person of unsound mind has been condemned to death, the execution is stayed by order of the Minister of Justice until the woman has given birth, or the person of unsound mind has recovered.

In addition to the Criminal Code, the National Security Law (Law No. 549, 1960, as amended) lays down heavy penalties for the offence of organizing "an association or group for the purpose of assuming a title of the government, or disturbing the State". A "ringleader" of such an "anti-State organization" is to be sentenced to death or life imprisonment; "leaders or those engaged in duties of leadership" in such an organization are to be sentenced to death or imprisonment for not less than five years (Chapter 1, Article 1). Acting under instruction from an "anti-State organization", if this involves finding out, collecting or divulging national secrets, or using explosives, committing homicide, arson or forging currency (Article 3) is likewise punishable by death.

Capital offences against the State are also specified in the Anti-Communist Law (Law No. 643, 1961, as amended). This law provides that an agent of an "anti-State organization" who infiltrates the Republic of Korea secretly, shall be punished by death, life imprisonment or hard labour for not less than five years (Article 6).

There is also provision in the National Security Law and the Anti-Communist Law for the death penalty to be applied, in certain circumstances, to people convicted for a second time under those laws or under a number of others covering offences against the State.

The National Security Law has been used by the Government to suppress political opposition. Its effect was further reinforced by a series of Presidential Emergency Decrees, of which No. 4 was especially harsh. It outlawed a student organization which had been vigorously critical of the administration of President Park Chung-hee, and prohibited any connection with that organization. Furthermore, it was "prohibited for any student to absent himself from school or refuse to attend classes or take examinations without legitimate cause; to hold an assembly, demonstration, rally, or any individual or collective sit-in, outside or inside the campus, except normal classes or research activities conducted under the guidance and supervision of the school authorities. However, customary non-political activities shall be excepted." Article 8 of Decree No. 4 specified that any person who violated this or any other of the listed prohibitions, or who "defamed" the

Emergency Decree, could be punished by death or imprisonment for not less than five years. The promulgation of this Emergency Decree, on 3 April 1974, was followed by the trials of 55 people. The military tribunals pronounced death sentences in July 1974 on 14 of the defendants, including the internationally-known poet, Kim Chi Ha. This provoked strong protest throughout the world and, on 20 July, the Defence Minister announced the commutation of five of the death sentences, including that of Kim Chi Ha. The Decree was eventually rescinded in August 1974.

In April 1975, the Supreme Court confirmed the death sentences passed on eight men accused of belonging to an "anti-State organization" allegedly involved in communist subversion. They were charged under a combination of the National Security Law, the Anti-Communist Law and the Emergency Decrees. An Amnesty International mission in Seoul at the time of the Supreme Court hearing found that torture had been used to extract false confessions, and that pre-trial irregularities prevented the defendants from presenting a full defence. The eight condemned men were hanged less than 24 hours after the Supreme Court had confirmed the death sentences, and were thus unlawfully denied the opportunity to pursue further appropriate avenues of appeal or to petition for clemency.

At intervals, the South Korean Central Intelligence Agency (KCIA) announces that it has apprehended North Korean spies. Under the National Security Law and the Anti-Communist Law there is provision for the death penalty for espionage. A recent example is the "November 22 espionage case" of 1975. The Korean CIA announced that it had arrested 21 North Korean spies, many of whom were Koreans who normally live in Japan, attending colleges in Seoul and Pusan. The KCIA said the members of the ring were North Korean agents who had entered the colleges, posing as visiting students, in order to carry out subversive activities. The trials began in March 1976 and, in May, five of the defendants were condemned to death. Four of the death sentences were confirmed by the Appeal Court, and one was commuted to life imprisonment. In at least one case, the Supreme Court has rejected an appeal against conviction and the death penalty. Bodies concerned over these trials, including the Tokyo Bar Association, have maintained that they were unsatisfactory – based in several cases mainly on confessions, and without concrete evidence of alleged subversive activity. Subsequently, the Tokyo Bar Association pointed to the availability of evidence of alibi, and appealed (unsuccessfully) to the South Korean Government for the cases to be reopened.

Apart from offences against the State, the Government passed a law in March 1977, which banned all smoking of and trafficking in marijuana, and specified penalties ranging from 10 years' imprisonment to death.

### *Laos (the People's Democratic Republic of)*

After the abolition of the monarchy in December 1975 and the proclamation of the Lao People's Democratic Republic, the Program of Actions of the new Government included a paragraph stressing cooperation "with the Supreme People's Assembly to study the questions concerning the elaboration of the new Constitution of the People's Democratic Republic to serve as the basis for political affairs, the setting-up of institutions, and concerning the questions of the revolutionary State's law". However, at the time of writing, the Constitution has not yet been published and no further information on the law is available to Amnesty International.

On 5 September 1975, the Central Supreme Court in Vientiane heard a case against "31 traitors who committed crimes against the people and fomented rebellion against the Nation". Twenty-six of the convicted men were sentenced to terms of imprisonment, and the others were sentenced to death *in absentia.* The latter were prominent members of the "rightist" faction in the former coalition Government, who had fled the country earlier.

On 17 April 1976, the official newspaper, *Sieng Prasasone,* reported that a people's court in Vientiane had sentenced to death six people on charges of "trying to sabotage Government property, including rice depots and power stations", and of being involved in an incident earlier in 1976, in which hand grenades were thrown at the Soviet and Cuban Embassies. Three of the men sentenced to death were tried *in absentia,* and were reported to be still at large a month later. The three others were, according to report, executed on 17 May 1976.

Ten people were condemned to death for their part in an alleged assassination plot directed against the Lao leadership, according to a statement issued on 17 November 1977 by a source close to the Lao Ministry of Justice. Additionally, the Bangkok daily newspaper, *Thai Rath*, reported that in the previous week, 13 members of a right-wing movement, including five Thai citizens, had been executed by firing squad.

No official information is available to Amnesty International on the number of death sentences and executions in the past three years (1975–77).

### *Malaysia (the Federation of)*

An examination of the Malaysian Penal Code reveals that the following offences may be punished by death: waging war against the Government (Section 121); intending hurt or death to or restraint of the President (mandatory under Section 121A); perjury resulting in execution of a person indicated on a capital charge (Section 194); abetting the suicide of a person under 18 or an "idiot... or insane or delirious person" (Section 305); kidnapping for murder or where the victim is placed "in danger of being murdered" (Section 364), and certain offences relating to mutiny in the armed forces (Section 132). An amendment to the Narcotics Act, approved by Parliament in April 1975, makes trafficking in narcotics a capital offence. The amended act also provides for life imprisonment and flogging for narcotics dealers. Before the amendment was adopted, the maximum penalty for offences under the Narcotics Act was seven years' imprisonment. By virtue of Section 275 of the Criminal Procedure Code 1970, a pregnant women shall be sentenced, not to death but to life imprisonment. Section 277 of the same Code provides that execution be carried out by hanging.

In September 1975, in an attempt to deter "anti-government activities", the Government announced its intention of imposing the death penalty on persons found possessing firearms, ammunition and explosives in any area declared a "security area". In such cases, the accused may be charged under Sections 57, 58 or 59 of the Internal Security Act 1960. Section 57 restricts the possession of such material within any security area without lawful excuse – and the onus of proving the excuse lawful is placed on the defence. Section 58 proscribes consorting with a person in breach of Section 57. Section 59 proscribes, among other things, possessing, receiving or providing any supplies from or to any other person in circumstances "which raise a reasonable presumption that he intends or is about to act, or has recently acted, in a manner prejudicial to public security or the maintenance of public order...".

The application of Section 59 is not confined to security areas. The death penalty is mandatory under Sections 57 and 59 (where the supplies consist of firearms, ammunition or explosives), and discretionary under Section 58. It does not apply to offences under Section 58 (2) which include consorting in circumstances where there is no reasonable presumption that the public security may be prejudiced.

In October 1975, the Malaysian Government introduced new emergency regulations, known as the Essential (Security Cases) Regulations 1975. These remove basic legal safeguards in cases certified by the Public Prosecutor as "security cases". The new law shifts the burden of proof on to the defence. It also permits witnesses for the prosecution to give evidence *in camera,* by affidavit or even while wearing a mask in court. Under the new regulations, appeals in security cases can no longer be made to the Judicial Committee of the Privy Council in London, and trials are held in special courts, without a jury. In addition, the judges have had their discretionary powers taken away, and are now obliged to impose whatever was previously the maximum penalty permitted by law for the offence. Section 3 (3) of these regulations reads: "Where a person is accused of or charged with a security offence, he shall, regardless of his age, be dealt with and tried in accordance with the provisions of these regulations and the Juvenile Courts Act 1947 shall not apply to such a person."

The incidence of communist insurgency threatening the security of Malaysia is the general explanation given by the Government when passing new laws such as the above, and increasing the number of offences liable to the death penalty. Official comment on the death penalty is rare. However, according to the BBC Summary of World Broadcasts, 24 November 1976, the Sultan of Selangor said that he would not grant clemency to anyone who had been sentenced to death. This was his conclusion after a briefing on the security situation in the State on 20 November 1976, at which the Chief Minister, the Chief Police Officer of the State, and the Commander of the Kuala Lumpur garrison were present.

A Reuters report of 18 April 1977 stated that a total of 13 people sentenced to death on various charges, including carrying illegal arms, were at that time waiting in prison for the sentences to be carried out. The cases below are among those reported in the press.

According to *Agence France Presse*, Kuala Lumpur, a Malaysian house painter, hanged on 6 January 1967 for shooting at two police officers (neither of whom had been hit by the shots), was the first person to be executed under a 1971 law increasing penalties for using firearms (item in the British newspaper, *The Times,* 7 January 1976).

A carpenter aged 32, Chai Yee Ken, was sentenced to death by the High Court on 14 December 1976, after being found guilty in February of that year of unlawfully possessing five pistols and 74 rounds of ammunition. According to the Malaysian newspaper, *New Straits Times* of 15 December 1976, his house was in a place which had been declared a security area on 11 February 1976. The newspaper also said that Chai had pleaded not guilty to the charges, which fell under Section 57 of the Internal Security Act.

At the end of March 1977 the Acting Deputy Public Prosecutor, Senior Federal Counsel P.M. Mahilingam, applied for the commital as a security case of Lim Woon Chong, aged 21, under the Essential (Security Cases) Regulations 1975. Lim, reportedly described as the leader of the Malaysian People's Liberation Army, was charged with the murder of the former Inspector General of Police in June 1974 and, together with another man, with the murder of the Deputy Commissioner of Police in Ipoh on 13 November 1975. The two men were due to be tried together for the latter murder in Ipoh in July 1977, and Lim was expected to be tried alone in the High Court on the first murder charge. Both men were also charged under the Internal Security Act with illegal possession of two pistols and seven rounds of ammunition.

The *Far Eastern Economic Review* correspondent in Kuala Lumpur, K. Das, reporting on these two cases on 8 April 1977, said that the number of people tried up to that date under the Essential Regulations was approximately 12.

The awesome implications of the Essential (Security Cases) Regulations 1975 became a reality in August 1977, when a fourteen-year-old boy was sentenced to death in Penang for possessing a firearm. He was sentenced under the Internal Security Act and tried under the new emergency regulations. The presiding judge, Mr Justice Arulanandon, stated that "It must be made clear that any juvenile, that is, any person who has attained the age of criminal responsibility described in Section 82 of the Penal Code, that is ten and under the age of eighteen, is liable to be sentenced to death if he is convicted under the Internal Security Act."

The sentence against the boy provoked grave disquiet in Malaysia and abroad. The Malaysian Bar Council protested strongly against the court's decision and against the Internal Security Act which gave rise to it. In October the boy had his sentence commuted to detention at the King's pleasure by the State Pardons Board. There is still serious concern in Malaysia over the implications of the Internal Security Act.

According to one report, quoting the *Straits Times* of 28 April 1977, 15 people were sentenced to death for possession of firearms between 1975 and February 1977. The report stated that this figure was given by the Deputy Law Minister, Encik Rais Yatim, who also revealed that a total of 366 people had been arrested for possession or use of firearms without permission in the same period. Apart from the 15 sentenced to death, 77 were reported to have been sentenced to various terms of imprisonment, 40 released due to lack of evidence, and 234 cases were still pending before the courts. In July 1977, the Minister of Home Affairs, Tan Sri Ghazali Shafie, stated that a total of 47 people had been sentenced to death by the High Courts of Malaysia between the beginning of 1976 and the end of June 1977. However, at the time of writing, none of them has yet been executed.

### ***Nepal** (the Kingdom of)*

Nepal is the only country in South Asia which Amnesty International knows to have abolished the death penalty for ordinary crimes. In 1931, the death penalty was suspended experimentally and in 1945 formally abolished by law. However, the State (Crime and Punishment) Act 1962 (the Raj-Kaj Act), enacted under

Article 93 of the Constitution, provides for the death penalty for the offences of physical attack on a member of the Royal Family (Section 2), violation of the chastity of the Queen or Princess (Section 3), insurrection against the State (Section 4 (1)), and collusion with a foreign state in a manner likely to undermine the independence, sovereignty and integrity of Nepal (Section 4 (1A) – this last Section being introduced on 24 April 1975). The death penalty is also retained for certain military offences covered by Section 27 of the Military Act 1959. The Raj-Kaj Act carries the death penalty for treason.

After the 1945 reforms, execution by beheading was discontinued. It is now by hanging or shooting. Sentence of death requires confirmation by the Supreme Court and may be recommended for revision by the Judicial Committee. Once it has been confirmed, execution takes place within 30 days.

Since 1945, Amnesty International knows of one execution, which took place in 1962 by hanging. Durganand Jha was executed following trial *in camera* by a Special Tribunal at which three people, including Jha, were sentenced to death on the charge of attempting to kill the King.

On 17 February 1977, the Supreme Court of Nepal confirmed the death sentences passed by Special Court on Yagya Bahadur Thapa, convicted of treason under Section 4 (1) of the Raj-Kaj Act, and on Bhim Narayan Shrestha, convicted of the same offence, under Section 2 of the Act. The court had found Thapa, a former army captain, guilty of promoting armed rebellion (insurrection) with the intention of setting up his own government in eastern districts of Nepal – the incident became known as the "incident of Okhaldhunga" – and Shrestha of an attempt on the life of the King in 1973 (he had thrown a grenade in the city of Biratnagar). Both sentences were confirmed by the Regional Court on 26 May 1976 and later, on 17 February 1977, by the Supreme Court. The two men petitioned the King for clemency.*

* Both prisoners were unexpectedly executed by shooting on 9 February 1979.

### New Zealand

The only capital offence specified in the New Zealand Crimes Act 1961 is treason. Section 73 of the Act specifies that a person convicted of treason shall be sentenced to death. The definition of treason includes: killing, wounding, doing grievous bodily harm to, or imprisoning the Monarch; levying war against New Zealand; assisting an enemy at war against New Zealand; inciting or assisting anyone to invade New Zealand with force; using force for the purpose of overthrowing the New Zealand Government (Section 74). Attempted treason is not punishable by death.

People exempted from the death penalty include pregnant women (who would be sentenced to life imprisonment) and anyone under the age of 18 when the offence was committed (they would be sentenced to detention until release at the discretion of the Government).

A person sentenced to death can appeal to the Court of Appeal, New Zealand's highest Court. The Governor General is able to exercise the prerogative of mercy or grant a free pardon.

Between 1951 and 1957, the death penalty was imposed 18 times for murder. There were seven further convictions for murder in the period 1958–61, but death sentences were not imposed. The death penalty for murder was abolished in 1962.

***Pakistan** (the Islamic Republic of)*

Under the provisions of the Pakistan Penal Code (PPC), sentence of death can be imposed for the following offences: waging war (or abetting the waging of war) against the State (Section 121, PPC); this is the only offence against the State punishable by death under the Penal Code; abetting mutiny (if mutiny is committed as a result) (Section 132, PPC); and murder (Sections 300–302, PPC). Sentence of death is mandatory if murder is committed by a person serving a sentence of life imprisonment (Section 303, PPC). The Code lists the circumstances in which culpable homicide is not murder–for example, grave provocation (Section 300). In addition, the death penalty can be imposed for kidnapping a person under the age of 10, if the intention is to murder or cause grievous hurt (Section 364-A), and *dacoity* (robbery by five or more persons) resulting in death, all participants in the act being punishable by death (Section 396). Furthermore, the Explosive Substances (Amendment) Act of 1975 provides for death or imprisonment for anyone convicted of keeping or using explosives contrary to the provisions of the Act.

Sentence of death can only be imposed by the High Court and sessions judges, and is subject to confirmation by the High Court. There is always the possibility of an appeal to the Supreme Court. Execution is by hanging. The High Court may order the execution of a pregnant woman to be postponed and may substitute a sentence of life imprisonment. Both the provincial Governments and the President have the power to commute the death sentence (Sections 401–402, Criminal Procedure Code).

If the powers of reprieve are exercised centrally (which is usually the case), the actual decision is taken in the Prime Minister's Secretariat on a recommendation of the Home Ministry and with the legal advice of the Law Ministry.

No information is available to Amnesty International about the number of cases in which the death penalty was imposed and carried out under the civilian administration in power until July 1977, but the civilian courts were apparently reluctant to impose the death penalty as a matter of course in cases of murder. The Supreme Court, in a judgment of 30 April 1976, noted "the marked propensity of the courts to avoid death penalty at the trial or allow unjustified commutation on appeal followed by frequent remissions of sentence". The Court observed that this practice is "bound to take away the sting of deterrence". In the case in question, the Court observed that the fact that the murder was a premeditated act which had been committed by several people did not constitute an extenuating or mitigating circumstance for any of them. It quoted a judgment of the Supreme Court in 1970 which listed some of the extenuating and mitigating circumstances usually taken into account by the courts. These include "extreme youth, sudden provocation, influence of an elder and a question of family honour".

During the period of civil disturbance which followed the outcome of the March 1977 general election, martial law was imposed in April 1977 in Karachi, Lahore and Hyderabad, by the civilian administration headed by Z.A. Bhutto. Martial Law Instructions Nos. 7 and 8 provided for offences (including those for which there was provision for the death penalty under the Pakistan Penal Code) to be tried by Field General Courts Martial and Summary Courts Martial. It is not known whether any sentence of death was imposed during this short period of martial law by martial law courts.

During the three months in which martial law operated, martial law regulations allowed for anyone breaking the curfew regulations imposed by the army to be "shot on sight" (Military Administrative Order No. 1 of 21 April 1977). There are reliable reports that at least 350 persons were killed during the period of civil unrest following the March 1977 elections, a considerable number of them shot by the army.

On 5 July 1977, a military take-over took place and the new martial law administration imposed harsh martial law orders. These provided the death penalty for *dacoity* (as defined in the Penal Code), for attacking, resisting or injuring any members of the civil or military forces, or for damaging, tampering or interfering with Government property (Martial Law Regulations 7, 9 and 10 of 1977). Martial Law Regulation 15 makes any incitement to seek "the territorial or administrative dismemberment of Pakistan" an offence punishable by death, and the same punishment can also be imposed for attempts to seduce members of the armed forces from their duty or allegiance to the Goviernment or the Chief Martial Law Administrator (Martial Law Regulation No. 16). Special martial law courts are able to impose the death penalty for contravention of these Regulations. Execution can only take place after confirmation of the sentence of death by the Chief Martial Law Administrator, whose decision is final. The method of execution is hanging (or whatever the Court directs in a particular case).

Only in few instances of political murder have there been any judicial proceedings. The *Amnesty International Report on Pakistan,* published in May 1977, states that:

> *"There is no doubt that, over recent years, a number of political assassinations have taken place in Pakistan. Leaders of both pro-government and of opposition parties have been victims. But, whereas when government officials are killed, judicial proceedings and trials are instituted and concluded without delay, when opposition politicians are killed, the cases frequently remain unresolved."*

Since the military take-over in July 1977, a number of cases have been brought before the courts, concerning political murders which occurred during the period of civil administration headed by Z.A. Bhutto. Mr Bhutto himself was arrested on 3 September 1977 for alleged complicity in the murder of Nawab Mohammed Ahmed Khan, the father of Ahmad Raza Kasuri, a dissident member of the Pakistan People's Party and a Member of the National Assembly. Mr Bhutto and four officials of the Federal Security Force were brought to trial before the full bench of the Lahore High Court on 10 October 1977. They were charged with conspiracy to murder under the provisions of the Pakistan Penal Code. The offence carries the death penalty.*

* Mr Bhutto and the other four defendants were sentenced to death. On 6 February 1979 the Pakistan Supreme Court upheld the sentences: in the case of Mr Bhutto by a bare majority of 4-3. (Recent official information states that about 800 people are executed annually.)

### *Philippines, The (the Republic of)*

Since martial law was imposed by President Ferdinand E. Marcos in September 1972, more than 800 people have been sentenced to death (Reuters, 18 April

1977). Of these, 658 were sentenced by civilian courts, the majority being convicted of murder. The remainder were sentenced by military courts.

Of those sentenced to death by civilian courts, the sentences on only 17 have been confirmed by the Philippine Supreme Court, and these people are reportedly awaiting execution. The remaining cases are still being reviewed by the Supreme Court. Philippine law requires that death sentences be reviewed by the Supreme Court and a death sentence may not be carried out unless confirmed by the votes of 10 members of the Supreme Court (Republic Act No. 296, Section 9; Resolution of the Supreme Court of 15 November 1973; Presidential Decree No. 1165, 24 June 1977).

On 24 November 1977, 642 male and 4 female prisoners were detained in national penitentiaries awaiting completion of the review of their death sentences by the Supreme Court; 22 others, one of them a woman, had had their sentences confirmed and awaited execution.

People sentenced to death may petition the President for clemency.

Since 1950, 66 death sentences have been carried out, 12 of them after martial law was imposed.

Apart from civilian courts, military tribunals set up under martial law have jurisdiction in cases of treason, espionage, provoking war, disloyalty in case of war, piracy, mutiny on the high seas, subversion, rebellion, sedition, distribution of subversive literature, illegal possession of firearms and crimes committed with illegally possessed firearms, and usurpation of military authority (General Order No. 59, 24 June 1977). The maximum penalty for many of these offences is death.

Military tribunals have reportedly sentenced more than 140 people to death by firing squad; of these, three have been reported executed. The remaining cases are under review, including the cases of three aeroplane hijackers convicted in 1976 (Reuters, 18 April 1977).

Under the Revised Penal Code (Public Act No. 3815, 1932), a discretionary death penalty exists for a wide range of offences. The first category, called crimes against national security, includes treason (Article 114), espionage (Article 120) and aggravated piracy (Article 123). For these offences, the courts may impose terms of imprisonment from 12 years to life as an alternative to the death penalty. However, under the Anti-Piracy and Anti-Highway Robbery Law of 1974 (Presidential Decree No. 532, 8 August 1974), when piracy is accompanied by murder, homicide or rape, and in certain other specific circumstances, the death penalty is mandatory.

The death penalty is also available in cases involving crimes against the person. The death penalty may be imposed for, among other things, premedidated murder; or murder by arson, poison, explosion; or where cruelty is exercised towards the victim or his or her corpse is mutilated (Article 248); or for the deliberate killing of a child less than three days old (Article 255). However, a mother or maternal grandparent who kills a child less than three days old "to hide the mother's dishonour" is not sentenced to death (Article 255). In cases involving kidnapping, the death penalty is discretionary; if the kidnapping is committed for the purpose of extorting ransom, the penalty is life imprisonment or death, whereas in other cases, the specified minimum sentence is from 12 to 20 years' imprisonment (Article 267).

The death penalty is also specified for a number of crimes against property.

These include robbery with violence resulting in death (Article 294), where the minimum sentence is life imprisonment. The death penalty is mandatory in cases of arson resulting in death (Article 326-A). Under the Anti-Cattle Rustling Law of 1974 (Presidential Decree No. 533, 8 August 1974), if a person is seriously injured or killed as a result of or on the occasion of cattle rustling, a sentence of life imprisonment or death shall be imposed.

The death penalty is available on a discretionary basis in cases of rape with the use of a deadly weapon, and rape committed by two or more persons. It is mandatory if the victim becomes insane as a result of the rape; or if homicide is committed in the act of rape or attempted rape. The specified sentence for other cases of rape is life imprisonment (Article 335).

The provisions of the Penal Code relating to capital offences have been reinforced by a number of other legislative provisions.

An Act passed in 1941 to protect national security (Commonwealth Act No. 616) specified the death penalty for espionage and related offences, and for participating in a conspiracy to commit those offences if, as a result of the conspiracy, an act of espionage is carried out (with a specified minimum sentence of up to 30 years' imprisonment).

The Anti-Subversion Act, 1957 (Republic Act No. 1700) outlawed the Philippine Communist Party, and made the death penalty available for any officer or ranking leader of the outlawed Party or its military wing (the *Hukbong Mapagpalayang Bayan*) or for members who took up arms against the Government. The Act further specified that no such person shall be convicted except on the testimony of at least two witnesses, or upon confession of the accused in open court. Under martial law, the two-witness requirement was done away with (Presidential Decree No. 885, 3 February 1976).

An Act was passed in 1971 "prohibiting certain acts inimical to civil aviation" (Republic Act No. 6235). It applies to anyone who compels a Philippines-registered aircraft to change its course or destination, or a foreign registered aircraft to land in the Philippines; or who seizes control of an aircraft whilst it is in flight. If the person concerned has fired a gun or exploded or attempted to explode a bomb in order to destroy the aircraft; or if the crime is accompanied by murder, homicide, serious physical injury or rape, the sentence may be death. The specified minimum sentence is 15 years' imprisonment.

A Presidential Decree (No. 532) of 1974, in addition to specifying the death sentence as mandatory in cases of piracy (see above), also specified it mandatory for cases of highway robbery, if this involved kidnapping for ransom or extortion; or murder or homicide, or if rape were committed as a result of or on occasion of the robbery.

Another Presidential Decree (1110-A, 29 March 1977) made the death penalty mandatory for any one making an attempt on, or conspiring against, the life of the President, of any member of his family, of any member of his Cabinet, or of any member of their respective families. The Decree does not define who is to be regarded as belonging to the family.

The Penal Code does not allow the death sentence to be imposed when the convicted person is more than 70 (Article 47). Moreover, the Code specifies that a woman shall not be executed within three years of the date of sentencing or while she is pregnant (Article 8).

A child under 9 years of age is exempt from all criminal liability (Article 12); minors under 18 are not sentenced unless, after being committed to a youth center, they prove to be incorrigible (Article 80, modified by Presidential Decree No. 603, The Child and Youth Welfare Code, 10 December 1974, as amended).

Death sentences imposed by the civilian courts are carried out by electrocution. The Penal Code allows the condemned to be anaesthetized when facing electrocution, if they request it (Article 81). Military tribunals order execution by firing squad.

Philippine law specifies a wide variety of capital offences, and cases recently reported indicate that the death penalty is frequently invoked by the courts. These cases include:

A military tribunal in November 1976 sentenced two soldiers to death by firing squad for the murder of a police patrolman. A military tribunal in November 1976 sentenced three men to death by firing squad for their part in the hijack of a Philippine airliner in which 10 passengers and three of the hijackers were killed.

A father was sentenced to death on 12 December 1976 for having raped his daughter, aged 14, at knife-point. Twelve people were sentenced by a military tribunal to death by firing squad in February 1977 for kidnapping a banker and taking a ransom of 300,000 *pesos*.

It would appear, on the basis of available information, that the majority of cases in which the death penalty has been imposed, involve homicide. An example of a trial on subversion charges, for which the death penalty may be imposed, is that of three people alleged to be leading members of the underground communist New People's Army, one of whom was the former Senator Benigno Aquino, a political opponent of President Marcos. On 25 November 1977, the three were sentenced to death by firing squad; but, following international protests against the sentences, President Marcos ordered the case to be reopened for the sole purpose of hearing evidence and arguments from the defence.

***Singapore** (the Republic of)*

The Singapore Penal Code provides that the following offences may be punished by death: waging war against the Government (Section 121); intending hurt or death to or restraint of the President (mandatory under Section 121A); perjury resulting in the execution of a person indicted on a capital charge (Section 194); murder (mandatory under Section 302); abetting the suicide of a person under 18 or an "idiot, insane or delirious person" (Section 305); kidnapping with intent to murder or where the victim is placed "in danger of being murdered" (Section 364); robbery by a gang of five or more (Section 396); certain offences relating to mutiny in the armed forces (Section 132).

An amendment to the Misuse of Drugs Act made in 1975 specifies that any person found trafficking in more than 30 grammes of morphine or heroin may be sentenced to death. The possession of certain types of arms is proscribed by the Arms Offences Act, which covers armed robbery and use of a firearm with intent to cause injury.

The Criminal Procedure Code provides that sentence of death shall not be passed on people under 18 or pregnant women (Section 203-4). By Section 206, the death sentence is to be carried out by hanging; by Section 228, the President has the power to exercise clemency.

Under the Criminal Procedure Code (Amendment) Act 1969, trial by jury for capital offences was abolished, largely because it was claimed that juries were reluctant to pass death sentences in murder trials. The Act states that offenders liable for the death penalty shall be tried by a court consisting of two judges of the High Court, one of whom shall be the presiding judge, and that the decision of the Court as to the guilt of the accused shall be arrived at unanimously.

The total number of people under sentence of death and of executions carried out in the period 1973–77 are not known. Executions are carried out by hanging in prison and are not always reported. However, a few cases have been made public since 1973, and some examples are given below.

The British newspaper, *The Times*, of 27 July 1973, reported that a woman and her husband, both sentenced to death in December 1970 for the murder of a Japanese woman, were hanged in Changi Prison, after a last appeal to the Judicial Committee of the Privy Council in London had been rejected.

In the same prison, 11 other executions were reported to have taken place in 1975. The first case concerned a group of eight men convicted of murder in 1971 and 1973, and hanged in prison on 28 February 1975. The eight men, aged from 21 to 35, included four Chinese, three Indians and one Malay. According to one report, quoting a prison source, they were hanged in three groups with hoods over their heads. A twenty-four-year-old convicted murderer, sentenced to death by the High Court in September 1973, was executed in the same prison in April 1975. The execution of two men, aged 25 and 29 respectively, who had been sentenced to death for a murder committed in 1972, was reported in June 1975.

In the summer of 1976, the High Court of Singapore sentenced to death three young men found guilty of seven charges under the Arms Offences Act. The charges included robbery in which guns were involved (Section 5), and use of a revolver with intention to cause injury (Section 4).

The first person to be sentenced to death under the amended Misuse of Drugs Act was a young Malaysian aged 25, Too Hook Seng. He was sentenced on 13 July 1976 after a seven-day hearing by the High Court, having been found guilty of trafficking in 46.38 grammes of morphine in January of the same year. Seventeen other people were awaiting trial under the same law at that time.

Four other death sentences for drug charges were reported in October and November 1976.

### *Sri Lanka (the Republic of)*

The death penalty was suspended in Ceylon (now Sri Lanka), from 1956 to 1959, but was re-introduced by the Suspension of Capital Punishment (Repeal) Act 1959. The late Prime Minister, S.W.R.D. Bandaranaike, played a leading role in the Cabinet decision to suspend the death penalty in 1956, pending full investigation by a Royal Commission. The Report of the Commission on Capital Punishment, known as the Norval Morris Commission, was published on 19 June 1959, and the majority of the Commission recommended that capital punishment remain suspended. The main conclusion of the commission was that there had been no observable increase in the rate of homicidal crime during the period of suspension of the death penalty. Despite this, the death penalty was re-introduced after the assassination of Mr Bandaranaike in 1959.

An Amnesty International delegation visiting Sri Lanka in January 1975 concluded that "on the face of the statistical evidence, it does appear that there has been a revival of hanging which in the recent past had begun to fall into disuse".* The *Report* quotes official figures indicating that between 1970 and 1974 there had been an increase in the executions carried out (as against total death sentences passed) of 27 per cent – from 1.6 per cent to 28.6 per cent. (In 1970, one in 65 sentenced to death was executed; in 1974, the figure was 24 (up to October 1974) out of 84 (up to December 1974).) The Ministry of Justice has explained that these figures merely disclosed "a marked speeding-up of disposal of appeals and quick decisions about the prerogative of mercy", but the Amnesty International mission concluded that "there had been a marked shift towards [favouring] the continued retention of the death penalty." However, in the following years the execution rate dropped dramatically: in 1975 four out of 67 people were executed, in 1976 one out of 53 (up to 21 July 1976).

The vast majority of those sentenced to death in Sri Lanka have been convicted for murder under the provisions of the Criminal Code. Among those awaiting a final decision on execution at the time of the Amnesty International mission were 12 prisoners who had taken part in the 1971 uprising; they had been convicted by the ordinary courts on charges of murder. So far as Amnesty International is aware at the time of writing, none of them had been executed.

The Emergency (Miscellaneous Provisions and Powers) Regulations in force in Sri Lanka until February 1977, made the death penalty applicable to several offences, including conspiracy to overthrow the Government, arson, trespass and looting, and participation in unlawful assemblies. The power to impose the death sentence was, however, limited to the High Court. Under Section 191 of the Criminal Code, perjury leading to the death by execution of another is itself punishable by death.

The President of Sri Lanka has the power to exercise the prerogative of mercy. The Law Minister, F.D. Bandaranaike, put on record the principles which had been followed in this matter since he assumed office in 1972:

> *"The position is that excepting where there is something particularly shocking to the conscience about the murder – in the nature of premeditation or a deliberately calculated, cold-blooded murder, where there has been extraordinary cruelty about the way in which a person has been killed, not merely the sad fact that a person has been killed but the way the murder has been committed – it is not the general policy of the State to order the execution of the death sentence. In those cases there is a routine followed where a death sentence is not executed but commuted to 20 years' imprisonment." (National Assembly Debates, 25 November 1975)*

In laying down a policy for clemency, the Law Ministry has stated that the political motivation of anyone committing a capital crime is not taken into consideration. On 25 November 1975, the Minister of Justice stated in the National Assembly that:

> *"I do not accept for a moment the argument that political prisoners should be treated differently from others. A man who commits a crime with a political motivation is not any less guilty than a man who commits a crime with some other motivation." (National Assembly Debates, 25 November 1975)*

* Report of an Amnesty International Mission to Sri Lanka, 9–15 January 1975.

Section 257 of the Administration of Justice Law 1973 provides that within 14 days of the imposition of a death sentence, the trial judge shall forward to the President of the Republic a copy of the notes of evidence taken at the trial, together with a report setting out any reasons why the defendant should not be executed. This clearly has great relevance in cases where the death penalty is mandatory.

Administrative delay, to which some appeals for clemency appear to be subject, is of serious concern. In 1963, both Government and opposition Members of Parliament demanded the appointment of a Select Committee to probe delays in the granting of reprieves. The committee was never set up. In 1975, the Minister of Justice himself cited a tragic case in which administrative delays had had fatal results, in that "[the] papers [of the man in question] had never reached the Ministry of Justice until the eleventh month after the sentence was imposed upon him. When the recommendation went to the President, the man had hanged himself inside the cell." (National Assembly Debates, 25 November 1975)

The death penalty is carried out by hanging. In one case, a prisoner is known to have been carried to the gallows on a stretcher. Deduwa Jayasinghe Siripala, known as "Maru Sira" (Killer Sira), was hanged on the morning of 5 August 1975 after prison guards had been unable to wake him. The inquiry into his execution revealed that he had been given an overdose of drugs on the evening before his execution, and that he was presumably unconscious at the time of his execution. According to the evidence of the doctor and the executioner, life had not been extinct until 18 minutes after the hanging had taken place.

According to *The Times* of Ceylon, dated 20 January 1975: "If there is any single question on which the leaders of all Sri Lanka's political parties are agreed, it is that the death penalty must go." A letter in the *Sunday Times*, Colombo, of 10 October 1976, stated: "In a predominantly Buddhist country like ours where *ahimsa* (non-killing) is much discussed, the death penalty cannot continue to have meaning."

The British newspaper, *The Times*, 23 May 1977, reported that President William Gopallawa commuted to life imprisonment the sentences of 144 men and six women sentenced to death. This was done to mark the 5th anniversary of the Republic of Sri Lanka. Fifteen prisoners awaiting execution were pardoned on 17 September 1977, their sentences being commuted at the occasion of the Prime Minister's birthday.

### ***Taiwan** (the Republic of China)*

The following laws of Taiwan (the Republic of China) refer to the death penalty: The Criminal Code (1935) (as amended); Statute for Punishment of Corruption during the Period of Communist Rebellion (1963); Provisional Statute for Punishment of Offenders against National General Mobilization (1942) (as amended); Martial Law (1934) (as amended); Criminal Law of the Armed Forces (1929) (as amended); Statute for the Punishment of Rebellion (adopted 1949) (as amended); Law of Wartime Military Discipline (1950) (additionally applicable during time of "rebellion").

Taken together with provisions of the current State of Siege (proclaimed 19 May 1949), this legislation reveals that the following are capital offences in Taiwan: kidnapping for ransom; murder; piracy; arson; rape; drug-trafficking; certain forms of sedition; espionage; spreading rumours and "beguiling" the public; incitement to rebellion or public riot; disrupting the money market; theft or robbery with violence; armed robbery; strikes by workers or traders which disrupt public order; encouragement of students to strike or public incitement of others to commit crimes; destruction of or theft from traffic or communications facilities; disruption of the supply of water, electricity or gas; certain offences involving corruption; causing fire or flood or endangering public safety; unlawful possession of arms, ammunition or explosives; unlawful misappropriation of public property or foodstuffs.

Under the Statute for the Punishment of Rebellion, treason, rebellion, and assistance to a "rebel" are punishable by a mandatory death penalty. Apart from overt acts of rebellion, the definition of the crime includes participation "in an organization or meeting for the purposes of rebellion", and the making of "propaganda beneficial to the rebels by written word, books or speeches" (Article 2). The definition includes "surrendering when in command of armed forces units" (Article 3).

Under Article 4 of this Statute, a discretionary death sentence is available for, among other things, "...[inducing]...a public official...to commit a breach of discipline".

Article 11 makes provision for summary execution, by "the highest military organ", of a person caught in a "war area" while engaged in an offence, the penalty for which is a mandatory death sentence under the Statute. The summary execution must be reported, and if it later transpires that "the facts or evidence are inconclusive", or that there has been "a serious mistake", all those concerned, including the most senior military officer, shall be "punished according to the law".

Under the Criminal Code 1935 as amended, those who communicate with a foreign state or its agent to "start war against the Republic of China" or to "subject territory of the Republic of China to such a state" or "bear arms against the Republic of China or any ally", may be sentenced to death or life imprisonment. The same applies to certain acts committed for the benefit of an enemy state. In addition to the above, special provision is made in the Criminal Law of the Armed Forces for the death penalty to be available for certain offences of "malfeasance and incompetence", wilful disobedience, unauthorized manufacture of firearms, looting, pillage, and desertion. By virtue of provisions of the Military Trial Law of 1956, the Criminal Law of the Armed Forces applies not only to serving members of the military, but also to the police corps and civil servants seconded to the military.

Whereas numerous executions of political opponents of the Government were reported in the 1950s and 1960s, there seem to have been few executions of political prisoners in recent years. However, executions of ordinary criminals have recently increased. At the end of 1975, the Government decided that, temporarily, cases involving crimes of violence (murder, rape and armed robbery) would be tried by military courts and not, as previously, by civilian courts.

In memory of President Chiang Kai-shek, who died in April 1975, the Government enacted a Bill to reduce the sentences of prisoners convicted of various offences. This Bill, which became law on 14 July 1975, was intended effectively to commute all death sentences to imprisonment for life. However, its terms did not apply to those who had committed overt acts of rebellion (or sedition) while belonging to the Communist Party, or who were convicted murderers, arsonists, kidnappers, or to Government officials guilty of major crimes of corruption.

In February 1977, Reuters reported that three young men and a boy aged 16 had been executed for armed robbery. This was said to bring the total number executed in Taiwan for a two-week period to 11. The British newspaper, *The Times,* reported on 31 December 1977 that, according to a police report, four Taiwanese seamen convicted of murdering seven fellow crewmen in a gambling dispute three years earlier had been executed. The total number of executions and death sentences in the past three years is not known to Amnesty International.

Execution is by firing squad.

***Thailand** (the Kingdom of)*

In Thailand the death penalty exists for murder and treason. Moreover, the Prime Minister is given sweeping constitutional powers to order execution without trial in cases which are considered to affect national security.

On 15 April 1977, acting under powers derived from Article 21 of the Constitution, the Prime Minister, Thanin Kraivichien, ordered the execution of a forty-four-year-old man accused of possessing 14 kilogrammes of heroin. The accused was killed by an executioner using a sub-machine gun. In a speech reported on the same day, the Prime Minister, a former judge, said that the Government was considering "much harder" punishment for narcotics offenders.

Six days after that execution, the Prime Minister ordered another summary execution without trial of a senior Thai General, accused of involvement in an abortive *coup* attempt the previous month. The General was also executed by machine gun. A Government announcement made that day said that he had murdered another General during the abortive *coup* attempt.

Under previous military Governments in Thailand, there have been public executions, usually held in a large field in the centre of Bangkok. In March 1965, a businessman arrested on charges of manufacturing and selling drugs was machine-gunned to death, and the execution was shown on Thai television. The then military Government – which has itself been accused of major involvement in drug-trafficking, since its collapse in October 1973 – had ordered his execution without trial. The last public executions took place under military rule in 1972, when 35 men were shot.

Apart from those executed by firing squad after military trial, and others whose executions are ordered by the Prime Minister, the death penalty in Thailand applies mainly to cases of murder. Thailand has an extremely high rate of murder: in 1975, there was an average of about 30 murders a day.

A research study conducted in 1972 showed that most of the criminals sentenced to death were men aged between 20 and 25; more than 70 per cent were unemployed.

There is an unkown number of people awaiting execution in Thai prisons. Death sentences may be commuted on appeal or by petitioning the King for clemency. Reprieves are often granted on special occasions, such as a royal birthday; one such occasion was the King's 48th birthday, on 5 December 1975, when commutation was announced for 40 people under sentence of death, who were among 10,000 prisoners freed in an amnesty.

According to one news report, a total of 26 people convicted of murder were executed between 1969 and 1975 (*Far Eastern Economic Review*, 23 July 1976). These figures do not include those executed by firing squad after military trial.

Under Thai law, a plea of guilty at any stage of the proceedings may reduce the maximum penalty to 50 years' or life imprisonment.

All executions except public executions have taken place at Bang Kwang Maximum Security Prison, approximately 16 kilometres north of Bangkok; a single executioner carries out the sentence with a sub-machine gun.

***Tonga** (the Kingdom of)*

According to information available to Amnesty International, the death penalty is discretionary for murder. In the 10 years up to 31 May 1977, out of 10 convictions for murder, 4 death sentences were imposed. Of these, three were commuted to life imprisonment; one execution took place.

***Vietnam** (the Socialist Republic of)*

On 23 March 1976, the official Saigon Press Agency announced that the Provisional Revolutionary Government (PRG) of South Vietnam was setting up people's tribunals and appeal jurisdictions, and was reorganizing police forces as a basis for a "democratic and progressive judiciary". Three decrees containing the basis of a future Penal Code put an end to the exceptional military jurisdictions which had been functioning since the end of the war in South Vietnam.

One of the decrees outlawed "counter-revolutionary crimes" (defined as all acts "endangering national defence, the national democratic people's revolution and the construction of socialism"), which could be punished by a term of imprisonment or the death penalty, depending on the gravity of the case.

North and South Vietnam were reunified in July 1976; Amnesty International does not know whether these decrees are still valid, or whether the penal system of the former Democratic Republic of Vietnam (North Vietnam) has been kept.

The information available to Amnesty International on death sentences or executions in the period 1975–77 concerns only the south of Vietnam.

In an interview published on 22 July 1975, the PRG Foreign Minister, Mrs Nguyen Thi Binh, stated that the PRG policy "is one of clemency, national concord, for those who repent ... but we are determined to punish all acts which affect the revolutionary power of the people. Unfortunately, there are also a few cases which we must punish severely at the command of the population." The expression, "punish severely", also used later by other Vietnamese officials, was sometimes interpreted by observers as referring to the death sentence.

In the first weeks after the change of government in 1975, the press reported several public executions of thieves, looters or former soldiers, who had engaged in clashes with the police in the Saigon area. According to the official Liberation Radio, on 4 July 1975, the Military Court of the Military Management Committee of Chau Doc City sentenced to death Le Nhat Thanh, formerly a First Lieutenant in the defeated army, for "counter-revolutionary activities" which included "hoarding arms and joining others to steal money and state property". During the trial, which was public and reportedly attended by 10,000 people, ex-Lieutenant Thanh was said to refuse to admit his guilt, in spite of his father's plea. The report did not say whether the sentence had been carried out. Later, in September of the same year, the Saigon newspaper *Giai Phong* announced that death sentences had been passed by military courts on two former intelligence agents in Can Tho, 120 kilometres south of Saigon, and on two "war criminals" in Rach-Gia, on the Gulf of Thailand, who were found guilty of murder on a number of counts.

According to the *Washington Post* of 24 May 1975, quoting Saigon Radio, several supporters of the former South Vietnamese Government were killed by villagers in An Nhan and An Phu Dong for failing to surrender their weapons and register themselves with the new Government. The report said that the broadcast did not give any further information, except that those killed were guilty of "committing crimes against the people".

In September 1976, a court in Ho Chi Minh City (formerly Saigon) sentenced to death three men, including a Roman Catholic priest and two ex-army personnel, who were among 14 people tried on charges of organizing "subversive forces, publishing counter-revolutionary leaflets and counterfeiting currency and official documents". The group was arrested after some of them were involved in a gun battle with the police at a suburban church in February. In November 1977, the death sentences on the three men were confirmed by the Appeal Court of Ho Chi Minh City.

No official statistics were available to Amnesty International on death sentences and executions in the past two years (1975–77). It is generally believed that few executions have taken place since the end of the war in April 1975. However, one Vietnamese refugee was quoted in the British paper *The Times* of 2 May 1977, as alleging that approximately 500 officials of the former régime had been executed in Phu Yen Province in 1975.

## EUROPE

At the end of 1977, Austria, Finland, the Federal Republic of Germany, Iceland, Portugal and Sweden had abolished the death penalty completely. Those countries which have abolished the death penalty for all offences committed in peacetime but have kept it for specific offences committed in time of war are Denmark, Italy, the Netherlands, Norway and Switzerland.*

All other European countries have retained the death penalty for certain offences committed in peacetime. Some of them have a long-standing policy against its use. In Luxembourg and Belgium, death sentences have automatically been commuted. In the United Kingdom, which abolished the death penalty for all other offences, certain treasonable acts and piracy are still technically punishable by death although no one has been sentenced to death for them for many years. However, there is good reason for caution in classifying as "abolitionist *in practice*" any country which keeps the death penalty *in law*: this is borne out by the example of Belgium – which has not had an execution for a civil offence since 1918 – where new laws were passed in 1975 and 1976, allowing for the use of the death penalty for certain offences in peacetime. Similarly, in the Republic of Ireland, where there has not been an execution since 1954, two people were sentenced to death in 1976, at a time when the Government indicated its readiness to apply the death penalty for terrorist murders. Although Greece has not had an execution since 1972, multiple death sentences were passed there in at least two cases in the period 1974–76. In Cyprus, the dominant tradition of commuting death sentences did not prevent the execution of three people in 1962.

The following states not only preserve the death penalty for peacetime offences, but have carried out executions in the period 1974–76: Albania, Bulgaria, Czechoslovakia, France, the German Democratic Republic (GDR), Hungary, Poland, Romania, Spain,* Turkey, Yugoslavia, and the Union of Soviet Socialist Republics.

In each of the countries in Europe which retain the death penalty, it may be passed and carried out only on a person convicted of an offence punishable in law by the death penalty. (Albania may be an exception to this.) In some countries, offences not involving acts of violence are punishable by death. In Turkey, for example, courts may impose the death penalty for leading a society aimed at establishing the domination of one social class over another. In the USSR, the death penalty is available in peacetime for treason, an offence which may, according to the law, consist merely of "flight abroad or refusal to return to the USSR from abroad". In the USSR, Poland and Romania, large-scale theft of state property is in itself punishable by death. In a number of states, the degree of repugnance of some crimes of violence is taken into consideration in imposing the death penalty – aggravated murder, murder in association with kidnapping or rape, rape under certain circumstances. In other countries, violent crimes are made punishable by death when committed against institutions or officials of the State.

Many retentionist countries keep the death penalty for crimes relating to State security. Throughout Eastern Europe such offences as "treason", "espionage", "endangering the independence of the State" and "hostile activities against the State" are punishable in peacetime by death, and several Western European states also have retained the death penalty for treason in peacetime.

With regard to the imposition and application of the death penalty in recent years, it is remarkable how many states have passed death sentences for offences not resulting in death. Of those sentenced to death in the USSR in each of 1974, 1975 and 1976, a certain number annually have been convicted only of theft of state property. In Romania and Bulgaria, in 1974 and 1975, people were sentenced to death for "espionage" not involving acts of violence. In Albania, in 1976, official sources indicated that certain defeated political figures among the country's leaders may have been executed (although it is not clear, here, whether any judicial process was involved). The most recent executions in Turkey were of left-wing guerillas who had not killed anyone, but who, in the course of other criminal offences, had used firearms. In Greece, the only death sentences passed in the period 1974–77 were on politically-motivated terrorists convicted of murder, and on former Government leaders convicted of treason. (All these sentences were commuted to imprisonment.) Of those sentenced to death in Spain in recent years, the only ones to be executed had been convicted of politically-motivated acts of violence: two people who were garrotted in 1974 and five who were shot in 1975. In the Republic of Ireland, only two people have been sentenced to death in the past two decades, convicted in 1976 of murdering a policeman. (If the victim had been a civilian, the death sentence could not have been passed; these two death sentences were finally reduced to imprisonment after an appeal court ruling that it remained unproven whether the defendants had known, at the time of the offence, that the victim was a policeman.)

* For more recent changes in Denmark and in Spain, see pp. 111 and 125.

In a number of European states, people may be sentenced to death under judicial procedures which diverge from the established standards and practices for safeguarding the rights of the accused which are applied in dealing with many less serious offences.

In Spain, "summary" proceedings may be held in military courts against civilians charged with certain crimes against the State. In 1975, the courts violated a number of rights to fair trial in sentencing 11 alleged terrorists to death, including one who was mentally unfit at the time of his hearing. In the Republic of Ireland, several offences for which the death penalty is available are liable to be tried in a special non-jury court. In the USSR, people sentenced to death have more limited opportunities for appeal than those convicted of most other types of offence not carrying the death penalty; in some Union Republics of the USSR, no possibility of appeal exists at all in cases involving the death penalty.

In every European state, the final decision as to whether or not a death sentence is to be carried out is taken by the head of state or by some other appointed government official or body. Procedures for deciding whether or not clemency is to be granted vary from state to state.

In some countries – Belgium and Luxembourg, for example – clemency is always granted, but in most states, there is no reliable way of predicting when, and in what manner of case, it will be granted.

Although all countries of Eastern Europe and the USSR are committed by certain elements of socialist legal theory to the ultimate abolition of the death penalty, they show no clear trend towards abolition. Over the past two decades, the USSR has steadily increased the number of offences for which the death penalty is applicable. The trend in some countries of Eastern Europe, on the other hand, is towards the introduction of new penal codes, reducing the number of offences for which the death penalty may be applied. Even so, the range of capital offences remains wide.

In Western Europe, there is no apparent trend towards more states abolishing the death penalty in the near future. The Government of the Republic of Ireland has clearly indicated its willingness to return to the use of the death penalty in the face of terrorism, an attitude which other governments may take. In France, widespread and outspoken support for abolition has not succeeded in preventing two executions sanctioned by a President who has avowed his personal opposition in principle to the death penalty. In France, too, a popular singer and even two Government ministers were able, apparently with impunity, to advocate in public the execution of a suspect who had not yet been tried in court.

***Albania** (the People's Socialist Republic of)*

On 1 October 1977 a new Penal Code came into force. The one previously in force provided a discretionary death sentence for 40 crimes, 25 of them political and military. Under the new Code, the Albanian courts can, at their discretion, impose the death sentence for 32 offences, of which 23 are political and military crimes.

In the new Penal Code a discretionary death sentence is available for the following crimes: treason to the fatherland (Article 47); espionage (Article 48); provoking war or the breaking off of diplomatic relations with the Socialist People's Republic of Albania (Article 49); terrorist acts (Article 50); organization of armed groups or participation therein (Article 51); diversion of socialist wealth by destruction or damage, by explosion, fire or other means, by poisons, by the spreading of epidemic epizootic diseases to weaken or undermine the people's Government (Article 52); sabotage (Article 53); genocide (Article 54); agitation and propaganda against the State (Article 55); incitement to hatred or quarrels between nationalities and races (Article 56); creation of a counter-revolutionary organization or participation therein (Article 57); hostile activity before the Liberation (Article 58); support [for an offender] after the commission of a crime against the State [that is, concealment of such an offender] (Article 59); activity against the revolutionary movement of the working class (Article 60); appropriation of socialist property if committed more than once or by an organized group or in large proportions (Article 62); theft of socialist property (Article 65); wilful destruction or damage of socialist wealth by fire or other means involving common danger (Article 67); forgery of currency (Article 76); wilful destruction of or damage to ways and means of communication (Article 78); wilful murder committed for, among other things, revenge or from jealousy towards two or more people, or on more than one occasion, when the person killed has no means of self-defence (Article 84); robbery (Article 102); dissemination of false information resulting in panic (Article 124); avoidance of military service (Article 139); failure to execute an order (Article 142); refusal to carry out a duty and coercing others to refuse (Article 144); misuse or destruction of or damage to military property (Article 147); destruction of means of combat (Article 152); disobeying orders to fight (Article 153); abandonment of the battlefield and surrender as a prisoner (Article 154); loss of the flag of a military unit in time of war through fear (Article 155); abandonment of a warship about to sink without an appropriate order from those in command (Article 156); appropriation of the possessions of those killed, wounded or captured (Article 157); violence against the population in areas of military operations (Article 159).

According to Article 22 of the new Penal Code:

*"The death penalty is an extraordinary punishment imposed solely for especially dangerous crimes.*

*"The death penalty will not be imposed upon persons who have not completed their eighteenth year at the time of the commission of the crime, or upon women who are pregnant at the time of the commission of the crime or the trial.*

*"A death sentence imposed upon a woman will not be carried out if she is found to be pregnant when the sentence is to be executed. This penalty will be replaced by the court by twenty-five years' imprisonment."*

Several reports from Albania allege that summary executions are still widespread but it is difficult to verify them.

According to one report, in April 1973, four ring-leaders of a prison riot in protest at insufficient food and insanitary conditions in the mines near Spac in which they worked, were executed in front of other prisoners.

There have been numerous allegations that local authorities have ordered the killing of clergy and active believers in Albania. One well-documented case is that of Father Shtefen Kurti. He was first sentenced to death in 1945 on charges of "espionage for the Vatican" because of his public opposition to Government action against the Roman Catholic Church in Albania. His sentence was commuted to life imprisonment and he was released after serving 18 years in strict confinement in 1963.

In the mid 1960s, shortly after his release, Father Kurti was reportedly arrested again by the police, severely beaten and sentenced by an *ad hoc* tribunal (which, as far as Amnesty International knows, had no authority in law). His sentence was a further 16 years' imprisonment for engaging in "illegal religious activities". In 1973, while serving the sentence in Lushnja prison camp, he is said to have baptized a new-born baby. Shortly afterwards he was taken to the local church, tried by a similar special tribunal and sentenced to death. According to report, he was executed by firing squad and his personal belongings distributed among the believers in the village.

According to press reports, in November 1976, Bequir Balluku, the former Defence Minister, and eight other high Government officials were charged with conspiring against the State and sentenced to death; the trials evidently took place after political struggles within the Government. Amnesty International does not know, at the time of writing, whether the death sentences were carried out.

***Austria** (the Republic of)*

The death penalty was abolished for all crimes in 1968. Article 85 of the Federal Constitution states that "The death penalty is abolished."

***Belgium** (the Kingdom of)*

The death penalty has been retained in Belgium, although no executions have been carried out since 242 collaborators were shot after the Second World War. These sentences were passed by councils of war or military tribunals. The last execution for a civil crime – namely, murder – was in 1918. Two crimes apart from crimes which fall under military jurisdiction have recently been made punishable by death: in June 1975, a law was passed providing a discretionary death penalty in cases of kidnapping in which the victim is killed or tortured. In June 1976 a law was passed providing the death penalty for the hijacking of an aircraft if death results.

In practice, death sentences are not carried out; to date applications for clemency have always been successful.

***Bulgaria** (the People's Republic of)*

The amended Bulgarian Penal Code of 1 May 1968, currently in force, considerably reduced the number of crimes which were punishable by death under the Penal Code of 1951 – from 50 to 29.*

A discretionary death penalty is provided for the following crimes, referred to in the Penal Code as "high treason": participation, with intent to overthrow the State system, in an attempted *coup* aimed at the forcible seizure of central or local power, or in armed uprising (Article 95); murder of a State or public official with the aim of undermining or weakening the power of the State (Article 96,

* The German translation of the 1968 Penal Code by T. Lyon and A. Lipowschek states on p.36 that there are 29 crimes punishable by death. A more recent study by T. Horvath, *Allam es Jogtudomany,* Vol. 18, No. 4, pp. 515-539, published in Budapest, lists only 26 crimes punishable by death.

paragraph 1); creating a public danger by poisoning water or food – with the aim of undermining or weakening the power of the State (Article 97); murder of a representative of a foreign state with the aim of bringing about war or international complications for the People's Republic (Article 99, paragraph 1); giving aid to the enemy, and participating in war against Bulgaria (Article 100); espionage (Article 104, paragraph 4); sabotage (Article 106); incitement to disaffection in the Bulgarian army with the intention of weakening the State's ability to defend itself, either in time of war or if grave consequences result (Article 102, paragraph 2).

Article 116 lists eleven different varieties of homicide punishable by the death penalty. They include premeditated murder; the killing of a Bulgarian official or an official of an ally; killing in certain aggravated circumstances, in which, for example, the victim is a relative, or someone helpless, or the method of murder is particularly cruel; killing for personal gain.

Other offences which may carry the death penalty include: robbery accompanied by attempted murder (Article 199); making plans to conduct a war of aggression (Article 409); war crimes (Article 410a and b); aggravated cases of war crimes against prisoners of war (Article 411a, b and c); aggravated cases of infringing specified provisions of the laws of war (Article 412a, b, c, d, e, f); use of prohibited methods of war or prohibited arms (Article 415, paragraph 2); genocide (Article 416a, b, c, d); occasioning damage to specific transport facilities, or allowing such damage to take place, if life or foreign-owned property is thereby jeopardized, or death results (Article 340); especially serious cases where there is loss of life caused or allowed by non-compliance, either deliberate or through negligence, with traffic or vehicle regulations in certain circumstances involving public transport; aggravated cases of disrupting public transport or traffic thereby causing death of a person or persons in charge of a vehicle (Article 342, paragraph 2[c]); causing death by deliberately poisoning water supplies (Article 349, paragraph 2); preparation of epidemic bacteria with the intention of causing infection in other people (Article 349, paragraph 3).

In addition to the above, five military crimes are punishable by death.

In Bulgaria, people under 20 (18 in wartime) and women pregnant at the time of the offence or trial are not sentenced to death; for a woman who subsequently becomes pregnant, a sentence of 20 years' imprisonment is substituted for the death sentence.

The Bulgarian Supreme Court is charged with examining the legality of the death sentence imposed by lower courts. People sentenced to death have the right of appeal to a higher court. (In serious cases involving political or economic offences, the trial proceedings may take place in the Supreme Court. After the final decision has been taken and the death sentence affirmed by the Supreme Court, the defendant has the right to petition for clemency. This is granted by the Presidency and the State Council, which have the power to commute a death sentence to 20 years' imprisonment. Execution is by firing squad (Article 131 of Code of Criminal Procedure).

In June 1974, Dr Heinrich Spetter, a fifty-three-year-old Bulgarian economist of Jewish descent, was condemned to death for alleged economic espionage. After an international campaign for commutation of the sentence, Dr Spetter was released on 22 August 1974 and expelled from Bulgaria.

In September 1974, Nicholas Stefanov Charmulisky, a high official in a co-operative, was arrested and charged with economic espionage, on the grounds of having contact with an employee at the Italian Embassy in Sofia, through whom he sent letters and documents to relatives in the United States of America. He was sentenced to death, but in August 1976 the sentence was commuted to 20 years' imprisonment.

In January 1977, Vasil Velev, convicted of a particularly brutal murder, was executed.

***Cyprus** (the Republic of)*

Article 205 of the Cyprus Penal Code provides for a mandatory death sentence in cases of premeditated murder. Article 53 of the 1960 Cyprus Constitution provides that the President or Vice-President of the Republic shall have the right to exercise the prerogative of mercy for condemned prisoners belonging to their respective communities. Where the victim of the murder and the offender are members of different communities, the prerogative of mercy shall be exercised by agreement between the President and Vice-President. In the event of disagreement, the vote for clemency prevails.

With only one exception, every application for clemency since the establishment of the Republic of Cyprus in 1960 has been successful. The exception occurred in 1962, when three people were executed while the President was out of the country, and the Vice-President declined to grant clemency.

In 1974 a Bill was introduced, providing the death penalty for people involved in arms trafficking. The provision has not yet become law.

Pregnant women and people under the age of 16 when the crime was committed may not be sentenced to death.

There have been no changes of law relating to the death penalty since 1965. At the time of writing, an important amendment to criminal law is being considered: it would give the court discretion to pass a lighter sentence than that specified for the offence (the death sentence) if the circumstances so warrant.

According to Article 7 (2) of the Constitution, the death penalty may be provided by law for cases of premeditated murder, high treason, piracy *jure gentium*, and for certain offences under military law.

***Czechoslovakia** (the Czechoslovak Socialist Republic)*

Under the 1973 Penal Code, the following crimes are punishable by a discretionary death sentence: high treason (Article 91); aggravated cases of violent acts against the State (Article 92, paragraph 2); terrorism (Articles 93 and 94, paragraph 3); deliberate or attempted homicide with the intention of causing damage to the socialist society and State (Article 93); killing or endangering the lives of several persons or causing extensive damage with the intention of deterring others from fulfilling their tasks in socialist society (Article 94, paragraph 3); aggravated cases of disruption of the State system or of its defence capability (Article 95, paragraph 2); disruption of the economy of the State in time of war (Article 96, paragraph 2); aggravated cases of sabotage (Article 97, paragraph 3); any of the above offences (apart from an offence under Article 91), if committed against allied socialist States (Article 99); aggravated cases of espionage (Article 105, paragraph 3); aggravated cases of espionage against other socialist countries

(Article 108); treason during war (Article 114); aggravated cases of endangering public security (Article 179, paragraph 3); hijacking (Articles 180A, paragraph 2 and 180C, paragraph 2); premeditated homicide (Article 219); genocide (Article 259); aggravated cases of the use of prohibited arms in war (Article 262, paragraph 3); wartime atrocities (Article 263, paragraph 2); exploitation of the situation on a battlefield, e.g., stealing from the dead (Article 264). In addition the Penal Code lists 13 military offences carrying a discretionary death sentence.

Pregnant women and people under 18 are exempt from the death penalty under Article 29, paragraph 4 of the Penal Code.

An execution can only take place after the Supreme Court has examined the case and confirmed the verdict, and after a petition for clemency has been refused (Article 317 of the Code of Criminal Procedure). The judge, prosecuting counsel, director of the prison, and a medical doctor must be present at the execution (Article 319, paragraph 1 of the Code of Criminal Procedure).

In the following cases, Amnesty International knows that the death sentence has been imposed. In April 1974, Olga Hepnerova was sentenced to death for the wilful murder of eight people in August 1973: she had driven a lorry into a group of people, killing eight of them. A report in the *Neue Züriche Zeitung* of 8 April 1974 did not say whether the sentence was carried out. On 20 October 1975, Ladislav Meszaros was executed for murdering a young girl in March 1973 and attempting to murder her brother. On 28 December 1975, Peter Richter, who had several previous convictions, was executed for killing a policeman who was attempting to arrest him for stealing firearms in August 1974. In January 1977, Ladislav Molnar was executed for the murder of his baby daughter and mother-in-law in 1976. In August 1977, K. Kalmer was executed for three attempts to murder "with tragic consequences" and for other criminal offences. In October 1977, Miroslav Z. was sentenced to death for strangling one woman and stabbing another to death, after attempting to rape them. A report by the Czechoslovak News Agency did not say whether the sentence was carried out.

### ***Denmark** (the Kingdom of)*

The death penalty was abolished for ordinary crimes in 1930, but is retained for certain crimes against the State in time of war.* The maximum penalty in ordinary criminal law for any crime, civil or political, even in wartime, is life imprisonment. The Military Criminal Code, however, retains the option of applying the death penalty to members of the armed forces and civilians for grave treasonable offences in time of war.

After the Second World War, penal legislation was temporarily suspended, and 46 collaborators were executed. The last execution took place in 1950.

### ***Finland** (the Republic of)*

The death penalty was abolished for all crimes in 1972. It had already been abolished for offences in peacetime in 1949.

### ***France** (the French Republic)*

The French Penal Code and the Code of Military Justice authorize the use of the

* The death penalty was abolished by the *Folketing* (Parliament) in April 1978. This amended the law relating to offences committed in time of war.

death penalty for a wide variety of civil and military crimes. Since 1959, 51 people have been condemned to death for ordinary crimes, of whom 14 have been executed. This figure does not include the four members of the OAS who were executed in the period 1962–63. In view of the number of death penalty cases in the last two decades, it is hardly surprising that the issue of the death penalty is of major public interest in France, and that both the retentionist and the abolitionist viewpoints have been most forcefully argued. At the time of writing, three people are under sentence of death. Although there are current cases of people condemned to death *in absentia*, under French law such cases have to be retried when and if the accused lands on French soil.

A mounting campaign against the death penalty has attracted support from important professional bodies and personalities, including the President of the Republic now in office, M. Valéry Giscard d'Estaing. On 11 April 1974, while still a candidate for the Presidency, M. Giscard d'Estaing expressed "une aversion profonde pour la peine de mort" (a profound aversion to the death penalty). He has stated, however, that there are two crimes for which he considers the use of the death penalty may possibly be justifiable: the premeditated kidnapping of children resulting in death, and lethal attacks on elderly people.

Among other legal and religious bodies, the *Syndicat de la Magistrature*, at its 9th Congress in November 1976, voted by 228 to 9 with 10 abstentions for the abolition of the death penalty. The *Syndicat* represents approximately 1,200 of the 4,500 (*magistrats*) in France. In addition, in July 1976 all the members of the Commission for the Revision of the Penal Code, declared their hostility to the principle of the death penalty and their desire for its removal from French legislation.

The churches also have taken a strong line. The Protestant churches have long expressed their doubts, and recently the attitude of the Roman Catholic Church has become clearer. On 23 January 1977, *L'Osservatore Romano*, the official daily newspaper published in the Vatican, argued that the right to life was inalienable, and that the State did not have the right to decide between the life and death of a human being.

Two methods of execution are authorized in France. All those sentenced to death for civil crimes are decapitated by the *guillotine*. Executions of people convicted of crimes against the State are carried out by firing squad. Pregnant women cannot be executed until after the delivery of the child. Anyone under the age of 18 has their status as a minor accepted as a mitigating circumstance by the court, unless this acceptance is withheld in special cases by express decision ("une délibération spéciale et motivée") of the court, and is not sentenced to death. Between the ages of 13 and 18 the accused, if found guilty of a capital crime, is normally sentenced to a prison term of between 10 and 20 years. However, under Article 66 of the Penal Code, the court may decide to set aside the status as a minor of a defendant aged between 16 and 18, if in its judgment the circumstances and character of the accused warrant it. The trial would be held in the *Cours d'Assises des Mineurs*, but could still result in a sentence of death. (See the case of "Bruno T." below). A person below the age of 13 may be charged with a capital crime, but is considered to lack responsibility (*Ordonnance du 2 février 1945*).

Broadly speaking, the offences for which the death penalty may be applied in

France fall into the following categories:

(a) where the death penalty is used to punish direct or indirect attempts upon human life. This would include, among other things, murder, infanticide, kidnapping of a minor resulting in death (Article 302 of the Penal Code, paragraphs 1 and 2; Article 312, paragraphs 10 and 11; Article 355, paragraph 4; Article 303; Article 316, paragraph 2; Article 304, paragraphs 1 and 2);

(b) where the death penalty may be applied in instances of most serious crimes carried out by dangerous criminals. This would include, among other offences, armed robbery, kidnapping with torture, arson (Articles 381; 344 and 361, paragraph 2; Article 434, paragraphs 1 and 2; Article 434, paragraph 10). Also in this category are destruction of railways, thus impeding convoys (Law of 15 July 1845), piracy (Law of 10 April 1825) and violation of sanitary regulations at frontiers (Decree of 5 October 1953);

(c) where the death penalty may be applied for crimes against the security of the State – for example, treason (Articles 70-72 of the Penal Code), espionage (Articles 70-73), attempts on the authority of the State, insurrection (Articles 86-91, 93-95 and 99);

(d) where the death penalty may be applied in times of war for military crimes – for example, desertion, mutilation, capitulation, treason (Articles 390, 398, 401, 403, 404, 408. 424, 428, 446 and 453 of the Code of Military Justice);

(e) where the death penalty may be applied for military crimes in times of both peace and war – for example, desertion, destruction of equipment (Articles 388 and 452 of the Code of Military Justice).

In the period 1974–77, death sentences have been passed only for the crimes of murder and kidnapping with aggravating crimes of torture, rape and theft. From 1974 to 1977, Presidential clemency was granted in all but three cases.

The power of the President of the Republic to grant clemency is of crucial importance. It stems from the absolute power of the monarch in the pre-revolutionary *ancien régime* and was legalized by an *ordonnance* of Louis XVIII in 1818. It is now codified in Article 17 of the French Constitution of October 1958, which states that: “le Président de la République a le droit de faire grâce” (the President of the Republic has the right to pardon). This power is theoretically unlimited in its application and includes the right to award clemency; however, on 22 April 1976, the President defined it as “the right to reduce penalties for humanitarian motives”.

All cases involving the death penalty for ordinary crimes are tried in the Assize Courts and those involving minors (see above) in the *Cours d’Assises des Mineurs*. These courts consist of three professional judges and a non-professional jury of nine citizens. Defence counsel may challenge five members of the jury and the prosecution three members. After presentation of the case by the prosecution, by the defence and, if necessary, by counsel representing third parties (*avocat de la partie civile*), judgment is reached by the court of 12 people (the three judges and nine jurors), who, in the case of a verdict of guilty, also decide on the sentence.

Sentences for which no reasons are given are not subject to appeal, but may be referred to the *Cour de Cassation*. This is the highest court. Its one function is to make sure that any judgment referred to it is in accordance with the law.

If the *Cour de Cassation* decides, on legal grounds, to set aside a judgment, a new trial in another Assize Court is convened. If, however, the verdict of the Assize Court is upheld, the only recourse open to the convicted person is to petition the President to exercise his right of clemency under Article 17. If clemency is granted, the sentence of death is commuted normally to life imprisonment.

Decision on clemency is reached by a complex process of consultation, involving the written opinion of the President of the Assize Court passing the sentence, the Advocate General who requested the sentence and, finally, the entire administrative council of the Ministry of Justice. Opinions are received orally from the lawyers for the convicted person and from the Superior Council of the Magistrature, in a meeting presided over by the President. On the basis of the advice he receives, the President takes his decision, which is countersigned by the Prime Minister, the Minister of Justice, and any other relevant Minister (Article 19 of the French Constitution, 1958), and then communicated to the person who has lodged the petition.

In the period 1974–76, the trials of the following people involved the death penalty: Robert Hennebert (aged 44) and Roger Davoine (aged 26) were convicted in November 1973 of murder while carrying out a theft in which the victim was an elderly person. They were granted clemency by the then President, M. Georges Pompidou, and their sentences were commuted in March 1974.

There were no convictions involving the death penalty in 1974. The first case involving the death penalty after M. Giscard d'Estaing became President was that of "Bruno T." (a minor whose full name was not made public). Bruno T., the first minor to be sentenced to death in France since 1929, was found guilty of murdering an old lady. The President commuted his sentence in February 1976. Moussa Benzhara, also found guilty of murdering an old lady, had his sentence commuted in August 1976. Joseph Keller and Marcellin Horneich, found guilty of robbing and murdering an English tourist couple, and also of raping a girl, had their sentences commuted in January 1977.

Christian Ranucci, aged 21, was sentenced to death on 10 March 1976, after being convicted of murdering an eight-year-old girl. After his petition had been rejected by the President, he was executed at dawn on 28 July 1976. In accordance with previous practice, the sentence was carried out promptly after rejection of his plea by the President. Six-and-a-half days elapsed before the execution, which took place in Baumettes Prison in the presence of the President of the Assize Court, the Assistant Procurator of the Republic, the *juge d'instruction* in the case, the Almoner of the prison, the prison doctor, the *contrôleur général*, the police inspector, and three lawyers.

Jérôme Carrein, at first sentenced to death in July 1976 after being convicted of attempted rape and the murder of a minor, had his sentence quashed by the *Cour de Cassation* in October 1976. He was found guilty in a new trial in the *Cour d'Assises du Nord* on 1 February 1977. His second plea to the *Cour de Cassation* was rejected in March 1977, and the President of the Republic refused to exercise his right to grant clemency. Carrein was executed by guillotine at dawn on 23 June 1977.

The case of Patrick Henry, a self-confessed kidnapper and murderer of an eight-year-old boy, for whom he was seeking a ransom of one million francs, is to be noted. There was intense interest throughout France during his trial in January 1977, and the issue was apparently badly prejudiced by statements in favour of the death penalty made by, among many others, the Minister of the Interior, M. Michel Poniatowski, and the Minister of Justice, M. Jean Lecanuet. Henry was sentenced to life imprisonment. This, in view of the extreme emotion which the case had aroused, occasioned general surprise. The verdict was held by some to reflect a movement away from the application of the death penalty. That view is, however, open to question as, since that time, the death penalty was carried out in three cases: that of Jérôme Carrein, already discussed, and two others. Hamida Djandoubi was condemned to death on 25 February 1977 for murder after premeditated torture, rape and assault; and Michel Bodin, found guilty, on 25 March 1977, of murder with premeditation of an old man and the use of torture to facilitate theft.

The sentence of death passed on Hamida Djandoubi on 25 February 1977 was carried out on 10 September 1977. The sentence passed on Michel Bodin on 25 March 1977 was quashed by the *Cour de Cassation* on 23 June. At a retrial, the court accepted his plea of extenuating circumstances and he was sentenced to life imprisonment.

The three people under sentence of death at the time of writing are Jean Portais, for double murder; Mohammed Yahiaoui, for double murder; Michel Rousseau, for the murder of a nine-year-old girl.

***German Democratic Republic** (the) (GDR)*

The law as it stands in the GDR today is the result of the third in a series of thoroughgoing legal reforms carried out successively in 1952, 1958 and 1963. The principles guiding this reform were expressed in Part One of the Decree on the Administration of Justice, the *Rechtspflegeerlass* of 4 April 1963.

The laws under which the death penalty may be passed are:

(a) the Penal Code at present in operation (which replaces the Bismarckian Penal Code of 1871), the *Strafgesetzbuch* of 12 January 1968, as amended by the *Gesetz zur Änderung des Strafgesetzbuches (Strafrechtsergänzungsgesetz)* of 20 January 1975 and the *Gesetz zur Änderung und Ergänzung straf- und strafverfahrensrechtlicher Bestimmungen (2. Strafrechtsänderungsgesetz)* of 14 April 1977;

(b) the rarely invoked law for the Protection of Peace, the *Gesetz zum Schutze des Friedens (Friedensschutzgesetz)* of 15 December 1950.

Under the Penal Code, a death sentence may be passed for the following offences: murder (Article 112 – specifies four variants of the offence, two of which are connected with political offences); political offences such as crimes against the sovereignty of the GDR, against peace, humanity, and human rights (*Menschenrechte*) (Articles 85 and 86 – aggression; Article 91 – genocide; Article 93 – war crimes); a further category of political offences which are specifically referred to as crimes against the State (Article 96 – high treason; Article 99 – treason; Article 97 – espionage; Articles 101 and 102 – terrorism; Article 103 – "diversion" [including economic and defence sabotage]; Article 104 – sabotage).

Military offences coming under the Penal Code and carrying a possible death sentence include: desertion (Article 254); evasion of military service (Article 256); insubordination (Article 257); mutiny (Article 259); cowardice – that is, surrendering voluntarily because of cowardice, cowardly behaviour in the face of the enemy, etc. (Article 260); attacking, resisting or coercing superiors, guards, patrols or other military personnel (Article 267); offences by military personnel who have fallen into enemy hands – specifically, serving under arms against the GDR and her allies (Article 276); assault and plunder (Article 277); pillage (Article 278).

Under the law for the Protection of Peace, Article 6, paragraph (2) provides for the death penalty.

The death sentence is not mandatory for any of the above offences. Alternative sentences range from one year's imprisonment (usually as a minimum) to life imprisonment. Article 8, paragraph (2) of the Law for the Protection of Peace specifies that a death sentence has to carry with it the confiscation of all property belonging to the condemned. Article 60, paragraph (1) of the Penal Code provides that the death sentence carry with it the permanent deprivation of all civic rights, and that execution be by shooting.

According to Article 60, paragraph (2) and Article 78, a death sentence must not be passed on anyone under the age of 18. It must not be carried out on a woman pregnant when the crime was committed, or at the time the sentence is pronounced or scheduled to be carried out. A death sentence may not be carried out on anyone who becomes mentally ill after sentence is pronounced.

There are no official statistics on the use of the death penalty. The official statistical yearbook, *Statistisches Jahrbuch der Deutschen Demokratischen Republik*, 1972, contains data under the heading of criminal jurisdiction (*Strafgerichtsbarkeit*), but no figures on death sentences. Since 1972, the statistical yearbook has omitted any reference to criminal jurisdiction, supplying data only on labour law, civil and family law, and divorce law proceedings.

From press reports, it appears that between 1973 and 1976, five death sentences were passed and carried out, three for murder and the others for genocide and espionage respectively.

Under the 1968 Constitution (Article 77), the Council of State, functioning collectively as Head of State, may exercise the right to grant amnesty and clemency. The relevant procedural laws, the Law on the Administration of the Courts, (*Gerichtsverfassungsgesetz*, 27 September 1974), the Criminal Trials Procedure Law, (*Strafprozessordnung*, 12 January 1968, as amended by the *Gesetz zur Änderung der Strafprozessordnung,* 19 December 1974), and the Criminal Register Law (*Strafregistergesetz*, 19 December 1974) contain only very brief references to appeal mechanisms, commutation procedure, and the execution of the death sentence. Precise details of the relevant procedure are not accessible to Amnesty International; Article 246, paragraph (4) of the *Strafprozessordnung* lays down that immediately after the judgment has been read out in court, the defendant is to be instructed verbally on the appeal and commutation procedures that are available. At the same time the defendant is to be handed a written statement of these procedures (*Rechtsmittelbelehrung*).

As for execution of sentence, the *Strafprozessordnung*, Article 348, paragraph (1) states that when a petition for a pardon has been filed and the decision on this is still pending, the execution is to be stayed. Article 339, paragraph (2) makes the officials of the Ministry of the Interior responsible for carrying out a death sentence; paragraph (5) specifies that detailed procedural regulations are to be made by separate procedural decrees. Such decrees do not appear to be published in the official law gazette (*Gesetzblatt*).

Each year in the GDR, an unknown number of people – probably less than 10 – are killed in attempts to leave the country illegally across the heavily fortified frontier, particularly the one with the Federal Republic of Germany. Under Article 213 of the Penal Code, crossing the border without permission is a crime punishable by a prison sentence of up to five years, yet the tactics of border guards and the anti-personnel devices on the frontier have proved so lethal that they may possibly constitute a form of Government-authorized murder or summary execution.

### *Germany, Federal Republic of*

The death penalty in the Federal Republic of Germany was abolished in 1949. Article 102 of the Basic Law of the Federal Republic of Germany, made public on 23 May 1949, reads "Capital punishment shall be abolished."

### *Greece (the Hellenic Republic)*

One article of the Greek Penal Code provides a mandatory death sentence – for treason, but the death penalty is applicable under seven other articles for crimes connected with high treason: killing or attempting to kill the Head of State (Article 134); treason, that is, detaching, or attempting by force to detach, territory from Greece (Article 138); negotiating with a foreign government to cause war (Article 139). According to Article 86 of the Greek Penal Code, the death penalty can be applied for murder only in certain instances: namely if the crime is particularly hideous and abhorrent because of the way in which it was carried out and the circumstances surrounding it, and if the criminal is considered dangerous to society.

The last execution to take place in Greece was for murder, on 25 August 1972, and on only two subsequent occasions known to Amnesty International have death sentences been passed. Two Palestinian terrorists were sentenced to death in January 1974, for murdering five people in an attack on Athens Airport. Their sentences were commuted to life imprisonment. In August 1975, three former leaders of the Greek *junta* were sentenced to death, but their sentences were almost immediately commuted to life imprisonment.

A Greek newspaper, *Athens News*, reported on 10 March 1976 that the death penalty was to be abolished in Greece, and that the Minister of Justice, Constantine Stefanakis, was soon to submit a draft Bill to Parliament to this end. At the time of writing, no action appears to have been taken, but in June 1977 Mr Stefanakis was quoted in the Greek press as saying that he planned to propose the abolition of the death penalty "soon".

### *Hungary (the People's Republic of)*

Socialist Law No. 1, concerning the imposition of the death penalty in the Hungarian People's Republic, was introduced in 1946. The death penalty became mandatory for conspiracy to overthrow or weaken the political régime and attempts on the life of the President.

Law No. 18 of 1947 prescribed the death sentence for war crimes and "crimes against mankind". Government Decree No. 8800/1946, No. 4/1950 and No. 24/1950 introduced a mandatory death penalty for crimes against the economy and social property. Law No. v/1961 provided that the death penalty, where discretionary, should be imposed only in the most serious instances of the crimes in question. According to Decree No. 28/1971, the death penalty was retained for crimes against property, and was also introduced for serious cases of hijacking.

According to the Hungarian Penal Code, the death sentence is discretionary, and courts may impose sentences of from 10 to 15 years or life imprisonment as an alternative.

At the time of writing, the following offences were punishable by the death penalty in peacetime: aggravated cases of conspiracy (Section 116, paragraph 3 and Section 113, paragraph 3); aggravated cases of rebellion (Section 120, paragraph 2); wilful damage (Section 124, paragraph 2); aggravated cases of destruction (Section 125, paragraph 2); assassination (Section 126, paragraph 1); treason (Section 129, paragraph 2); giving aid and comfort to the enemy (Section 130, paragraph 1); espionage (Section 131, paragraph 3); hijacking an aircraft (Section 192, paragraph 2); premeditated murder (Section 253, paragraph 2); genocide (Section 137, paragraph 1); atrocities in wartime (Section 139, paragraph 2); aggravated cases of prison riot (Section 186, paragraph 3).

The Hungarian Penal Code 1962 lists in addition 13 military crimes punishable by death.

Since the mid 1960s, the death penalty has been imposed mainly for cases of premeditated homicide. Hungarian statistics indicate that in the period 1960–69 there were only one or two cases in which the death penalty was imposed for crimes other than those against the person. The total number of executions in 1960–75, excluding those for military crimes was 104. To Amnesty International's knowledge, no statistics are made public on military crimes. The highest annual rate of executions within this period (1960–75) was in 1961, when 14 persons were executed, mainly on charges of aggravated murder. According to official statistics, six people were executed in 1970, three in 1971, six in 1972, three in 1973, four in 1974 and three in 1975.

In Hungary, the death penalty may not be passed on people under 20 or on pregnant women.

The Hungarian Supreme Court examines the legality of death sentences imposed by lower courts. All those sentenced to death have the right of appeal to a higher court. After the death sentence has been upheld by the Supreme Court, the defendant has the right to petition for clemency. This may be granted by the State Council, who may commute the death sentence to imprisonment for 20 years. In such cases, the court may decide on the infliction of supplementary punishments, such as loss of civil liberties and confiscation of property.

Execution is carried out by hanging in peacetime, and by firing squad in wartime.

On 6 May 1976, Geza Horvath, an army sergeant, was executed after being found guilty of shooting and killing three people. In December 1976, Imre Miskei was sentenced to death for raping and murdering a twelve-year-old girl. His execution took place on 29 March 1977, after his petition for clemency had been refused.

***Iceland** (the Republic of)*

The death penalty was abolished in 1928. The Penal Code of 1940 states that the maximum punishment permitted is life imprisonment.

***Ireland** (the Republic of) [Eire]*

In the Republic of Ireland the death penalty was abolished in 1964 for all but a few restricted categories of crime. These are contained in the Criminal Justice Act 1964. This Act retains the mandatory death penalty for a number of specified categories of murder (described in the Act as "capital murder"), and the discretionary death penalty for treason under the Treason Act 1939 and for offences committed by persons subject to military law under certain sections of the Defence Act 1954.

Capital murder is defined in Section 1 of the Criminal Justice Act as "murder of a member of the *Garda Siochana* [police force] acting in the course of his duty"; "murder of a prison officer acting in the course of his duty"; or "murder, committed within the State for a political motive, of the head of a foreign State or a member of the Government of, or a diplomatic officer of, a foreign State".

Capital murder is also defined in Section 1 (b) (iii) of the Criminal Justice Act as murder in the course of committing certain offences against the State. These are contained in Sections 6, 7, 8 and 9 of the Offences Against the State Act 1939, and relate to offences such as usurpation or unlawful exercise of any function of Government (Section 6); obstruction of Government by force of arms or other violent means (Section 7); obstruction of the exercise or performance by the President of any of his functions, powers or duties (Section 8) or interference with military or other employees of the State (Section 9). Section 1 (b) (iii) of the Criminal Justice Act further defines capital murder as murder committed in the course of furthering the aims of an unlawful organization, itself an offence under Section 18 of the Offences Against the State Act 1939.

The Defence Act of 1954 provides the death penalty for certain military offences under Sections 124, 125, 127 and 128. These include refusal by a commanding officer to engage the enemy; treacherous desertion or surrender; aiding the enemy or prisoners of war; and mutiny with violence.

Military tribunals have power to pass sentence of death during a state of war or armed rebellion or when a member of the defence forces on active service is before them as defendant.

A charge of capital murder under the Criminal Justice Act falls within the jurisdiction of the Central Criminal Court, which sits with a judge and jury. However, in practice, charges related to terrorism are tried in the Special Criminal Court which sits with three judges and no jury. Acting under powers conferred by the Offences Against the State Act, special criminal courts may be employed whenever the Government is satisfied that the ordinary courts are inadequate to secure the effective administration of justice and the preservation of public peace and order. The Special Criminal Court was reintroduced in 1972, specifically to try offences under the Offences Against the State Act, although the Director of Public Prosecutions has the power to refer to the court any case which he has certified as being of such a nature that ordinary courts are inadequate in the terms described above. This was done in the Murray case (see below).

Two people have been sentenced to death in the Republic of Ireland since

1964, when the Criminal Justice Act was passed. At the time of writing there have been no executions under the Act. Noel Murray (aged 27) and Marie Murray (aged 28), a married couple, were sentenced to death in the Special Criminal Court in Dublin in June 1976. They were convicted under Section 1 (b) (i) of the Criminal Justice Act for murdering a policeman in the course of his duty, but the Supreme Court quashed the capital murder convictions.

Noel and Marie Murray were the first persons to be tried on capital murder charges under the current legislation, and their case was seen by the courts as a test case for interpretation of the Criminal Justice Act. The question of law involved was whether, for a conviction of capital murder, it was necessary to show that the defendants were aware that the victim was a policeman acting in the course of his duty. By a majority of four to one the Supreme Court held that if it could be shown that the defendants either knew, or were reckless of the possibility, that the victim was a member of the police force, then a conviction for capital murder could stand. If neither of these factors was present (as the Court finally held in both these cases), the conviction would be for ordinary murder, for which the death sentence is not available.

The right exists in all cases for a person condemned to death to petition the President for clemency. In such cases, the President always acts on the advice of the Government.

The death penalty became a contentious political issue during 1975 and 1976. The abolitionist lobby of that period included several jurists who emphasized the broad scope of the capital punishment legislation, in particular Section 1 (b) (iii) of the Criminal Justice Act.

Section 18 of the Offences Against the State Act, relating to the furtherance of the aims of an unlawful organization, is very broadly framed. When, in October 1975, a group of people kidnapped a Dutch businessman, Dr Tiede Herrema, the Government announced its intention, in the eventuality of murder, to prosecute the kidnappers under Section 18 of the Offences Against the State Act and Section 1 (b) (iii) of the Criminal Justice Act. The death penalty would therefore be available.

People under sentence of death in the Republic of Ireland must have two prison officers present at all times until execution. The prisoner may have unrestricted access to the prison chaplain or to any clergyman. The prisoner may also be visited by any relatives, friends and legal advisers he or she may wish to see, but only if authorization is given in writing by either the Minister for Justice or a member of the prison visiting committee. Even these concessions may be withdrawn at any time by the Minister for Justice under powers given him by Statutory Instrument in 1976. This allows the Minister to refuse admittance to a prison to any visitor, including the prisoner's legal adviser, where he considers it necessary in the interests of the security of the prison or of the State. Whilst under sentence of death, Noel and Marie Murray were allowed visits only from Noel's parents and one brother and from their legal adviser, despite requests for visits from friends and other relatives.

Execution is carried out by hanging.

### *Italy (the Italian Republic)*

In Italy the death penalty was abolished by Legislative Decree of the Lieutenant of the Realm No. 224 of 10 August 1944 for all offences specified in the Penal Code. Subsequently, Article 27 of the Constitution of the Italian Republic specified that "the death penalty shall be applied only in the cases laid down by the military laws of war". The death penalty under military penal laws in peacetime was replaced, in 1948, by penal servitude for life.

The President of the Republic is empowered by Article 87 of the Constitution to grant clemency and commutation of sentence to all those under sentence of death in wartime.

***Liechtenstein** (the Principality of)*

Under the provisions of the Austrian Criminal Code of 1852, as applied in the Principality of Liechtenstein, the death penalty exists for high treason, damage to property leading forseeably to the death of a person and murder. (Active accomplices to murder may also be sentenced to death.)

On 25 November 1977, Hans Frich was sentenced to death for the murder of his wife and two of his children. The appeal proceedings before the Superior Court (*Obergericht*) were stayed indefinitely after psychiatric evidence was heard. Hanz Frich was the first person to be sentenced to death in Liechtenstein since 1785.

Execution in the Principality is carried out by hanging.

***Luxembourg** (the Grand Duchy of)*

The death penalty has been retained in Luxembourg for crimes such as the assassination of the Grand Duke or the Heir Apparent, and for certain categories of murder. A further list of articles making the death penalty available was inserted into the Penal Code relating to offences committed during the German occupation of the country in the Second World War.

In Luxembourg all death sentences are commuted automatically.

***Netherlands** (the) (Kingdom of the)*

The death penalty was abolished by statute in 1870 for all civil crimes, including murder, but remained in the Military Penal Code for certain grave crimes committed in time of war. However, it could only be pronounced if, in the opinion of a majority of the judges hearing a case, the security of the State required the defendant to be executed.

By Royal Order (*Koninklijk Besluit*) of 22 December 1943, the death penalty was reintroduced for war crimes committed during the German occupation in the Second World War. This was replaced by a statute in July 1952. Crimes normally carrying a maximum sentence of not less than 15 years may carry the death penalty if committted by collaborators during enemy occupation. The trial would be held before a special independent criminal court, and the death penalty could only be imposed by unanimous verdict of the judges. This applies also to trials under the Military Penal Code.

Since 1952 there have been no executions. At the time of writing, two men are on trial in a special court for war crimes.

In 1977, the outgoing Government announced in the Queen's Speech that the death penalty would be completely abolished. At the time of writing, this had not been accomplished.

*Norway (the Kingdom of)*

The death penalty for ordinary crimes was abolished in Norway in 1905, and the maximum punishment is life imprisonment. However, the Military Penal Code retains the death penalty for acts of treason during time of war or national emergency.

After the Second World War, 38 collaborators, including Vidkun Quisling, were executed.

***Poland** (the Polish People's Republic)*

The Polish Penal Code of 1889 abolished the death sentence, at the end of lengthy parliamentary discussion, which had begun early in the nineteenth century.

After the establishment of an independent Polish Republic in 1918, the death penalty was reintroduced by Decree No. 2008, enacted on 23 September 1926. The application of the death penalty was extended by a decree in 1930 which prescribed this punishment for serious crimes against the State.

The Polish Penal Code of 1932, which remained in effect until 1970, prescribed the death penalty for several offences. A decree of 10 August 1944, made public in 1946, introduced the death penalty for grave atrocities during the Second World War, collaboration with the German occupation forces, and causing loss of life or other serious damage to the Polish State. A decree of 22 January 1948 introduced the death penalty for political offences and crimes against property committed in peacetime.

The latest Polish Penal Code of 1970 lists six crimes against the State which carry a discretionary death sentence: aggravated cases of treason aimed at overthrowing the system by force in collaboration with foreign powers (Article 122); activities aimed at depriving Poland of independence (Article 123); espionage (Article 124); violent attempt upon the life of an official of the State, made with purposes hostile to Poland (Article 126, paragraph 1); aggravated economic sabotage (Article 127); usurpation of property of great value in collaboration with others; disturbing the national economy (Article 134, paragraph 2); murder (Article 148, paragraph 1).

The Polish Penal Code of 1970 lists in addition one military crime punishable by death: for a member of the armed forces to fail or refuse to carry out an order during combat (Article 310).

Between 1970 and 1976, the death sentence in Poland was passed mainly on people convicted of murder, but a few other cases are known to Amnesty International. These include the execution of leaders of the meat industry in Warsaw, who were charged with organizing usurpation of property of great value and causing serious disturbances in the functioning of the national economy. In another case, the brothers Kowalczyk were sentenced to death in the early 1970s for putting a bomb in a school building in which police meetings were regularly held. The sentences were commuted by the Supreme Court in Warsaw, probably as a consequence of the circumstances in which the bomb explosion happened: it was thought that the explosion did not involve an attempt on life but was meant as a demonstration against such meetings in public buildings.

According to official Polish statistics, 10 people were executed in 1970, 9 in 1971, 15 in 1972, 18 in 1973, 8 in 1974, and 18 in 1975.

The death sentence in Poland cannot be imposed on people under 18, on anyone who is physically or mentally ill or on pregnant women. It is not specified whether the facts upon which the exemptions rest must exist at the time of the commission of the offence, or at the time of sentencing or when the execution is due to take place.

The Supreme Court examines the legality of the death sentences imposed by lower courts at the district or regional level. After a death sentence has been upheld by the Supreme Court, the defendant has the right to petition for clemency. This may be granted by the State Council, which may commute the death sentence to 25 years' imprisonment.

Execution is by hanging; military personnel, however, are executed by firing squad. Article 110, paragraph 2 of the law governing punishments (*Kodeks Karny Wykonavczy*) states that the defendant may ask for a representative of the clergy or legal counsel to be present at the execution. The Public Procurator, governor of the prison and an authorized medical doctor attend the execution.

In 1976 there were several press reports of the death penalty being imposed. The leader of a gang of four was sentenced to death for murdering a Roman Catholic priest. The trial took place in Przemysl on 23 April 1976. In May 1976, a twenty-four-year-old man was sentenced to death for sexual murder of two young girls. He had attempted to murder a third girl. Amnesty International does not know whether or not the death sentences were commuted or carried out.

Zdislaw Marchwiseki, a fifty-year-old ex-miner from Katowice, known as the "vampire" of Katowice and convicted of beating 14 women to death, was executed in May 1977. He confessed to whipping the women, aged between 16 and 57, with steel and leather thongs. His brother, Jan Marchwiseki, was executed with him for the same offence.

***Portugal** (the Portuguese Republic)*

Portugal abolished the death penalty in 1867. Article 25 of the 1976 Constitution states that human life is inviolable and that under no circumstances should the death penalty be imposed.

However, the Military Penal Code retained the death penalty for some crimes, until it was changed in April 1977.

***Romania** (the Socialist Republic of)*

After the establishment of a socialist government in Romania at the end of the Second World War, Law No. 16, 1949, introduced the death penalty for a number of civil crimes. Previously it could only be used in time of war. Decree No. 469 of 30 September 1957 and Decree No. 318 of 21 July 1958, considerably extended the range of crimes punishable by death. The death penalty was mandatory for a number of offences until 1968, when alternative punishments were introduced.

Although the death penalty is treated in theory as an "exceptional punishment", all the following offences carry a discretionary death sentence under the Penal Code which has been in force since 1 January 1969: high treason (Article 155); treason – aiding the enemy (Article 156); treason – disclosure and transmission of secrets to foreign agents or groups (Article 157); hostile activities against the State by foreigners residing in Romania and by Romanian citizens (Article 158); espionage – with reference to Article 157 (Article 159); attempted assassination of an official, thereby endangering the security of the State (Article 160); attempted mass murder with the object of weakening the State (Article 161); undermining the power of the State through armed action (Article 162); sabotage (Article 163); sabotage – with reference to Article 248 (2) (Article 164); undermining the economy and thereby causing significant loss (Article 165); conspiracy in the form of leading, establishing, belonging to or supporting a group amongst whose goals is the commission of crimes against the State under Articles 155-165 (Article 167); murder "when committed with cruelty" or by two or more persons or by someone who has previously committed a murder or in order to conceal a robbery or piracy at sea, or when the victim is a pregnant woman (Article 176); the taking, use or embezzlement of public property by an official if very serious consequences result (Article 223); the theft of public property if very serious consequences result (Article 224); robbery of public property which results in death or in other serious consequences (Article 225); cruel and inhuman treatment of prisoners of war or other persons in the custody of the perpetrator (Article 358). In addition, the Romanian Penal Code of 1969 lists seven military crimes punishable by death. People under 18 and pregnant women are exempted from execution. The Penal Code contains provision for the death sentence to be commuted to 25 years' imprisonment in the case of mothers of children who are below the age of three. Anyone ruled to be insane, either at the time the offence was committed or at the time of their trial, is also exempted from the death penalty.

The death sentence may be imposed by regional or district courts. The jurisdiction of the district court is of a local nature. Amnesty International does not know which of the above crimes fall solely within the jurisdiction of the regional court.

A death sentence imposed by a district court may be appealed to the regional court; if the sentence is upheld a further appeal may be made to the Supreme Court. Death sentences imposed in the first instance by the regional court may be appealed to the Supreme Court.

Article 424 of the Penal Code provides that if a death penalty is upheld after all avenues of appeal, review and petition for clemency are exhausted, the case will be referred back to the court that first imposed the sentence and execution be carried out on the order of the president of that court.

A person sentenced to death has the right of appeal to a higher court. There is right of appeal to the Romanian Supreme Court from a sentence of death imposed by a lower court. If the death sentence is upheld by the Supreme Court, the person sentenced has the right to petition for clemency within five days of the death sentence having been confirmed by the Supreme Court.

The prison governor, in the presence of a member of the State Procuracy, is obliged to inform the condemned person of their right to petition for clemency. The State Council is entitled to grant clemency after an appeal has been formally submitted through the Ministry of Justice (Article 31 of Law No. 23/69 as amended on 2 March 1973). The president of the district court in the area to which the prison belongs, the president of the State Procuracy of the same district, the governor of the prison and a medical doctor must be present at the execution (Article 32 of Law No. 23/69 as amended on 2 March 1973).

Execution is by firing squad.

Richard Szattinger, a Romanian citizen of German origin, was arrested in October 1974 and sentenced to death on charges of economic espionage. The charges related to the content of talks which he had had with a representative of an Austro-American firm in his own capacity as a representative of a Romanian industrial company. Although the sentence imposed on Richard Szattinger was formally for an economic crime, it was also of political relevance. In November 1975, after considerable reaction abroad, the sentence was commuted to 18 years' rigorous imprisonment. In the summer of 1977, Mr Szattinger was released.

A few cases of the application of the death sentence in the period 1973–77 are known to Amnesty International. Two men, B. Iorgolescu and I. Ilies, both industrial managers, were sentenced to death in the summer of 1976 for disclosing State economic secrets. In November 1976 both sentences were commuted to life imprisonment by President Ceausescu.

***Spain** (the Spanish State)*

During the period covered by this *Report* (1974–77)*, substantial changes were made with respect to Spanish court procedure and sentencing for political crimes which carry the death penalty. Arguably the most important of these was the law ordering the use of the most "summary" (*sumarisimo*) trial procedure, decreed in August 1975 by Generalisimo Franco. Its major features were modified in February 1976 and allowed to lapse entirely in February 1977.

The death penalty was in continuous use in Spain until 1932, when it was abolished in the reform of the Penal Code carried out under the Second Republic. It was reinstated for certain crimes of terrorism in October 1934. It was not until 1938 that the Government led by the late Generalisimo Franco fully reinstated it. The preamble to the 1938 law gives an accurate idea of the views of the Government on the function of the penalty. Since that time, the death penalty was used increasingly in political cases, and this practice reached its peak in August 1975 with the provision for mandatory death sentences in the Anti-Terrorism Law (*Decreto-Ley 10/1975, del 26 de agosto, sobre prevención del terrorismo*).

The 1938 law stated:

> *"The following law which is promulgated is one that does not require either explanation or justification, as it is reality which imposes it and prescribes it. The penal codes of nearly all countries are impressive witnesses to this, including those who like to decorate themselves with the title of democracy. As a result of a manifestly false sentimentalism which ill becomes the dignity of a strong and just State, the General Scale of Penalties of the penal code of the ill-fated Republic was cut down, eliminating the death penalty..."*

From the allusions to a "strong state" and the "ill-fated Republic", it is clear that the 1938 law, promulgated during the 1936–39 Civil War, was designed to serve, if required, as a political weapon. Whereas the major part of legislation from the Civil War period and its immediate aftermath has been amended or removed from the statutes, this was not the case with the death penalty.

* Article 15 of the Constitution, approved by the referendum of December 1978, abolishes the death penalty, except where laid down in the Code of Military Justice. The Code was amended by Decree Law on 23 December 1978 so as to substitute a sentence of 30 years' imprisonment for all offences which might hitherto have carried the death penalty, except for those committed in time of war.

The continued use of the death penalty as a political weapon stretches right up to the period under review. Indeed, the law was changed in August 1975 by Generalisimo Franco's Government to permit speedier trials of people accused of capital crimes with a political motive. However, there have been no executions since Generalisimo Franco's death in November 1975, and the Anti-Terrorism Law was substantially amended in February 1976.

An examination of the number of death sentences passed in the period 1959–77, carried out in relation to the type of court concerned with the case and the relevant jurisdiction, establishes three facts:

(a) Although many death sentences have been passed by Spanish civilian courts, no one convicted in these courts has been executed in Spain since 1959. All have been commuted by the Head of State.

(b) Owing to the unique extent to which military jurisdiction has extended its competence to cover ordinary crimes, military courts are able to assert the supremacy of their jurisdiction over the civilian courts in any case construed by military authorities – and (by implication) the Government – as "political".

(c) The only executions to have taken place in the period under review have been those of political activists of the Left charged with killing policemen. The trial procedure in such cases is extraordinary: this was justified by the Government on grounds that it was required to combat the "virulent wave of terrorism" facing the country.

The conclusion is inescapable: that, while the death penalty has been passed for a wide variety of offences in both military and civil courts, it has only ever been used as an exemplary weapon against political opponents of the régime, who may also be violent.

The procedure for trying ordinary crimes is simple. All cases go before an *audiencia provincial*, a court covering a specific judicial geographical area, for trial after an examining magistrate has assembled a dossier of the facts. The state prosecutor (*fiscal*), the private prosecutor (*acusador particular*) and the defence counsel present their cases, after which the court decides on the sentence. If required, appeal may be made to the Supreme Court (*Tribunal Supremo*), and finally, if the death sentence has been upheld, the cabinet in full session must be informed. The Head of State may, if he so wishes, exercise his right to pardon or commute. The executions in 1959 by sentence of a civil court involved a man named Jarabo, who was condemned to death for the murder of four people.

Crimes for which the Penal Code prescribes the death penalty are as follows: treason (Articles 120-122); murder of foreign heads of state while in Spain (Article 136); piracy (Article 139); crimes against the internal security of the State (Articles 142-144); crimes aimed at changing the form of Government (Article 163); rebellion (Articles 214 and 215, in connection with Article 163, paragraph 1); sedition (Articles 218 and 219); attacks against the Head of State, ministers or other officials in their official capacity (Articles 233 and 234); terrorism (Articles 260 to 262); murder of a member of one's family (Article 405); assassination (Article 406); robbery with violence if it results in death (Article 501, paragraph 1). The death penalty is not mandatory for any of these offences, and is imposed only if aggravating offences exist.

In Spain, it is the power of the military courts, and their competence to judge civilians according to the Code of Military Justice, which is of the most importance. This competence steadily increased under the Government of Generalisimo Franco, although it has been a feature of the Spanish legal structure for more than a century. An example of the breadth of competence of military justice may be drawn from the 1976 metro strike in Madrid, during which all metro workers were drafted into the armed forces, thereby becoming subject to military discipline.

The following are crimes liable to a mandatory death sentence under the Military Code of Justice: treason (Article 258); rebellion (Article 287); sedition (Article 295); insults – with physical or armed force – to sentries, security or armed forces (Article 306); insubordination – with physical or armed force – (insult to a superior or disobedience) (Articles 319, 320 and 327); crimes against military honour (Article 338); crimes against the aims and methods of action of the army (Articles 358 and 360); crimes against the duties of sentries (Article 361).

The Military Penal Code also makes the following offences punishable by death, but for these offences the death penalty is discretionary: treason (as defined in Articles 259-263, 270 and 271); espionage (Article 272); acts of unjustifiable aggression against a foreign power, violation of a treaty or armistice, capitulation, etc., to an enemy with serious results, unauthorized destruction of military material, sacking of towns and similar offences (Articles 279 and 280); rebellion (as defined in Article 288); insubordination (as defined in Articles 307 and 308); attacks and threats (as defined in Article 314); crimes against military discipline, and disobedience (as defined in Article 330); crimes against military honour (as defined in Articles 339, 340, 342, 344, 345, 347 and 348); crimes against the aims and methods of action of the army (Article 359); crimes against the duties of sentries (Articles 362 and 364); desertion (as defined in Articles 365, 367, 375 and 376); refusal to help (as defined in Article 384); negligence (as defined in Articles 388 and 392).

In August 1975, an Anti-Terrorist Decree Law was published. This brought together under a most summary court procedure the most important provisions relating to the punishment of political offenders. The death penalty was included in the scale of penalties. The new Decree Law made reference to Articles 260-264 of the Penal Code and Article 294 *bis* of the Code of Military Justice. The Decree Law laid down a scale of penalties up to death for the following broad categories of offences:

(a) attempted crimes affecting the public peace which would be carried out by causing, among other things, fires, explosions or disruption of communications;

(b) attacks for political motives on persons who may be part of organizations preserving the public peace and maintaining communications;

(c) attacks on property having as their aim the collection of funds to benefit groups or organizations which threaten the unity of Spain or the institutional order, or the giving of aid in any way to the aims of such groups or organizations.

All these crimes, whether committed by military personnel or civilians, are tried by a military court (*consejo de guerra*), which consists of seven serving officers of whom only one, the *ponente*, is obliged to have any knowledge of the law whatsoever. The *ponente* draws up the judgment of the court and, in addition, there are two *suplentes* (adjuncts), the President who holds the rank of colonel or higher and three other officers (*vocales*) who hold the rank of captain or higher. The composition of the court is completed by a prosecutor and counsel for the defence. Once the sentence has been passed, it is communicated to the Captain General of the appropriate military region via the *Coronel Auditor*. In cases in which the death penalty is involved, the Captain General passes the decision of the court (*consejo*) and all the appropriate documents to the *Consejo Supremo de Justicia Militar*.

The Supreme Council of Military Justice is made up of three officers from the judicial corps of the army, one each from the navy and air force, and a further post which is held by rota (all of whom are of the rank of divisional or brigade general and on active service). The appointments to this Council are made by the Government. Finally, the judgment is passed to the Council of Ministers (*Consejo de Ministros*) who have the power to make a recommendation for the sentence to be either confirmed or commuted and this recommendation is passed to the Head of State to be acted upon.

It was under this pre-August 1975 military system, with its restricted procedure and largely legally unqualified officers, that Salvador Puig Antich and Heinz Chez were executed by the garrotte on 2 March 1974. Puig Antich was a member of the *Movimiento Ibérico de Liberación* (an anarchist group) and was found guilty of killing an inspector of the Political Social Brigade during a bank raid in Barcelona in September 1973. Heinz Chez was executed in Tarragona at the same time for the murder of a civil guard and for robbing a bar.

On 27 August 1975, the law was substantially changed by the Anti-Terrorist Decree Law to provide a new and far more stringent code which, among other things, widened the list of offences, and provided a mandatory death penalty for killing an official, a member of the armed forces or state security, or other public employees. Similarly, the crime of kidnapping resulting in death was made a capital offence.

Equally drastic was the introduction of summary (*sumarisimo*) trial procedures in political cases. This procedure was substantially amended in February 1976. One example will suffice to demonstrate the absence of impartiality and safeguards from the former system.

On 16 August 1975, Lieutenant Pose of the Civil Guard was shot dead in Madrid. Six people, four men and two women, belonging to the *Frente Revolucionario Antifascista y Patriota* (Revolutionary Anti-Fascist and Patriotic Front, *FRAP*), a splinter group of the Communist Party of Spain, were put on trial by a council of war (*consejo de guerra*) in ordinary summary proceedings, trial number 310/75. However, with the subsequent passing of the new *sumarisimo* law, the case was transferred to a new court, where it was tried retroactively under the new procedure (as trial No. 1/75). The court consisted of a president, four other judges and two deputies. The defence lawyers attempted at first to challenge the case on procedural grounds – namely, that they had only been given the papers on which to prepare a case at 10.00 p.m. the day before, and they naturally required to consult with their clients. Their application that, without such facilities, the trial would be invalid, was dismissed, but the judge did agree to postpone the hearings until 4.30 p.m. Only one of the lawyers managed to present a written defence, but, even so the trial went ahead. The lawyers protested strongly that six people were being tried on a capital charge and proper legal representation was effectively denied them. As a result, five lawyers were excluded from the court, and army officers were appointed as counsel in their place. The officers, with no legal training, were given two hours to familiarize themselves with the case. The hearings having ended at 9.00 p.m., the verdict was given at 8.00 a.m. the next day. Of the six defendants, five, two of whom were women (who claimed to be pregnant), were sentenced to death. (Spanish law provides that no pregnant woman can be executed until 40 days after giving birth.) The sixth defendant was given 30 years' imprisonment. Under the new August 1975 law, the death sentences could be carried out if the Captain General of the region signed them all and informed the Cabinet through his superior officer, the Army Minister. Once the decision had been made public, 12 hours remained in which the Head of State might commute the sentences before they were carried out. Only if the Captain General did not concur with the verdict could the case be referred to a higher court – the Supreme Court of Military Justice. The defence was permitted just two hours in which to prepare petitions. Three of the defendants were awarded clemency by the Head of State; two were executed.

On 17 September 1975, five men were shot by firing squad despite worldwide petitions for clemency: Angel Otaegui Etcheverría, a member of *Euzkadi Ta Azkatasuna* (Basque Homeland and Liberty, *ETA*), tried with José Ignacio Garmendia Artola for the murder near San Sebastián of the local chief of the Intelligence Service in April 1974; Garmendia had his sentence commuted; José Luis Sanchez-Bravo Sollas, 21 years old, and Ramón García Sanz, 27 years old, both of whom were tried in *sumarisimo* 1/75 mentioned above. Their co-defendants had their sentences commuted; Juán Paredes Manot, an *ETA* member tried in *sumarisimo* 100/75 and convicted of killing a policeman in the course of a bank robbery in June 1975; and José Humberto Baena Alonso, a *FRAP* member accused of killing a policeman in July 1975 (his two co-defendants, who had been sentenced to death, had their sentences commuted).

The traditional method of executing civilians in Spain is the garrotte.

In 1977, there was a significant change in the law whereby a separation of jurisdiction between the civil and military systems was decreed. This could mean that crimes carrying the death penalty would no longer be tried by a military court. A new superior court, the *Audiencia Nacional*, would have jurisdiction over civil offences.

### **Sweden** *(the Kingdom of)*

The death penalty for ordinary crimes was abolished in Sweden in 1921, even though it was retained for crimes of high treason in wartime. It was abolished for this offence in 1973. Article 1 of Chapter 8 of the present Constitution, which came into force on 1 January 1975, stipulates that no law or other regulation must imply that the death penalty can be imposed.

### **Switzerland** *(the Swiss Confederation)*

The Swiss Penal Code introduced in 1942 does not allow use of the death penalty. However, the provisions of Military Law can be applied in time of war and temporarily during States of Emergency. The Military Penal Code lists the crimes for which the death penalty is applicable as being disobedience, mutiny, cowardice and capitulation to the enemy, and betrayal of military secrets.

*Turkey (the Republic of)*

Thirteen articles of the Turkish Penal Code of 1926, as amended, provide a mandatory death penalty for crimes against the State, the Government or the Constitution. They include: acts designed to put Turkey under the sovereignty of a foreign state; a Turkish citizen commanding the armed forces of a foreign state; collaboration with the enemy during time of war; acts of destruction that jeopardize Turkey's war preparations or military capability; espionage; a Government official using classified scientific or technical inventions which he has encountered in the course of his duties for the benefit of a state at war with Turkey; setting up, or attempting to set up, or conducting or administering more than one society aiming at establishing domination of one social class over another; or aiming at exterminating a certain social class; or aiming at overthrowing the basic economic or social order of the State; attempting to abolish or alter by force the Turkish Constitution; attempting to overthrow the Council of Ministers or the Grand National Assembly, or to prevent them from functioning; starting armed revolt, or killing during the course of it (Article 149); unauthorized taking over of the command of a military unit or installation (Article 152).

By Article 450 murder is a capital crime if, among other things, it was premeditated; or of certain specific members of one's family, or of a member of the Grand National Assembly; or of several persons, if accompanied by torture or the infliction of grave injuries, or if committed in the course of arson, deliberate flooding or shipwreck.

Execution is by hanging. Pregnant women may not be executed until after having given birth.

Death sentences, if upheld by the Court of Appeal, are subject to ratification by Parliament and then confirmation by the President, who may commute the sentence only on the grounds of the age or the ill-health of the defendant.

The only executions of politically motivated prisoners to have taken place in recent years were in May 1972, when three members of an extreme left-wing urban guerrilla group were hanged. They had not killed, but were convicted of shooting at people, bank robbery and kidnapping.

Amnesty International has no figures for executions of ordinary criminals.

In May 1975, the Turkish Parliament voted overwhelmingly to retain the death penalty. The Republican People's Party had introduced a Bill to abolish the death penalty for many offences, but it was rejected by the Justice Commission of Parliament, and this decision was endorsed by Parliament itself.

***Union of Soviet Socialist Republics** (the) (USSR)*

In the USSR, the death penalty may be imposed for 18 different offences in peacetime, among them offences not involving the use of violence. While there are no published official statistics on the number of death sentences and executions in the USSR, the Soviet press has published reports on the passing of the death sentence on about 30 people in each year in 1974, 1975 and 1976. In several cases in those years, the press has disclosed that people sentenced to death were executed.

Much of classical socialist doctrine rejected the use of the death penalty, as had Russian rulers and legislators on a number of occasions before the fall of the Tsarist system. In conformity with socialist principles, Soviet criminal and penal theory since the founding of the Soviet State has tended formally to give preference to correction and re-education rather than to punishment as the means of dealing with offenders and criminality. However, the death penalty has been in use throughout most of the history of the Soviet State.

The death penalty has been formally abolished in Soviet law on a number of occasions since the Revolution of 1917. After the February Revolution, the Provisional Government abolished it within ten days of coming to office, only to restore its use several months later for offences at the battle front. The Bolshevik-dominated Government which came to power in October 1917 likewise formally abolished the death penalty almost immediately, and restored it in mid 1918. The use of judicial execution was again abolished in January 1920 and again restored several months later. The most recent occasion on which the death penalty was abolished was in 1947.

In 1950, the death penalty was restored for the politically-motivated offences of treason, espionage and sabotage. In 1954, the list of offences punishable by death was extended to include deliberate murder with aggravating circumstances; banditry was added in 1958. In that year, the old criminal legislation of the USSR, dating back to 1927, was replaced by new criminal legislation which is still in effect. This dates from 1958, when new Fundamentals of Criminal Legislation of the USSR and Union Republics became law. On the basis of the Fundamentals, each of the USSR's 15 Union Republics passed its own Criminal Code within three years of 1958. These Criminal Codes list all criminal offences and the maximum penalties for each. For convenience, the present study will refer only to the Criminal Code (and other relevant Codes) of the Russian Socialist Federated Soviet Republic (RSFSR), the largest of the Union Republics, since there are no relevant differences between the criminal legislation of the RSFSR and that of the other Union Republics.

The 1958 Fundamentals and the subsequent Union Republic Criminal Codes preserved the death sentence. Article 23 of the RSFSR Criminal Code described the death penalty as "an exceptional measure of punishment", to be retained "until its abolition". The official Commentary (1971) to Article 23 further emphasizes the transitional character of the use of the death penalty, saying that its temporary retention is "dictated by necessity" ("*vynuzhdennaya*") and that it is "liable to complete abolition as soon as the conditions for this come into existence, that is, even before the final liquidation of criminality and the replacement of punishment by methods of social influence".

The death penalty is carried out in the USSR by shooting. A death sentence may be passed only by a court, and only on conviction for a crime liable to punishment by death. Civilians charged with such offences (or any other) are tried in the country's civil courts. Cases of espionage are the single exception: they are heard by military tribunals. Cases of crimes by military personnel and by personnel of the state security authorities (the *KGB*), and service crimes by officers of corrective labor institutions are also tried by military tribunals. Civilian co-defendants in such cases are also tried by military tribunals. Military tribunals apply the same Criminal Codes as do civil courts, and they are bound by the same codes of criminal procedure. Apart from their separate jurisdiction, military tribunals differ from civil courts in their personnel and in the fact that they are not within Union Republic jurisdiction but directly within that of the USSR Supreme Court and other

USSR justice agencies (see the Edict of the USSR Supreme Soviet "On Military Tribunals", 25 December 1958).

When it came into force on 1 January 1961, the RSFSR Criminal Code kept the death penalty for a number of offences. In 1961 and 1962, the Criminal Codes of the Union Republics were amended to extend the list of offences punishable by the death penalty. Murder or attempted murder of a policeman acting in the course of his duties, when committed with aggravating circumstances, became punishable by death, as did rape under certain circumstances (when committed by a group, or against a minor, or with particularly serious consequences for the victim, or by an "especially dangerous recidivist").

Amendments in 1961 and 1962 also made a number of economic offences punishable by death. These amendments were part of a vigorous official campaign against economic corruption in the form of persistent large-scale theft of State property and through embezzlement and speculation. About 250 people are known to have been executed for economic offences in the period 1961–64. Although the incidence of death sentences for such offences declined after that time, reports indicate that the use of the death penalty to deter economic corruption increased again in the early 1970s, particularly in the Union Republics of the Trans-Caucasus (Armenia, Georgia and Azerbaidzhan).

The RSFSR Criminal Code was further amended in 1962 to allow courts to pass the death sentence for "actions disrupting the work of corrective labour institutions" when committed by "especially dangerous recidivists or persons convicted of grave crimes" (Article 77-1 of the RSFSR Criminal Code). In 1973, the RSFSR Criminal Code was further amended to provide the death penalty for aircraft hijacking when the offence led to loss of life or the infliction of serious injuries.

Through the amendments to the RSFSR Criminal Code (and to the criminal codes of the other Union Republics) cited above, there has been an undisturbed increase in the number of offences for which the death penalty may be applied. Furthermore, in 1965, a special edict was issued by the Presidium of the USSR Supreme Soviet to enable the passing of death sentences on persons just recently apprehended and convicted for "crimes against peace and humanity and war crimes, irrespective of the date of commission of the crimes"; specifically, for people convicted of war crimes committed in the period 1941–45 (Decree of the Presidium of the Supreme Soviet of the USSR, 4 March 1965). The RSFSR Criminal Code (Article 48) provides that criminal proceedings may not be instituted against a person if 15 years have elapsed since the time when the crime was committed and if the period of limitation has not been interrupted by the commission of a new crime. Article 48 provides that the court may use its discretion over whether to apply the period of limitation in a case involving a possible death sentence, but states that even if the court does not apply it, it may not impose the death sentence. (Article 49 reiterates the provision that the death penalty may not be imposed on a person convicted of a crime committed more than 15 years before the initiation of criminal proceedings.) The 1965 Supreme Soviet Decree excluded war criminals from the application of any period of limitation, saying: "Nazi criminals guilty of very grave, heinous crimes against peace and humanity and of war crimes are liable to trial and punishment irrespective of the time elapsed since the commission of their crimes." The official Commentary to Article 5 of the RSFSR Code of Criminal Procedure makes known that this applies not only to

"Nazi criminals" convicted of these offences but also to "Soviet citizens who during the Great Patriotic War of 1941–1945 actively carried out punitive activity, who personally took part in murdering and torturing people."

At present, the following offences committed in peacetime are punishable by death in the RSFSR: treason (Article 64); espionage (Article 65); terrorism (if the offence includes the killing of an official) (Article 66); terrorism against representative of foreign State (if the offence includes the killing of such a representative "for the purpose of provoking war or international complications") (Article 67); sabotage (Article 68); organizing the commission of any of the above-named offences (Article 72); commission of any of the above-named offences against other Working People's State (Article 73); banditry (Article 77); actions disrupting the work of corrective labour institutions (Article 77-1); making or passing counterfeit money or securities (when the offence is committed as a form of business) (Article 87); violation of rules for currency transactions (when committed as a form of business or on a large scale, or by a person previously convicted under this Article) (Article 88); stealing of State property on an especially large scale, regardless of the manner of stealing (Article 93-1); intentional homicide with aggravating circumstances (Article 102); rape, when committed by a group of persons or by an especially dangerous recidivist, or resulting in especially grave consequences, or the rape of a minor (Article 117); taking a bribe, with especially aggravating circumstances (Article 173); infringing the life of a policeman or People's Guard, with aggravating circumstances (Article 191-2); hijacking an aircraft, if the offence results in death or serious physical injuries (Article 213-2); resisting a superior or compelling him to violate official duties, an offence applicable only to military personnel, and carrying the death penalty in peacetime if committed in conjunction with intentional homicide of a superior or any other person performing military duties (Article 240).

The same offences are punishable by death in all 15 Union Republics of the USSR.

According to Article 23 of the RSFSR Criminal Code, the death sentence may not be passed on anyone who at the time the offence is committed or the sentence passed is under 18, or who is pregnant, and the death sentence must be commuted in the case of a woman who is pregnant at the due time of execution. The death penalty may not be applied to a person ruled to have been insane at the time of commission of the offence or at the time of the court judgment of the case.

Under USSR criminal legislation, defence counsel is required to take part in cases involving a possible death sentence (Article 22 of the Fundamentals of Criminal Legislation of the USSR and Union Republics, as amended by Edicts of the Presidium of the USSR Supreme Soviet of 31 August 1970 and 3 February 1972), although (as in all criminal cases) defence counsel may not participate in the case until after completion of the preliminary investigation, except by permission of the Procuracy or if the accused person is a minor or mentally or physically handicapped.

Cases involving a possible death sentence may not be heard in the first instance at the lowest court level, but are reserved for the competence of courts at the intermediate (city, regional or territorial) level or above. In the five Union Republics which are not subdivided into regions or territories, such cases are heard at the Union Republic Supreme Court level. The USSR Supreme Court may at its discretion serve as the court of first instance in any case of extreme complexity or particular national importance.

The only exceptions to these jurisdictional rules arise in cases of espionage, cases of offences committed by military personnel or by state security personnel and cases of service offences by officers of corrective labour institutions, all of which are tried by military tribunals.

Official Soviet commentators avow that the death sentence is not mandatory for any offence in the USSR. This is generally true, but is questionable regarding the offence "Infringing the Life of a Policeman or People's Guard" (Article 191-2 of the RSFSR Criminal Code). This offence, which may involve either homicide or attempted homicide, is punishable only by death if the court finds that it was committed "with aggravating circumstances". Article 39 of the RSFSR Criminal Code lists 12 "circumstances aggravating responsibility"; for example, "commission of the crime by a person who has previously committed any kind of crime", "the causing of grave consequences by the crime", and "commission of the crime by an organized group". In cases under Article 191-2 where the indictment charges that the offence was committed with one or more of these specified circumstances, the court must decide whether or not these circumstances were present; it must likewise decide whether the defendant committed the basic offence. If, on finding the defendant guilty, the court also finds one of the 12 "aggravating circumstances" present, then, in passing sentence, it will have no alternative but to impose the death penalty.

According to the official Commentary to Article 23 of the RSFSR Criminal Code, a court may pass the death sentence "only when its necessity is indicated by special circumstances aggravating the culprit's responsibility and by the exceptional dangerousness of his character". The death penalty may be passed by a majority verdict: that is, by two of the three people usually comprising the bench in a Soviet court (Article 306 of the RSFSR Code of Criminal Procedure). Only one of the three members of the bench of a court at the city, regional or territorial level is a professional judge, the other two being laymen ("people's assessors"), who serve on the bench for at most two weeks each year over a period of two years. Trials held at the Union Republic or USSR Supreme Court level in the first instance are heard by a similar bench. Some Soviet jurists have made implicit criticism of both the majority-vote principle and the lack of judicial training of the people's assessors as being incompatible with the need for verdicts reached with special care in cases involving the death penalty.

In cases of the death sentence, the normal rules for appeals and review provided by Soviet criminal legislation apply; no special provisions are made for such cases, and the sections of the RSFSR Code of Criminal Procedure dealing with appeals (Section 4: Articles 325-355) and with review of judgments (Section 6: Articles 371-390) do not make any specific mention of death sentence.

A person sentenced to death, or to any other criminal punishment, may lodge an appeal against the verdict or sentence passed by the court of first instance. The appeal must be lodged within seven days of the prisoner's receiving a written copy of the judgment, although the trial court may in law allow an extension of time and, in any event, the appeal court has discretion to consider an appeal irrespective of its date of submission. The lodging of an appeal suspends execution of the sentence. Appeal is to the next higher court. Since cases involving the death penalty are heard in the first instance at the intermediate (city, regional or territorial) level or above, appeals in such cases may be heard only at the Union Republic Supreme Court level, the next higher level, beyond which there is no appeal. The Union Republic Supreme Court must consider the appeal within 20 days of receiving it. The appeal hearing, as with the trial of first instance, must, according to law, be held in public except in certain exclusive circumstances, specifically defined. The appellant may attend the appeal hearing only if the appeal court so decides.

The court of appeal may reduce the sentence of the lower court, but not increase it. Among the grounds for reducing the death sentence (or any other sentence) is "lack of correspondence of the punishment assigned [by the lower court —Amnesty International note] with the gravity of the crime or the personality of the convicted person" (Article 342 of the RSFSR Code of Criminal Procedure).

As indicated above, appeals against the death sentence may be heard only by the Supreme Court of the Union Republic, and there is no legal possibility of appealing against its decision. So, unlike people sentenced for many offences not liable to punishment by death, those who are sentenced to death have at most only one possibility of appeal. However, citizens of five Union Republics (Latvia, Lithuania, Estonia, Moldavia and Armenia) do not have even this one possibility of appeal, since in those Republics courts at intermediate (city, regional or territorial) level do not exist, and the Union Republic Supreme Court serves as the court of first instance in all cases involving a possible death sentence.

A second possibility for alteration of a death sentence is provided by the procedure of judicial review, which may be undertaken at a higher court level on receipt of a protest against the judgment of the court of first instance or the court of appeal. Such a protest may be brought only by a Procurator or a court chairman, whose levels of competence in this matter are laid down in Article 371 of the RSFSR Code of Criminal Procedure. Any court judgment, including that of a Union Republic Supreme Court, may be subjected to review in this way, and the review court may, among other things, vacate the judgment of the lower court, order a fresh appeal hearing or reduce the sentence. If the review court finds that the assigned punishment is too mild, it may order a fresh trial, but it may not itself increase the punishment. Procurators and court chairmen at appointed levels have the right to suspend the execution of a protested judgment until its review has been carried out. They may be obliged to exercise this right in cases where a judgment including a death sentence is under protest, but the law does not spell this out.

Soviet law also provides a mechanism for reopening cases on the basis of newly discovered circumstances "which prove" the innocence of the convicted person, or that he or she is guilty of a less grave crime than that for which he or she was convicted. A case may be reopened in this way at any time. According to Article 385 of the RSFSR Code of Criminal Procedure: "The death of a convicted person shall not obstruct the reopening of a case concerning him on the basis of newly discovered circumstances for the purpose of rehabilitating such a convicted person."

If a death sentence remains in legal force after the available possibilities of appeal and review described above have been exhausted, the sentenced person may still benefit from an act of pardon (*pomilovaniye*)*. The Fundamentals and Codes

* Official Soviet translations of legal texts invariably translate this legal term as "pardon". As far as Amnesty International knows, it corresponds to what is generally understood by "clemency".

of Criminal Procedure do not give details of this mechanism, which is rather vaguely defined in Soviet law. The right of pardon is exercised, according to Article 121 of the USSR Constitution (1977), by the Presidium of the USSR Supreme Soviet, which may change a sentence from death to imprisonment. Anyone sentenced to death who seeks commutation by way of pardon, must petition for it. Evidently, the execution of the death penalty is suspended until the Presidium of the USSR Supreme Soviet decides whether or not to commute the sentence.

If a convicted person does not submit an appeal against sentence or petition for pardon, the sentence may be carried out within seven days of a copy of the judgment of the court being given to him or her. If a death sentence remains in force after the exhaustion of the appeal, pardon and review procedures, it may be executed. (The carrying out of some other types of sentence may be postponed in certain specified circumstances where immediate serving of the sentence could be particularly damaging to the defendant: for example, if the convicted person is seriously ill, if there is grave illness or a death in the defendant's family or "in view of fire or other natural calamities". However, people sentenced to death are deliberately excluded from this provision – see Article 361 of the RSFSR Code of Criminal Procedure.) In cases tried in the first instance at the Union Republic Supreme Court level or heard on appeal at that level, the sentence may be executed immediately after the Supreme Court has passed or upheld the death sentence (Article 357 of the RSFSR Code of Criminal Procedure).

If the death penalty is overturned by one of the above-mentioned procedures, it is normally replaced by a sentence of 15 years' imprisonment, the maximum term of imprisonment provided by Soviet criminal law. All offences for which the death penalty may be imposed in peacetime are qualified as "grave crimes", and people imprisoned for them are sent to serve their sentences in colonies which have "reinforced" or "strict" régime (Article 24 of the RSFSR Criminal Code). They are not subsequently eligible for parole (known in Soviet law as "conditional early release from punishment") or replacement of their punishment with a lesser form of punishment (Article 44-1 of the Fundamentals of Criminal Legislation of the USSR and Union Republics).

The Soviet authorities do not make public statistics on the use of the death sentence in the USSR. Information on individual cases of people being sentenced to death or executed comes mainly from reports in the Soviet press.* Some such reports appear in local newspapers which are not readily accessible abroad, and therefore their contents are known to Amnesty International only second hand, through reports on them by non-Soviet media.

Often the official report of a death sentence in the USSR is limited to one newspaper item. Almost invariably such reports, sparse in detail, do not describe in detail either the proceedings and findings of the trial or the submission of appeals and protests against the court's judgment. The Soviet press only occasionally reports

* Sources which Amnesty International has not studied systematically for the present report include the regular *Bulletins* of the USSR and RSFSR Supreme Courts, which publish information on some of the cases which come before them. These *Bulletins* are of little help in efforts to compile statistics on the use of the death penalty in the USSR, but do report on some cases which would not otherwise become known. Other sources essential for a comprehensive study include officially-published monographs and journal articles by Soviet jurists and criminologists on a variety of related subjects and especially on official efforts to combat certain types of crimes punishable by the death penalty.

that a death sentence has been carried out, or that one has been commuted.

It is known that the Soviet media make public only some of the death sentences passed in the country. Soviet "dissenters" who make an estimate of the number of death sentences passed each year in the USSR normally put it in the hundreds, but these estimates are not based on official statistics.

Approximately 30 death sentences in each of the years 1974, 1975 and 1976 are known to have been reported in the Soviet media. These figures correspond to those for earlier years in the 1970s, and also for 1977. The information given below on individual cases is only for the period 1974–76 inclusive.

Among the reported cases known to Amnesty International, death sentences during this period were more often passed on people convicted of war crimes (committed during the Second World War, invariably involving victims killed by violent means) than on any other category. At least 40 were sentenced to death for war crimes during the period 1974–76. Groups of as many as seven were tried together for war crimes and sentenced to death. In a number of cases, people were tried and sentenced to death for war crimes by military tribunals. The Soviet media stated explicitly with regard to ten people in this category that death sentences had been carried out. In other cases, the media made it clear that death sentences had been carried out by stating that those convicted had "been brought to account", or that they had "received the punishment they deserved", or that their execution was "inevitable".

Amnesty International knows of 17 reported cases of death sentences being passed in 1974–76 on people convicted of economic crimes not involving any use of violence. Here again, in some cases, groups of people were sentenced to death together. The Soviet media are known to have reported the execution of two in this category.*

Amnesty International knows of 20 reported cases of people being sentenced to death for murder during 1974–76. Seven executions in this category are known to have been reported in the official press.

During this period one man, N.G. Kalinin, is known to have been executed for treason in the form of espionage for a foreign government.

Finally, it has been reported by *emigré* sources that a number of participants in a mutiny on board the Soviet military vessel *Storozhevoi* in November 1975 were tried within days of suppression of the mutiny, and executed. Amnesty International knows of no report in official Soviet media on these alleged executions.

Thus, of the approximately 90 people known to have been sentenced to death in the period 1974–76, 19 were reported to have been executed in the Soviet press. These must be regarded as minimum figures. No women were among those reported to have been executed or sentenced to death. Amnesty International knows of only two cases in which the Soviet media reported that a death sentence had been commuted: a Georgian, who had taken up Canadian citizenship and had been apprehended on a trip to the USSR, tried, and sentenced to death for war crimes, had his death sentence commuted by way of pardon in 1975. Canadian Government representatives expressed the view that the commutation was "a sign of intense Soviet interest in maintaining good relations with Canada". Mikhail

* A third, Yury Sosnovsky, who was sentenced to death in 1975 for economic crimes, was executed in early 1977. His execution was apparently not reported in the Soviet media, but was learned of when officials informed his family that he had been executed.

Leviev, a Jew sentenced to death for economic crimes, was granted a commutation to 15 years' imprisonment after considerable international interest had been expressed in his case. Mikhail Leviev had appealed unsuccessfully against the death sentence. His was the only case during this period in which Amnesty International knows that a judicial review was undertaken. That, too, did not result in the alteration of his sentence, which was effected by an act of pardon.

It is not possible to give a general account of the length of time between sentencing and execution or commutation, since such details cannot be found in Soviet media reports. Yury Sosnovsky, sentenced in March 1975 for economic offences, was not executed until February 1977. Mikhail Leviev was sentenced to death in December 1974 and had his sentence commuted by decree of the Presidium of the USSR Supreme Soviet only in June 1976. On the other hand the *Storozhevoi* mutineers were allegedly executed within a short time of their apprehension, and it appears that some convicted war criminals have likewise been executed fairly soon after sentence has been passed.

There may have been political motivation behind the offences for which a number of people were sentenced to death, although Amnesty International does not have details to that effect. For example, the *Storozhevoi* mutineers may have wanted only to leave the USSR when they mutinied, and it was reported abroad that their leader was a "dissident Jew". Nationalist motives may have played a part in the activities of some of those sentenced to death for war crimes. A considerable proportion of them were allegedly members of nationalist partisan organizations, seeking independence for their own nationalities during the Second World War. Political motivation may have been involved in the espionage for which N.G. Kalinin was executed in 1975.*

While Soviet legal texts and official commentaries on them express in some degree a negative evaluation of the death penalty as a transient measure, retained only out of necessity, the general Soviet media do not reflect this view. In a number of reports on trials, Soviet newspapers and agencies have commented that the convicted person "deserved" the punishment, or reported that when the death sentence was passed the audience "cheered" or "greeted the sentence with approval".

Particularly illustrative was a report by Radio Moscow in July 1975 about the case and trial of two Latvians who were convicted for murder. The report told of a film shown on Moscow television, evidently within weeks of the conclusion of the trial. The film included footage of the two arrested men being questioned during the investigation of the case. The television film also included footage of the trial itself, about which Radio Moscow commented: "We also saw the mothers of both killers who stared in mute disbelief at their sons as if wondering 'Did I bring that into the world?', and we saw them faint when the death sentence was pronounced."

Some Soviet jurists have criticized the way in which death sentence cases are

* A more recent case in which the death sentence was passed for politically motivated offences was that of Vladimir Zhvania, a Georgian. He was tried by the Supreme Court of the Georgian Soviet Socialist Republic during January and February 1977 on charges including "sabotage" and "anti-Soviet agitation and propaganda". He was convicted of causing several explosions, in one of which a person was killed. At his trial he reportedly admitted causing the explosions, stated that he had not intended any loss of life and said that his actions had been "the wrong path for the liberation of Georgia". He was sentenced to death. The local Georgian press indicated in December 1977 that Vladimir Zhvania had been executed.

treated by the Soviet media, noting that some newspapers (especially local provincial ones) sometimes "pass the death sentence" even before the court has given its judgment. This phenomenon, and the even more striking one of judges citing "public demand" as one of the grounds for their judgment and the death sentence, have on occasion been condemned as incompatible both with Soviet legal standards and with the officially proclaimed ethic of "socialist humanism".

By contrast with the official publication of such reports, with their implicit approval of the use of the death penalty, no public debate is allowed to take place in the USSR on the question of abolishing the death penalty, except sporadically by implication rather than openly in specialist legal journals. Evidently the matter has been debated within relevant institutions among jurists, other specialists and legislators.

It is known that some jurists have criticized the existing procedural standards as they apply to death penalty cases, arguing that they are inadequate for cases with the "irreversible penalty". Among the subjects of criticism have been the lack of special, stronger guarantees of legality and fairness for defendants in such cases; the inadequacy of most court benches in their present composition to handle such cases expertly and humanely; the likelihood of courts being influenced by public opinion; the inadequacy of defence rights of defendants in such cases, and the inadequacy of their appeal and review possibilities. However, these criticisms are scarcely publicized in the USSR. Arguments openly in favour of outright abolition do not appear, even in the specialized legal journals and, as far as Amnesty International knows, have in recent years been made publicly only by a number of Soviet "dissenters".

### *United Kingdom of Great Britain and Northern Ireland (the)*

The Murder (Abolition of Death Penalty) Act 1965 suspended the death penalty for murder for an experimental period. The abolition in Great Britain of the death penalty for murder was made permanent by resolutions of both Houses of Parliament in 1969. A motion to reintroduce the death penalty for terrorist offences involving murder was defeated in the House of Commons in December 1975.

Sentence of death may only be passed for treason and certain forms of piracy.

The death penalty still exists under the Army Act 1955, the Airforce Act 1955 and the Naval Discipline Act 1957 for offences committed by members of the armed forces during wartime. The offences relate to the notion of intending to aid the enemy, and include mutiny and communication of intelligence material.

A death sentence may not be passed on any person who, at the time of the offence, was under 18, nor may it be passed on a pregnant woman.

No execution has taken place in Britain since 1964.

The Northern Ireland (Emergency Provisions) Act 1973, abolished the distinction between murder and capital murder previously obtaining in Northern Ireland and provided that the maximum penalty for the crime of murder be imprisonment for life. The death penalty for murder remains in the law of the Isle of Man. It was imposed on James Richard Lunney in 1973 but the sentence was commuted by the Crown to life imprisonment.

The Royal Prerogative of mercy is exercised by the Queen on the advice of the Home Secretary.

*Yugoslavia (the Socialist Federal Republic of)*

On 21 July 1977, a new Penal Code came into force in Yugoslavia, which increased the total number of capital offences. In line with a policy of devolution of administrative and legislative power, ordinary crimes now fall under the jurisdiction of the six constituent Republics and two Autonomous Regions of the Federation. Jurisdiction over political offences known as "criminal offences against the fundamental tenets of the socialist self-management system and the security of the Socialist Federal Republic of Yugoslavia" remains at the federal level.

The Federal Penal Code of 1951, as amended, provided a discretionary death sentence for 30 offences against the "people and the State" (including 12 military offences and crimes in time of war) and six ordinary offences; the latter included murder with one of four types of aggravating circumstance, and robbery or theft where death is intentionally caused. Murder, if it were not one of the four specified forms, was not a capital offence unless "several homicides" had been committed.

As shown below, under the new Penal Code (1977), a discretionary death sentence is provided in forty-five articles for crimes including military offences and the type of crime which was referred to by the previous Penal Code (1951) as crimes against the "people and the State"; it covers offences committed in peace and war.

Article 37 states that the death sentence may never be mandatory and should only be imposed for the most serious cases of the offence in question.

In the new Penal Code, a discretionary death sentence exists for the following offences: counter-revolutionary attack endangering the social order (Article 114); acceptance of capitulation and occupation (Article 115); aggravated cases of endangering Yugoslav territorial integrity in time of peace or war (Article 116); aggravated cases of endangering the independence of the State in time of war (Article 117); aggravated cases of dissuading others from combatting the enemy in time of war (Article 118); service in an enemy's army (Article 119); assisting the enemy (Article 120); undermining the military and defence capability of the State (Article 121); murder with the aim of harming the State (Article 122); aggravated cases of violence with the aim of harming the State in time of peace or war (Article 123); aggravated cases of armed rebellion in time of peace or war (Article 124); aggravated cases of terrorism in time of peace or war (Article 125); aggravated cases of destruction of objects important to the national economy in time of peace or war (Article 126); aggravated cases of sabotage in time of peace or war (Article 127); aggravated cases of espionage in time of peace or war (Article 128); infiltration or smuggling of armed groups, weapons and ammunition into the Socialist Federal Republic of Yugoslavia in time of war or in time of immediate danger of war (Article 132); association with the aim of carrying out hostile activities against the State in time of war or in time of immediate danger of war (Article 136).

"Crimes against humanity and mankind" which may be punished by death are: genocide (Article 141); war crimes against civilian population (Article 142); war crimes against the wounded and ill (Article 143); war crimes against prisoners of war (Article 144); illegally killing or wounding the enemy (Article 146); use of illegal means of combat (Article 148).

Military crimes which may be punished by death are: refusal to carry out an order in time of war or in time of immediate danger of war (Article 201); refusal to accept using weapons during time of war or in time of immediate danger of war (Article 202); mutiny (Article 203); attack against military personnel on duty (Article 206); infringement of regulations covering specified duties in time of war or in time of immediate danger of war (Article 209); infringement of regulations regarding the defence of State frontiers in time of war or in time of immediate danger of war (Article 210); evasion of and refusal to undertake military service in time of war or in time of immediate danger of war (Article 214); evasion of military service through self injury or deception in time of war or in time of immediate danger of war (Article 215); desertion in time of war or in time of immediate danger of war (Article 216); voluntary departure and escape from the armed forces in time of war or in time of immediate danger of war (Article 217); careless production and handling of military material during time of war or in time of immediate danger of war (Article 220); theft of weapons or other means of combat during time of war or in time of immediate danger of war (Article 223); passing on military secrets during time of war or in time of immediate danger of war (Article 224); surrendering to the enemy (Article 227); non-fulfilment of duties during combat (Article 228); desertion from duty during combat (Article 229); leaving a post contrary to orders (Article 230); prematurely leaving a damaged ship or aeroplane (Article 231); activity designed to lower morale in time of war or in time of immediate danger of war (Article 233); guarding a military unit insufficiently in time of war or in time of immediate danger of war (Article 234); disobeying an order to mobilize during time of war or in time of immediate danger of war (Article 236); endangering an aeroplane in flight, thereby causing the death of other persons (Article 241).

The courts of the six Republics and two Autonomous Regions have power to impose the death penalty for premeditated murder and for incitement to suicide of minors under the age of 14 or helpless persons or persons whose mental faculties are such as to prevent them from being aware of what is happening to them.

The courts of the Republics of Macedonia, Montenegro, Serbia and Bosnia-Hercegovina and of the Autonomous Regions of Vojvodina and Kosovo have power to impose the death penalty on anyone convicted of committing aggravated offences of armed robbery resulting in the death of another person. This does not apply in the Republics of Croatia and Slovenia.

Statistics published under the auspices of the Federal Ministry of Justice indicate that during the period 1966–75, 23 people were executed in Yugoslavia.

In 1965, there were three executions of people convicted of aggravated murder. In 1966, out of a total of five executions, four were for aggravated murder and one for an offence involving violence against public and private property. In 1967, no executions took place; in 1968 there were two, one of which was for aggravated murder and one for terrorist activities and in 1969 there were four executions following convictions for aggravated murder. The years 1970 and 1971 saw no executions but there were four in 1972, one of which was for aggravated murder and three of which reportedly involved terrorism. Executions held in 1973, 1974 and 1975 were all of people convicted of aggravated murder and numbered three, one and four respectively.

Published official statistics do not normally indicate the number of death sentences commuted to terms of imprisonment but on 21 October 1971 the official paper *Vecernje Novosti* reported that of 243 cases of aggravated murder registered "during the mid 1960s" with the Office of the Public Prosecutor, 50 sentences of death were imposed, of which 10 were carried out.

The Yugoslav Supreme Court reviews the appropriateness in law of death sentences imposed by lower courts. A person sentenced to death has the right of appeal to a higher court. If the first court of appeal is a Republic Supreme Court, the defendant may then appeal to the Yugoslav Supreme Court. A defendant sentenced to death by the Supreme Military Court of Yugoslavia has the right of appeal to the Yugoslav Supreme Court. After all avenues of appeal have been exhausted and a death sentence upheld, a defendant has the right to petition for clemency. The President may grant clemency, and has the power to commute a death sentence to 20 years' imprisonment.

The death sentence cannot be passed upon a person who at the time the offence was committed was less than 18, or upon a pregnant woman. The death penalty may be imposed upon an adult who at the time the offence was committed was between 18 and 20, if the offence is one "against the fundamental tenets of the socialist self-management system and security of the Socialist Federal Republic of Yugoslavia", against humanity, international law or against the armed forces of the Socialist Federal Republic of Yugoslavia.

The death sentence is carried out by firing squad.

Miljenko Hrkac, a Yugoslav worker, then 28 years old, was sentenced to death in 1969 by the district court of Belgrade for allegedly causing two bomb explosions resulting in the death of one person and severe injuries to a young girl. As a result of new evidence which became available in 1971, shortly after the sentence was reviewed by the Serbian Supreme Court, the case was remanded for retrial to another district court, which also imposed the death sentence. Following a hearing before the Yugoslav Supreme Court where complex and contradictory new evidence was called, this Court ordered another retrial at regional court level.

This new trial took place in Belgrade at Christmas 1975, with little public attendance. Miljenko Hrkac apparently died in prison at the beginning of 1978.

In July 1976, Vladimir Dapcevic, former Secretary General of the Yugoslav Communist Party, was sentenced to death by the district court in Belgrade for his alleged activities abroad as a leading "Cominformist" (Stalinist) opponent of the present Yugoslav leadership. Part of the trial was held *in camera*. Mr Dapecevic alleged that he was kidnapped by Yugoslav officials from Romania in the summer of 1975. His death sentence was immediately commuted to 20 years' imprisonment.

In June 1976, the Zagreb district court sentenced five people (Milos Tvrtko, 33 years old, Antun Zinko 34, Josip Preknic 54, Djuro Perica 35, and Branko Viducek 29) to death for allegedly collaborating with a foreign-based *ustacha* organization and causing bomb explosions with the aim of killing President Tito. No one was killed or injured in the explosions. The death sentences were commuted by the Yugoslav Supreme Court to 20 years' imprisonment. Lesser known cases in 1976 include that of a twenty-nine year old Yugoslav citizen, Milan Sekulic, who was executed in March 1976 for the murder of a police station chief and the attempted murder of another policeman. A Mr Kajrazovic, a forty-seven year old tradesman, was sentenced to death after appeal in July 1976 on charges of murdering two men in Nis. In November 1976, two civilians from the province of Kosovo were sentenced to death for a vendetta killing.

## LATIN AMERICA, THE ENGLISH-SPEAKING CARIBBEAN, CANADA AND THE UNITED STATES

### LATIN AMERICA

Many Latin American countries abolished the death penalty in the 19th or early 20th century. Ecuador became abolitionist for political crimes in 1852, and for all crimes in 1897; Venezuela abolished the death penalty for political crimes in 1857 and for all crimes in 1863; Costa Rica and Uruguay abolished it at the end of the 19th century; Colombia in 1910. These countries still have no death penalty for any crime; the Venezuelan Constitution of 1961 prohibits the death penalty in the following terms: "The right to life is inviolable. No law may establish the death penalty or any authority carry it out."

In countries where the death penalty exists at the present time and where death sentences are passed, they are rarely carried out. According to Amnesty International's information, there were two judicial executions in the period 1956–72 in Guatemala, and seven in Peru between 1973 and 1976.

In Latin America recently there has been a tendency towards reintroduction of the death penalty in times of political upheaval, particularly following a military *coup*, such as occurred in Argentina, Bolivia, Brazil and Chile in the 1960s and early 1970s. The impact of political crisis is also reflected in the inclusion amongst capital offences of attacks against military personnel (Argentina, Bolivia and Peru). When the initial upheaval has subsided, it is not unusual for the death penalty to be abolished for political crimes and for the sentence of death to be less frequently carried out. Thus, in Chile, for example, during the first six months after the military *coup d'état* of September 1973, there were reportedly several thousand executions, following summary trials before military tribunals and often carried out by the commanders of the military zones. Later, the death sentences passed by military courts were generally commuted to imprisonment. In Cuba, numerous summary executions took place in the period immediately following the revolution of 1959.

With the exception of Haiti, executions have generally not been made public spectacles in Latin America. They can, however, be carried out after very summary proceedings, with inadequate provision for appeal machinery. In such circumstances adequate facilities to prepare and present a case for the defence or an appeal submission are not allowed. In Argentina, the law stipulates that execution is to be carried out within 48 hours of the sentence being passed. In Peru, the latest Decree (1971) regulating the death penalty reduced the total time lapse for "investigation, judgment and the execution of the sentence" to 48 hours.

Haiti, with a legal system based on the French model, is the exception to the general rule in largely abolitionist Latin America. In addition to crimes against the security of the state and serious common-law crimes, "communist activities of any kind" are punishable by death.

The death penalty in Latin America cannot be seen only in terms of sentences which are judicially imposed. Para-military groups, the existence of which are condoned or actively supported by the authorities, as well as units of official security forces, carry out murders and illegal detentions in a number of Latin American countries, particularly Argentina and Guatemala. Detentions not officially acknowledged, known as disappearances, as well as killings, are also grave matters in Chile, Nicaragua, Uruguay, Paraguay, Brazil, El Salvador and the Dominican Republic. A further concern is the concept of the *Ley de Fuga* (Law of Escape), whereby authorities are empowered to shoot prisoners attempting to escape. It has been cited in justification of the murder of prisoners. Death under torture is another related concern (see Chapter IV).

***Argentina** (the Republic of)*

The law relating to the death penalty has been changed many times in the last 50 years. The death penalty was completely abolished in 1921. Nearly 30 years later, Act No. 13.985 of October 1950 introduced the death penalty for espionage and sabotage. Act 14.117 of October 1951 extended it to other cases provided in the Code of Military Justice, making it applicable to ring-leaders of rebellions. When the first Peronist Government fell, these acts were repealed by Legislative Decree No. 8315 of December 1955.

Fifteen years later, a military Government reintroduced the death penalty for political crimes by Decree No. 18.701 of June 1970. This Decree was repealed the next year by Decree No. 18.593 of March 1971, which, however, retained the death penalty and reintroduced it into the Penal Code. Argentine jurists were almost unanimous in their opposition to the reintroduction. They were supported by other sectors of public opinion in taking this position, and this led, once again, to the complete abolition of the death penalty, by Decree No. 20.043 in December 1972.

On 24 March 1976, the military seized power, and immediately reintroduced the death penalty, by Decree No. 21.264, for certain violent crimes. Article 5 of the Decree authorized the security forces to use firearms when a person apprehended *"in flagrante delicto*... does not stop upon the first warning or uses arms against the officers of the peace". Attacks against public transport, communications and other public services are punishable by "imprisonment for a fixed period or death". This Decree determined that the death penalty would apply to everyone over 16 years of age. Article 16 of the Argentinian Constitution expressly forbids the death penalty for political offences.

Decree No. 21.272, also of 24 March 1976, established the death penalty for anyone causing serious injuries or death to military personnel or to members of the security forces and police, whether or not they were carrying out their duty.

Finally, Decree No. 21.338, introduced on 25 June 1976, modified the existing Penal Code by introducing the death penalty by firing squad within 48 hours of sentence being pronounced. So far, however, the military tribunals set up under the Code of Military Justice to try people suspected of involvement in subversive activities, have not sentenced anyone to death.

The number of political deaths in Argentina is very high. In 1976, the number of people to have died as a result of political violence was put officially at 1,354. In the first four months of 1977, newspaper sources stated that a total of 293 people had been killed; most were guerilla suspects. There is considerable doubt about the accuracy of the official explanations for such deaths: these usually claim that the people concerned died in clashes with security forces. There is evidence that in many instances people who had been abducted or even officially detained were later said by the authorities to have been killed in such clashes;

there are, moreover, almost no reported casualties among the security forces. This inevitably gives rise to concern that unofficial executions are being carried out as a matter of routine. Summary executions of political prisoners have occurred in at least two prisons in Argentina: the penitentiary in Cordoba, where, between May and October 1976, at least 17 prisoners were alleged to have been shot during transfer while trying to escape; and the La Plata Prison where, since 5 January 1977, two political prisoners have been removed from their cells and shot during "transfers". The security forces cite the *Ley de Fuga* (the Law of Escape) as a justification for these killings; however, as all prisoners are handcuffed during transfers, are obviously unarmed and under heavy escort, the need to shoot to kill rather than to inflict a slight wound is hard to explain. (Cellmates of the dead political prisoners have alleged that they, too, were threatened with death.)

Details of murder committed or acquiesced in by the Government in Argentina are given in Chapter IV.

### **Bolivia** *(the Republic of)*

Two months after General Hugo Banzer Suárez occupied the Bolivian presidency as a result of a successful *coup d'état*, the Decree Law of 5 November 1971 was promulgated, establishing the death penalty for crimes of terrorism resulting in death. Terrorism is defined to mean: "Attacks on the lives of dignitaries of the State and members of the armed forces of the Nation and of the Public Order, for political motives", kidnappings and armed uprisings "in urban or rural areas".

In 1972, a Penal Code came into effect which had been drafted and promulgated by the Banzer Government, but which did not retain the death penalty provisions of the Decree Law of 5 November 1971. It did, however, provide the death penalty for crimes of parricide, murder (*asesinato*) and espionage.

Treason and espionage, defined as crimes against the *external* security of the State, in collaboration with foreign enemies, are punishable by death. But crimes against the *internal* security of the nation were now to be punished by imprisonment (for example, Article 121, "armed uprisings against the security and sovereignty of the State"; Article 123, sedition; Article 128, "attempts against the President and other dignitaries of the State".

### **Brazil** *(the Federative Republic of)*

The death penalty was abolished in Brazil in 1882 on the occasion of the nation's gaining independence, and did not exist in modern Brazilian legal history until 29 September 1969, when the military, who had seized power in 1964, promulgated the Fourth Law of National Security, or Decree Law 898. This reintroduced the death penalty for political crimes alone; it is still in force.*

Under Decree Law 898, the death penalty applies for any political act resulting in a death, such as sabotage of public services. It also applies for acts of violence motivated by factional or socio-political "non-conformism" which may lead to the death of people in authority. Furthermore, it applies for any act of violence against visiting heads of state which may result in their injury or death.

On each occasion that a death sentence has been pronounced in Brazil, there have been worldwide protests. Thus, the first such sentence, passed in March 1971

* In January 1979, the death penalty was abolished in Brazil, when changes to the Law of National Security were brought into effect.

against Teodomiro Romeiro dos Santos, 19 years old, was commuted to life imprisonment. In November 1971, death sentences were pronounced on Ariston de Oliveira Lucena, Diogenes Sobrosa do Sousa, and Gilberto Faria Lima. They were commuted in June 1972, and there is some reason to believe that international opinion was influential in this decision.

Over the past 12 years, death squads have killed many political activists, but the vast majority of their victims have been petty criminals and tramps (*marginais*).

***Chile** (the Republic of)*

The death penalty exists for civilians and military alike for crimes of treason and parricide, and for certain other crimes when accompanied by aggravating circumstances. This legislation derives from the Constitution of 1925 (amended by the Constitutional Acts of 11 September 1976), from the Penal Code of 1874 (enforced as applicable during the period under review), and from the Code of Military Justice of 1952 (as amended up to 1975). The last text defines the functions and attributes of the military courts, as well as the cases in which the death penalty may be employed by these courts (treason, rebellion or military uprising, sedition).

After the *coup* of September 1973, a high percentage of executions resulted from hasty military trials in private session, during which the Military Code of Justice was supposedly applied.

According to some sources, more than 5,000 people were executed in Chile in the first three months after the *coup*. In October 1973 the *Junta* acknowledged a total of 81 executions. In some cases, people originally condemned to prison sentences were retried (sometimes at the initiative of General Sergio Arellano Stark), condemned to death and executed. This occurred in the cases of Carlos Aleagaya, Roberto Guzmán Santa Cruz, and Hipólito Cortés Alvarez. There were, in all, 15 similar executions at the prison of La Serena. Aleagaya was originally condemned to 20 years' imprisonment and the other two to five years' imprisonment.

Between February and August 1974, the Chilean authorities did not officially acknowledge any executions. The death sentences passed by the military courts were generally commuted to sentences of imprisonment for life or for a fixed term. Commutation to life imprisonment occurred in the cases of members of the Socialist Party: Héctor Fuentes Araos, a student; José Balaguer Jara, a student; Humberto Vargas Vargas, a peasant leader; Miguel López González, a peasant leader and Nelson González Pobiete, a former local leader of agrarian reform. All were condemned to death on 29 April 1974 by a military court in San Fernando after having been charged with organizing an armed resistance group. In August 1974, the following people, originally condemned to death, also had their sentences commuted: Air Force Colonel Ernesto Galaz, Air Force Captain Raúl Vergara, Air Force Sergeant Belarmino Constanzo, Eric Schnake (former Socialist Senator) and Carlos Lazo (President of a bank).

Since August 1974, Amnesty International has not recorded any case where the death penalty, occasionally still demanded by the prosecution, has been passed in Chile for either political or civil crimes. However, executions without trial, deaths under torture, and "disappearances" of political prisoners continued to a disturbing degree. During 1975 and 1976, the instances of murder committed or acquiesced in by government were principally the work of the *DINA* (*Dirección de Inteligencia*

*Nacional*) the intelligence service of the régime, which was accountable only to the President of the Republic for its actions. On 13 August 1977, the *DINA* was replaced by the *CNI* (Central Nacional de Informaciones) which, in fact, is a replica of the *DINA*. Since that date, Amnesty International has continued to receive reports of arbitrary arrests, torture and disappearances in which *CNI* involvement has been alleged. By late 1977, Amnesty International estimated that over 1,500 people had "disappeared" since the *coup* of September 1973, many of whom are presumed or known to be dead.

***Colombia** (the Republic of)*

The death penalty was abolished in Colombia in 1910, when its prohibition was incorporated by an amendment to the Constitution of 1887. The same Constitution is still in force. Article 29 guarantees "that the law cannot impose capital punishment for any crime, and that this provision cannot be immediately modified", and the Penal Code of 1936 does not provide for the death penalty for any crime. The maximum sentence is penal servitude for 24 years.

***Costa Rica** (the Republic of)*

The death penalty was first abolished in 1882. Article 21 of Costa Rica's present Constitution (1949) maintains the abolition: "Human life is inviolable."

***Cuba** (the Republic of)*

One of the first Decrees of the Revolution was Law No. 425 promulgated on 7 July 1959, which defined the extent of counter-revolutionary activity and authorized the use of the death penalty in a wide range of cases. Law 425 divided counter-revolutionary offences into two basic categories: (1) those against the integrity and stability of the nation (*contra la integridad y estabilidad de la nación*) and (2) those against the powers of the State (*contra los poderes del Estado*). Article 2 defined 14 offences in category (1), the first 10 of which were punishable by penalties ranging from 20 years' imprisonment to death.

Law 988 of 29 November 1961, entitled "Death Penalty sanctions for those who carry out counter-revolutionary acts" was a reaction to the events of 1961, including the April Bay of Pigs invasion. It is no longer in force.

No official statistics on death sentences carried out have ever been published. The death penalty was used widely in the early years of the Revolution, and legislative amendments encouraged this wide use. In November 1977 the Cuban Supreme Court judge with specific responsibility for death penalty cases informed Amnesty International representatives that there had been about three executions per year in recent years.

Under the provisions of the Code of Social Defence (*Código de Defensa Social*) 1973 edition, the death penalty may be imposed for the following offences: committing actions against the independence of the nation and in collaboration with a foreign power (Article 128); promoting war against the nation (Article 129); taking up arms against the nation (Article 130); surrendering arms to the enemy (Article 131); divulging military, political or economic secrets concerning State security (Article 135); promoting armed rebellion against the State (Article 148); unauthorized taking of command over military emplacements or personnel (Article 154); organizing armed groups against the nation (Article 158); piracy

– at sea or in flight – causing death (Article 168); embezzlement of public funds (Articles 420 and 427); aggravated homicide – that is, when committed, for example, with premeditation or "perversity" (Article 43); parricide – the definition includes father, mother and child (Article 432); arson of a public building, meeting place or storage facilities for inflammable substances (Article 465); use of explosives against individuals (Articles 468 and 469); sexual intercourse with girls under the age of 12 (Article 482); homosexual assault with violence (Article 483); theft causing death (Article 517). Rape, armed robbery and setting fire to a sugar plantation also carry the death penalty.*

Executions which are carried out at present are believed to be of ordinary (non-political) prisoners and not those convicted of crimes against the State.

* The provisions of the new Cuban Penal Code, approved by the National Assembly in December 1978, are essentially similar to the provisions given in the text above.

### *Dominican Republic (the)*

Article 8 of the Constitution of the Dominican Republic, promulgated in 1966, rejects the death penalty, and guarantees "the inviolability of life ... under no circumstances will it be possible to establish, pronounce or enforce the death penalty. . . . Therefore neither the death penalty, torture, nor any other punishment or oppressive procedure or penalty that implies loss or diminution of the physical integrity or health of the individual may be established."

The frequency with which political murders and "disappearances" of people arrested by the forces responsible for order continue to take place in the Dominican Republic is disturbing. Circumstances surrounding the deaths of a number of people suggest that responsibility might lie with police authorities. For example, Ernesto Canela Cabral, detained in the prison of San Juan de la Maguana, was transferred to a hospital after being severely maltreated. He died in hospital on 8 February 1975.

### *Ecuador (the Republic of)*

On 26 June 1897 the Ecuadorian Parliament passed legislation abolishing the death penalty. It has not existed in law since that time. The Constitution of 1967 incorporates the 1897 law in its Article 28, paragraph 2, which guarantees "the inviolability of life; there is no death penalty."

The 1897 law abolishing the death penalty was the culmination of a fifty-year trend towards a restriction of the number of crimes punishable by death, and of the application of the death sentence as the maximum penalty. In 1852, Ecuador had banned the death penalty for "political crimes", and by 1897 the death penalty was only infrequently applied for other crimes.

### *El Salvador (the Republic of)*

The Constitution of 1962 provides in its Article 168 that "The death penalty can only be imposed for the crimes of rebellion or desertion in action *in time of war;* for treason and espionage, and for the crimes of parricide, murder, robbery or arson if a death should occur." Execution is by firing squad.

The Penal Code of 1973 provides for the death penalty to be imposed in place of the maximum prison sentence for cases of parricide or aggravated or premeditated murder (*asesinato*), "if in the circumstances of the act, the manner of realizing it and the determining motives, the agent should be deemed to have acted with a particular degree of perversity" ("... *si por las circunstancias del hecho, la manera de realizarlo y los móviles determinantes, dedujere mayor perversidad del agente*") (Article 154). *Asesinato* is defined as "murder with treachery (*alevosía*) or premeditation; with poison or other insidious means; using means likely to produce great destruction (*estragos*) or common danger, for a price or promise of remuneration ..." (Article 153).

Amnesty International has examined a number of cases in which Salvadoreans, generally *campesinos* (small farmers) were murdered, has disappeared or were detained in violation of law. There was evidence that the killings were officially sanctioned. Fifteen such cases were examined in 1976.

In 1977 the frequency of illegal detentions and killings apparently by security forces increased greatly. In most cases of "disappearance", where the authorities deny that the detentions occurred, those taking the victims into custody have been clearly identified as members of the *Guardia Nacional,* the *Guardia de Hacienda,* the *Policía Nacional,* and the para-military organization, *ORDEN*. This is the *Organización Democrática Nacionalista*; it is composed of civilians and commanded by the President of the Republic. In many cases, individual members of all these forces who have detained people have been named.

The victims are mainly *campesinos,* especially those involved in lay Roman Catholic groups, such as the movement *Cursillistas de Cristiandad*, or Roman Catholic catechists. Similarly, leaders and supporters of *campesino* trade union organizations have also been victims. In the course of 1977, Amnesty International investigated the cases of 28 *campesinos* who have been found dead after detention by security forces, or who had been shot outright. The bodies of some showed signs of mutilation, including flaying and amputation.

Forty-nine cases of "disappearance" in detention during 1977, including those of 35 *campesinos*, were under investigation in February 1978; it is feared that many of the people died in custody. There is considerable concern that there may be a further increase in killings carried out by security forces and in "disappearances", especially in rural areas.

In contrast to other Latin American countries where officially sanctioned murder occurs, the killings in El Salvador are generally attributed to formally established security forces, and to the official body, *ORDEN*, and not to semi-independent groups of civilians (vigilantes) who function elsewhere with only the knowledge and passive acquiescence of authorities.

***Guatemala*** *(the Republic of)*

The Guatemalan Constitution of 1965 provides, in Article 54, that "the death penalty shall be considered extraordinary"; it may not be imposed on women, minors, people over 70, people guilty of political crimes, or whose extradition to Guatemala has been granted on that condition. Article 131 of the Penal Code of 1973, now in force, provides the death penalty only for aggravated or premeditated murder (*asesinato*):

> *"The prisoner [convicted of] murder will be sentenced to 20 to 30 years' imprisonment; nonetheless, the death penalty will be imposed in place of the maximum [term of] imprisonment, if in the circumstances of the act and the occasion, the manner of carrying it out, and the determining motives, a greater or special degree of dangerousness of the agent should be revealed".*

In practice, however, the application of the judicial death penalty has been infrequent in Guatemala. In response to a United Nations survey, Guatemala stated on 9 March 1972 that since 1956 only two men had been executed. Those condemned were José Ixcajo Revolorio and Julio Roldán Godínez, both sentenced for the rape and murder of a minor under eight years of age.

Two executions were carried out on 16 April 1975 which had serious political implications. Two ex-patrolmen of the National Police, Lauro Alvarado y Alvarado and Marco Tulio Osorio, were detained and sentenced to death for the shooting of María Etelvina Flores Herrera, a killing that may not in itself have been of a political nature. After trial proceedings began, Alvarado smuggled from prison a declaration in which he spoke of arresting, "on superior orders", a number of people with left-wing views who, after being turned over to higher police authorities, had "disappeared" and later been found dead. Alvarado also claimed to have prepared a tape recording in which he gave details of police involvement in other political murders. He threatened to name specific officers.

Although opposition leaders appealed for a stay of execution until allegations could be investigated, both men were executed by firing squad at El Pavón prison farm on 16 April 1975.

Two people were executed in June 1975 for the murder of a shopkeeper, Rocael Ortiz and Héctor Mazariegos. To Amnesty International's knowledge, no other judicial executions have been carried out since that date. Murder attributed to security forces and to para-military groups, appearing to rely on the collaboration or close cooperation of certain governmental authorities, is reported almost daily in Guatemala (see Chapter IV).

### *Haiti* (*the Republic of*)

The laws of Haiti, a former French colony, are modelled on French legislation. The death penalty existed in colonial times, and was maintained in the Penal Code of 1835 after Haiti became an independent republic.

The death penalty is prescribed for certain crimes of both a political and ordinary criminal nature. The political crimes essentially concern the maintenance of state security: attempting to overthrow the Government by force of arms; leading movements whose aim is to overthrow the Government; sheltering spies; wishing to change the Government by force; provoking internal unrest and civil war; ordering, in the capacity of military commander, the uprising of troops against the Government; leading armed groups against the Government (Penal Code of 1953).

The special "anti-communist" law of April 1969 provides for trial by court martial and the death penalty for those who have engaged in "communist activities of any kind", including private spoken statements of communist beliefs. The law covers those who have in any way assisted such offenders.

The criminal offences punishable by death include certain types of homicide: premeditated killing or murder; parricide, infanticide and murder by poisoning (Article 247 of the Penal Code). Murder accompanied by another crime or offence is also punishable by death (Article 249).

The Penal Code of 1953 established that a person sentenced to death shall be executed by firing squad in a public square; this method of execution replaces the former practice of beheading. According to the current Constitution and laws of Haiti, anyone condemned to death has the right of appeal to the *Cour de Cassation*, in session or in chambers. The President has the power to grant clemency to anyone sentenced to death. Defence lawyers are sometimes provided by the court, but political trials are in secret, and facilities for defence and appeal proceedings are not known.

In a closed society such as Haiti, information is not readily available, and Amnesty International data are therefore incomplete. It is, however, reported that people sentenced to death in Haiti traditionally often remain in prison, and that executions are not carried out, even where there has been no formal commutation of the sentence. On the other hand, there are also reports of occasional summary executions of political offenders in and out of prison, without trial and in secret.

During the thirty-year period preceding the Presidency of Dr François Duvalier, there were few periods of political unrest and few executions. The dictatorial rule of Dr Duvalier (1957–1971) faced internal opposition, both peaceful and violent. The numerous death sentences imposed during the period are reported often to have followed summary trials, with inadequate time and facilities for appeal, and with the executions made into public spectacles. In 1964, the public execution by firing squad of two guerillas was witnessed by about 2,000 people, including several hundred children especially let out of school for the occasion.

According to information received by Amnesty International, the last judicially imposed death sentence for political offences was passed in April 1971, when 17 out of 38 defendants were sentenced by military court on charges of subversion. The charges covered invasions and plots between 1968 and 1970. The trial may have been mounted to give an appearance of strength to the régime during the last days of the dying President. The death sentences were not carried out.

Records kept by Amnesty International show that about six death sentences for murder are passed by courts throughout the country each year. Some of the defendants have been pardoned and freed, while others are still in jail, unlikely to be executed. The last known judicial executions were of two convicted murderers, who had killed and robbed an American priest. They were executed by firing squad on 12 January 1972, in Les Cayes, before 4,000 people, including the Justice Minister and the local bishop. This spectacle may have been connected with an attempt to assert the power of the Government over the local warlords, the *tonton macoutes.* The convicted murderers were connected with the local *tonton macoute* chieftain, a figure of some power. The interval between their conviction and execution was four weeks.

In cases of ordinary murder, death penalties are sometimes commuted by the exercise of Presidential clemency. On 27 December 1976, an official communiqué announced that two people sentenced to death by the *Tribunal criminel* of Port au Prince in July 1975, had had their sentences commuted to 15 years' imprisonment. The same communiqué made reference to nine people sentenced to death between 1968 and 1975 who had already had their sentences commuted to terms of imprisonment in the period 1971–75. In these cases, the longest period between sentence and commutation was three years: no lapse of time was shorter than eight months.

Unlike those of most Latin American countries, the laws of Haiti provide for the death penalty for political crimes. There is also a high incidence of death in custody. Moreover, the total absence of legal safeguards, the lack of proper formality in legal proceedings, and the complete isolation from the outside world of the great majority of those arrested for alleged political motives, make it impossible for even the families of detainees to establish whether they are alive or dead.

After the Presidential amnesty of 105 political prisoners in September 1977, the Government declared that there were no more political prisoners in Haiti. The question of what had become of the thousands of political prisoners unaccounted for throughout the Duvalier régime was answered in part by a group of prisoners who were expelled from the country immediately after their release. In addition to providing a list of 150 prisoners, whose death they attributed to tuberculosis and other serious illnesses, they reported that a number of executions without trial had taken place in the prisons of Port au Prince between 1971 and 1976.

***Honduras** (the Republic of)*

The death penalty was abolished in the Republic of Honduras by Article 56 of the Constitution of 1965, which declares that "The inviolability of human life is guaranteed, and capital punishment may not be established or applied by any law or by mandate of any authority."

***Mexico** (the United Mexican States)*

Article 22, paragraph 3 of the Political Constitution of the United Mexican States (1917) in essence provides that the death penalty for political offences be prohibited. The penalty exists for treason committed during a foreign war; parricide; homicide with perfidy, homicide which is premeditated or committed for profit; arson; kidnapping; highway robbery; piracy and the most serious military offences. Of the 31 Mexican States, 25 have abolished the death penalty, and the Penal Code covering the Federal Jurisdiction has also abolished it. According to Government sources, the death penalty has not been employed "for many years".

However, the police and the military use a considerable degree of force when carrying out arrests, and the frequent result of this is the death of suspects and bystanders. Recently, lawyers at the State University of Guerrero published a list of 257 people who had disappeared in the past four years during anti-subversive operations in the mountains conducted by the army. The lawyers maintain that the missing people are either being held incommunicado by the police or military, or have died in illegal detention.

***Nicaragua** (the Republic of)*

The Constitution of Nicaragua (1974) provides, in Article 38, that "Human life is inviolable." However, the death penalty is provided for the following crimes: high treason committed during a war against a foreign enemy; serious military offences; and the crimes of murder, parricide, arson or robbery resulting in death and aggravated by serious circumstances determined by law. The present Penal Code (1974) does not provide the death penalty for any crime. In a formal response to a United Nations survey of the death penalty (4 June 1969), Nicaragua reported that the death penalty was maintained, but not applied, as it had been "regulated" (*reglamentada*).

No cases of the use of the judicial death penalty have been reported during the period under review (1973–77). There have, however, been numerous reports that detentions carried out by National Guard troops in the northern areas of Nicaragua have been followed by arbitrary execution without trial. Roman Catholic Church sources have reported over 200 detentions and subsequent "disappearances". In January 1977 the seven Roman Catholic bishops of Nicaragua protested in a pastoral letter against alleged massive "executions" carried out by the National Guard, and against "terror and extermination".

Dr Pedro Joaquín Chamorro, Director of the newspaper *La Prensa* and the principal Nicaraguan opposition leader, was murdered in Managua on 10 January 1978 by three men firing sub-machine guns. It has been confirmed that an investigation into the killing would be made exclusively by the combined military and police force, the National Guard.

### ***Panama** (the Republic of)*

At the foundation of the Republic of Panama in 1903, the death penalty was abolished. Article 29 of Panama's present Constitution (1946) holds that: "There is no death penalty."

### ***Paraguay** (the Republic of)*

Like the Constitution of 1940 before it, the 1967 Constitution provides that "In no case shall the death penalty be applied for political considerations." However, the death penalty for "political considerations" was temporarily reintroduced in the 1940s for offences against the security of the state during the dictatorship of General Higinio Morinigo. According to some sources, the crime of sedition can be tried before a military tribunal and, consequently, punished by death.

The Penal Code provides for the death penalty for certain criminal offences – for example, killing in order to rob. This has led to a limited number of executions during this century. The Bill of the "Law for the Defence of Public Peace and Liberty of Persons" included a provision which authorized police to kill people who resisted a police raid on their homes. This caused general protest, particularly from the Roman Catholic Church and the College of Lawyers, and the article embodying the provision was removed before the Bill became law in 1970.

In Paraguay, both political and criminal prisoners have died as a result of torture or been murdered. In the late 1950s and early 1960s, the tortured and mutilated bodies of prisoners, with hands tied behind their backs, were washed on to the Argentinian shores of the River Paraná. During the period 1973–77, a number of people were killed while being arrested or died in custody as a result of torture. In 1977, several of the victims were peasant leaders.

### ***Peru** (the Republic of)*

From 1925 to 1933 in Peru, the death penalty was effectively abolished: the Penal Code of 1924 substituted lengthy imprisonment for crimes previously punishable by death. In 1933, however, a new Constitution, which is still in force, re-established the death penalty for "treason to the nation and homicide (*homicidio calificado*) and for all crimes so indicated by the law". Later modifications to the Penal Code made the death penalty available for parricide (Article 151), murder for profit, murder by poison, fire, explosions or "other means that might harm a great number of persons", or murder in which there was evidence of exceptional cruelty (Article 152).

Decree Law 18968 of 21 September 1971 modified Articles 151 and 152 of the Penal Code, limiting the application of the death penalty to the crimes of treason and kidnapping minors resulting in death. On 30 November 1971, however, Decree Law No. 19049 provided the death penalty for those who "through explosives or bombs cause death, injury, damage or serious destruction". On 30 January 1973, Decree Law No. 19910 was promulgated, widening the legal application of the death penalty still further, as well as establishing special summary trial proceedings in certain cases. Its preamble referred to "the alarming increase in criminality" and stated that "with increasing frequency criminal acts have caused the death of members of the Police Forces and other persons"; that, consequently, it had inevitably become "necessary ... to repress and sanction criminals with the maximum severity"; and that "the sanction should be imposed without delay, so that justice will fulfil its commitment, for which reason it should be administered, in certain cases, through the use of special summary proceedings". The Decree re-establishes the death penalty for crimes covered by Article 152 (see above), as well as establishing the death penalty for armed robbery resulting in death.

Those charged under this Law are tried by the Council of War in the appropriate zone of military justice (Article 2). Article 3 specifies that proceedings are to be carried out in accordance with Book II, Title 2, Section XI of the Military Code of Justice dealing with "Extraordinary Trials" (*juicios extraordinarios*); this established procedures for trial by Special Councils of War.

Title 2, entitled "Trials in the Theatre of Operations", provides the following time-limits for trial proceedings: 12 hours for study of the case dossier and the drafting of an accusation by the military prosecutor, and 12 hours for the defence to study the case dossier and the accusation (Articles 736 and 738, Military Code of Justice). The hearing (*audiencia*) then follows and, after judgment by the Special Council of War, the sentence should, according to the Military Code of Justice, immediately and automatically go to the Supreme Council of Military Justice for final review. There is no statutory right to appeal beyond the Supreme Council of Military Justice; in the past, the Supreme Court of Justice, constitutionally the highest court in the land, has not ruled against the supremacy of the military courts in matters of jurisdiction. Article 3 (of Decree Law No. 19910) also provides an exceptional procedure for the (mandatory) review of the death sentence by the Supreme Council of Military Justice, with a strict time-limit for each stage of the appeal.

Following review and ratification by the Supreme Council of Military Justice, the death sentence is carried out 24 hours after it is published; the execution, in peace time, "se verificará de día y, cuando más tarde, a las 24 horas de la publicación de la condena en la Orden General respectiva".

Decree Law 20.583 of 9 April 1974 made the death penalty applicable to those who carry out "the sexual act or analogous acts with a minor seven years old or less".

On 1 December 1974, General Javier Tantaleán, the Minister of Fisheries, and General Guillermo Arbulú, were wounded by gunfire in an unsuccessful assassination attempt against the then Prime Minister, General Edgardo Mercado Jarrín, who was travelling with them. Two days later, on 3 December, Decree Law No. 20.828 was promulgated to suppress "political terrorism". The preamble of the Law specified that the sanction must be "rapid, intimidating and exemplary", while the sentences should be "drastic, the procedures summary and the execution of sentence immediate".

Article 1 provides the death penalty for "those who for political purposes make attempts on the lives of persons, or who damage property, employing whatsoever means ... if death, or injuries, whatever their gravity, should be the outcome".

Article 2 provides for the application of the same sentence to "the authors, co-authors, accomplices and *encubridores* [accessories]".

Article 3 stipulates that Permanent Councils of War shall have jurisdiction over these crimes, as well as those indicated in Decree Law 19049; and that, in both cases, procedures are to be in accordance with those established in the Military Code of Justice for special courts in the "Theatre of Operations" (as for murder of a member of the police forces under Decree Law 19910). It further provides that the already summary proceedings specified in the Military Code be yet further reduced, so that "the investigation, the judgment and the execution of sentence should take place within 48 hours of the initiation of the investigation [*instrucción*]".

It is unclear whether the Supreme Council of Military Justice would be required to ratify sentences passed by the Councils of War before the execution of sentences; Article 7 of the Decree Law declares that "the norms of the Penal Codes and of Military Justice, as well as of the pertinent laws, are suspended to the extent that they oppose this law", and, consequently, there appears to be no appeal against sentences imposed in these circumstances.

From 1973 until February 1976, seven men were executed for the murder of members of police forces, apparently under Decree Law No. 19910, rather than Decree Law No. 20.828. On 29 November 1973, Alejandro Lastra Villa Vicencio, a former policeman, and Gerardo Pinto Sulcahuaman, were executed for their part in a bank robbery in which a policeman and a bank employee were killed. José Murillo Andrade, aged 21, was executed on 18 December 1976 for the murder of a police detective, although it seems that he was not yet 21 at the time of the crime. (Article 9 of Decree Law No. 19910 refers to Article 148 of the Penal Code, which provides for lesser penalties for offenders between the ages of 18 and 21.)

Juan Machare Zapata was executed on 19 June 1974, apparently for killing a policeman. Miguel Salazar Valdivia, aged 25, a labourer, was executed on 23 January 1974 for killing a policeman while robbing a store.

On 4 February 1976, Alfredo Benítez Caldas, aged 25, and Luis Uscuvilca Patino, were executed. Both had taken part in a bank robbery in which a member of the Civil Guard was killed. The court found that death was caused by one bullet, but was unable to determine which of the prisoners had fired it; the two men accused each other of responsibility. They were both condemned and executed in accordance with Article 8 of the Decree Law, which holds that "when it is not known who carried out the actions or who individually caused the death, all the protagonists of the criminal act will be taken as authors".

All the executions were carried out by military firing squad on the island of El Frontón, near the port of Callao.

### *Uruguay (the Eastern Republic of)*

The last execution in Uruguay took place publicly in a Montevideo square at the end of the 19th century. The indignation and protests it aroused finally led to the abolition of the death penalty by the *Law 3.238* of 1907. Article 1 of this Law abolishes the death penalty in both the Penal Code and the Military Code. This provision was upheld in later Constitutions. The Constitution of 1967, which is now in force, states in Article 26: "No one shall be sentenced to death." At the time of writing, a new Constitution is being drafted in Uruguay.

Despite increasingly severe security laws and their application by military tribunals, it appears that the death penalty will not be re-introduced.

The political crisis that began in the late 1960s has led to a gradual increase in political violence and to a serious erosion of the rule of law in Uruguay. Politically motivated killings have been committed by urban guerillas, by the armed forces and the police and by para-military and para-police groups, operating both in Uruguay itself and among Uruguayan refugees and exiles in neighbouring Argentina. In the years 1973–77 more than 35 people have died in police custody as a result of torture.

***Venezuela*** *(the Republic of)*

Venezuela abolished the death penalty in 1863. The present Constitution (1961) prohibits the death penalty in its Article 58: "The right to life is inviolable. No law may establish the death penalty or any authority carry it out."

## THE ENGLISH-SPEAKING CARIBBEAN

The following countries – all members of the Commonwealth – comprise the English-speaking Caribbean: Antigua, Bahama Islands, Barbados, Belize, Bermuda, Cayman Islands, Dominica, Grenada, Guyana, Jamaica, Monserrat, St Christopher-Nevis-Anguilla, St Lucia, St Vincent, Trinidad and Tobago, Turks and Caicos Islands and the British Virgin Islands. The status of these countries within the Commonwealth varies: Guyana and Trinidad and Tobago are republics, each with a President as Head of State; the Bahamas, Barbados, Grenada, and Jamaica are sovereign, independent states which recognize Queen Elizabeth II as Queen and Head of State: Antigua, Dominica, St Christopher-Nevis-Anguilla, St Lucia, and St Vincent, are Associated States; Belize, Bermuda, the British Virgin Islands, the Cayman Islands, Monserrat and the Turks and Caicos Islands are British Dependent Territories.

All the laws of these territories are based on English common law; their legislation concerning the death penalty is in many cases identical with English law as it stood before 1965. All have a mandatory death sentence for murder. The Bahamas, Bermuda, Guyana, St Lucia, St Vincent, Trinidad and Tobago, and Grenada have a mandatory death sentence for treason. In addition, the Bahamas and Bermuda have a mandatory death sentence for piracy with violence, and St Lucia has a mandatory death sentence for attempting to commit murder while under sentence of imprisonment for three years or more. Guyana and Jamaica provide a discretionary death sentence for those subject to military law who assist the enemy, participate in a mutiny involving violence, or fail to report, endeavour to suppress or prevent such a mutiny; while Trinidad and Tobago provides a possible death sentence for those who assist the enemy or participate in a mutiny involving violence.

In practice, only the legislation concerning murder is relevant to this report, because, to the knowledge of Amnesty International, the death penalty has not been imposed in recent years for treason, piracy, mutiny or assisting the enemy. However, in several of these Caribbean countries, executions for murder have taken place, and in others there are people at present under sentence of death for the same offence.

In all these countries, except Bermuda, Belize, Grenada, St Lucia, St Vincent, and Trinidad and Tobago, the law stipulates that pregnant women shall not be sentenced to death; in all except Barbados, Bermuda, Belize, the Cayman Islands, St Vincent, and Trinidad and Tobago, there is a stipulation that the death sentence may not be pronounced on anyone under 18 at the time the offence was committed. All these Caribbean countries except Guyana allow recourse to the Judicial Committee of the Privy Council in London as a final court of appeal on certain questions of law. Similarly, in all except Guyana and Trinidad and Tobago, death sentences may be commuted by the Crown; in those two exceptions, death sentences may be commuted by the President.

The following survey of individual countries within the English-speaking Caribbean covers only those countries for which Amnesty International has information about death sentences and executions in recent years. If a country is not mentioned, this should not be taken to imply that no death sentence has been passed. In other cases, the information may not be complete: for example, it is not always known whether death sentences which have been passed have been carried out.

***Antigua***

On 19 November 1975, Charles Joseph was executed for murder.

***Bahamas*** *(the Commonwealth of the)*

According to UN Document E/5616 of 12 February 1975, during the period 1969–73, of a group of 17 men sentenced to death in the Bahamas, four were executed; the sentence was commuted in 11 cases, and two cases were still under consideration.

In October 1974, two men were hanged for their part in a murder with political motives during the General Election campaign of 1972. On 3 February 1976, Earol Dean was hanged for the murder of a police inspector in 1974. In October 1976, Michaiah Schobek, an American, was hanged for the murder of three fellow American tourists. In connection with this execution a Bahamian Government spokesman said: "If we didn't hang people occasionally, the society would fall apart."

***Barbados***

No executions have taken place in Barbados since 10 June 1975, but on 1 February 1978, four people were under sentence of death, one of whom, David Walton, was convicted on 17 November 1974.

***Bermuda***

On 2 December 1977, Erskine Burrows and Larry Winfield Tacklyn were hanged, the first people to be executed in Bermuda for more than 30 years. The hangings were preceded by much publicity in the United Kingdom, in particular because of the circumstances of the trial and the convictions of the two men and because of the refusal of the United Kingdom Secretary of State for Foreign and Commonwealth Affairs, Dr David Owen, to intervene, even though Bermuda is a British Dependent Territory. The two men, who were Black, were convicted by a special jury selected on the basis of educational and other similar qualifications. Of the 12 jurors, 9 were White and only 3 Black and the decision to convict was arrived at by a majority of 9 members of the jury.

### *British Virgin Islands*

In October 1977, Sylvester Gaston was convicted of murder and sentenced to death. His appeal against his conviction was refused in January 1978. At the time of writing, he was seeking leave to appeal to the Judicial Committee of the Privy Council in London.

### *Dominica*

Since 1967, two executions have taken place in Dominica, the most recent of a person convicted of murder in 1973. Since 1973, there have been two convictions for murder, in 1974 and 1975, but in both cases the mandatory death sentences were commuted to life imprisonment in 1976. The 1974 conviction was of Desmond Trotter, who was alleged to have killed an American tourist. His case has received much publicity because he was a leader of a group known as "The Dreads", who were opposed to the policies of the Government. Desmond Trotter has repeatedly affirmed his innocence and claimed that his political activities were the reason for his arrest and conviction.

### *Grenada*

On 17 November 1977, four men were executed for the murder of a young girl in 1976, the first executions to take place on the island of Grenada since 31 May 1962. Amnesty International has received information that five or six other men were under sentence of death in Grenada at the time of those executions.

### *Guyana (the Republic of)*

On 11 June 1974, the High Commissioner for Guyana in London informed Amnesty International that the last occasion on which the death penalty had been carried out was on 3 March 1970, for the crime of murder. In a letter of 11 June 1974, he had already stated that the general policy of Guyana toward the death penalty was that all death sentences should be commuted unless there were compelling reasons to the contrary.

### *Jamaica*

In November 1977, there were 51 men under sentence of death in Jamaica's St Catherine District Prison. Many of them had been convicted several years earlier but remained on Death Row, awaiting the results of their appeals.

In December 1974, at which time there were 36 men on Death Row, an incident occurred which was described by the prison authorities as an "attempted mass break-out" and by the condemned men as a "demonstration against injustice and oppression". As a result, a Commission of Inquiry was set up by the Prime Minister, Mr Michael Manley, to investigate the circumstances which led to the incident. In its report the Commission provided information about the ages of the condemned men and the length of time spent in prison. Of the 36 men, 30 (83 per cent) were under 30 at the time of arrest, and 29 (80 per cent) were under 25. Fourteen (38 per cent) were aged 20 or less at the time of arrest. The average length of stay in the condemned cells was 20 months; the maximum time spent there being four-and-a-half years and the minimum time two months. Thirty of the men had spent over one year awaiting death by hanging. For eight of the 36 men the date of execution had actually been set; they had spent a varying number of days in the special cell used exclusively by men whose execution was imminent. All these men received a stay of execution within days of the date set for their hanging. Two received the stay of execution after 11 days in the death cell, three after nine days, two after six days; in one case, the period of time spent in the death cell is unknown.

The psychological stress created by this treatment can be deduced from that part of the Commission's report which describes the attitude of the condemned men to execution. It states that "Despite the fact that none of the men has actually witnessed a hanging, the men all have a horror in their minds associated with the *procedure* of hanging." In their conclusions the Commission states:

> *"What has emerged from our Investigation is that:*
>
> *(1) the condemned men are in terror of the prospect of hanging. Quote – 'There is not just the fear of death – it's how one's going to die.'*
>
> *(2) These men have spent up to four-and-a-half years waiting in condemned cells, in the belief that they will be assaulted and may even be beaten to death on the way to the gallows.*
>
> *(3) In an emotionally charged atmosphere rumours are escalated into terrifying fantasies, e.g. 'the warders lick* [sic] *your teeth before they hang you. And when they come back, they torture you, tell you you are going to hang next . . . .'*
>
> *"Fantasy is given credence, and the men's fears are reinforced and magnified, by the physical beatings, taunts and threats they regularly receive from the warders."*

In its recommendation the Commission says:

> *"This team questions fundamentally the use of hanging as a deterrent against murder, or a deterrent against violent crime. We feel that most men who commit the crime of murder can be adequately rehabilitated to lead normal productive lives. It is felt by this team that hanging as a punishment is regarded by most people as a revenge and does not serve the purpose for which it was devised."*

In 1974, 1975 and 1976, Amnesty International appealed to the Governor-General of Jamaica for the commutation of death sentences passed on young men who had been sentenced for crimes committed when they were under the age of 18 years. All the men concerned subsequently had their sentences commuted to life imprisonment, and on 20 April 1976, the Governor-General, Florizel Glasspole, wrote to Amnesty International, saying that new legislation had been introduced which prevents the death sentence being carried out in all cases where the offender was under 18 when the offence was committed.

Thirty-seven executions took place in Jamaica during the years 1968–77 (inclusive), the most recent in April 1976.

*. :ncent*

On 26 January 1978, three men were hanged for murder, the first executions to take place on St Vincent since November 1970.

***Trinidad and Tobago*** *(the Republic of)*

In February 1977, there were 26 prisoners, including one woman, on Death Row in the Royal Gaol, Port of Spain. All had been sentenced to hang. Some of them had exhausted every avenue of appeal, while others had appeals pending to the local Court of Appeal or the Judicial Committee of the Privy Council in London. In one case, the condemned man had been convicted as long ago as 1972; in two cases, conviction was in 1973; in four cases, 1974; and in 13 cases 1975. Of the remaining six cases, five were convicted in 1976, and the date of conviction of one is not known. A Trinidadian lawyer, Ramesh Maharaj, in a paper submitted to the Attorney-General of Trinidad and Tobago and to local and international bodies concerned with human rights, stated that:

> *"It must be a rule of elementary justice that people on criminal charges, especially capital charges, ought to be given speedy trials. After conviction of murder and whilst the appeals are pending the prisoners are kept in the death cells. When one sees these prisoners in death cells one is reminded of seeing animals caged in the Zoo, the only difference is that the cages in the Zoo are larger and more airy."*

During the years 1968–77 (inclusive), 62 executions have taken place in Trinidad, the most recent in August 1977.

## CANADA AND THE UNITED STATES OF AMERICA

***Canada***

The death penalty for murder, treason and piracy was abolished in Canada by an amendment to the Penal Code (Bill C-84) in July 1976. However, a number of capital offences remain under the National Defence Act, including espionage, mutiny, offences in relation to convoy of vessels, and certain other categories of offence committed by military personnel in time of war and where the defendant has acted "traitorously".

Canada temporarily suspended the death penalty for civilian (as opposed to military) offences for a five-year trial period from 1967 to 1972. The Criminal Law Amendment (Capital Punishment) Act, 1973, which came into force on 1 January 1974, temporarily abolished the death penalty for a further period until 31 December 1977. The abolition has been made permanent by the 1976 amendment.

***United States of America*** *(the)*

The death penalty in the USA is an issue over which the judicial, legislative and executive branches of government at both State and Federal level interact. In the years under review (1973–77), the death penalty was very widely discussed; as a result, there was a great deal of legislative action, litigation in the courts and, at State level, pronouncements of executive policy. They tended to create a somewhat uncertain atmosphere; nevertheless, there was and is a firm trend in favour of the death penalty. Abolitionist States are in a minority; there has been much death penalty legislation in recent years; the federal jurisdiction is retentionist and judicial decision has allowed the first execution to take place since 1967.

All State and Federal law imposing the death penalty must be consistent with provisions of the United States' Constitution. In addition, all State laws must be consistent with the Constitution of the State in question. However, litigation over the issue is mainly in terms of the Federal Constitution, and it is that body of legal principles which is most relevant to this survey. The 8th Amendment to the Federal Constitution provides that no "cruel and unusual punishments [may be] inflicted", and the courts have often had to determine whether the imposition of the sentence of death is in breach of this provision. Any law which is determined to be in breach of what is laid down in the Constitution is invalid. If, therefore, a death penalty statute is unconstitutional, the death penalty may not be applied.

Legal argument has centred round the issues of whether the death penalty is inherently "cruel and unusual" and/or whether it deprives its intended victims of the constitutional guarantees of "due process of law" or the "equal protection of the laws".*

In judicial decisions on 2 and 6 July 1976,† affirmed on 4 October 1976, the United States Supreme Court held by seven votes to two that the punishment of death *for murder* did not invariably constitute "cruel and unusual punishment", and therefore did not in all circumstances violate the Constitution of the United States.

However, the US Supreme Court held, by five votes to four, that a death sentence passed by a court in accordance with a law imposing a *mandatory* death penalty for a broad category of offences of homicide, did constitute "cruel and unusual punishment", and was therefore unconstitutional. This decision was based on the finding that mandatory death sentences provide no "objective standards to guide, regularize and make rationally reviewable the process for imposing a sentence of death" (a due process issue). The US Supreme Court also held that death penalty statutes which gave to judge or jury the power to decide, according to stated "aggravating and mitigating" features of a case, whether or not a sentence of death should be imposed, could be valid. In such instances, the wording of the statutes (known as "guided-discretion statutes") was held to provide necessary and adequate guidance for those whose duty it is to impose punishment.

A further US Supreme Court decision in June 1977 followed this line of reasoning, and held that a Louisiana statute which provided a mandatory death penalty for anyone convicted of the murder of a police officer was unconstitutional.

On 29 June 1977, the Supreme Court ruled that the death penalty, "unique in its severity and irreversibility", was too great a punishment for non-homicidal rape. This ruling may indicate that the death penalty is unconstitutional if imposed for crimes which do not involve loss of life.

Although the basic question of whether the death penalty might *ever* be imposed had been raised and considered in a case in 1972,** it was not resolved by

* "Due process of law" may be understood in general terms as "compliance with the fundamental rules for fair and orderly proceedings"; "equal protection of the laws" may be similarly understood as "a guarantee of uniformity of treatment under law of all persons in like circumstances".

† Gregg v. State of Georgia 429 US 1301 (1976).

** Furman v. State of Georgia 408 US 238 (1972).

the court. Five out of nine justices held in 1972 that the death penalty as then administered was unconstitutional; only two held that it would be so in any form. Each of those who concurred or dissented filed separate opinions and the disagreements between them made the long-term consequences of the judgment very unclear. Central to the 1972 case, was the finding that a jury should not have "arbitrary and wanton" discretion to impose the death sentence: such "unguided" discretion was itself held to be a violation of "due process" and "equal protection".

The issue of discrimination was taken up in some of the 1972 opinions. Justice Douglas stated that "the discretion of judges and juries in imposing the death penalty enables the penalty to be selectively applied, feeding prejudices against the accused if he is poor and despised, and lacking political clout, or if he is a member of a suspect or unpopular minority, and saving those who by social position may be in a more protected position."

The 1976 cases arose because, in 1972, the Supreme Court had decided only one limited issue: that unbridled jury discretion in the imposition of the death penalty was unconstitutional. As a result of legal decisions, many States then enacted new death penalty laws which provided different procedures for sentencing people to death. No one sentenced under these new laws was executed, because the States concerned awaited a US Supreme Court decision on whether the new state laws were constitutional. It was this particular issue, as well as the general one of whether the death penalty was inherently "cruel and unusual", which was determined in 1976.

A synthesis of the 1972 and 1976 decisions provides the following basic outline of the probable current state of the law:

(1) The death penalty is only constitutional if it is imposed after a separate sentencing hearing (which is itself subsequent to conviction for a capital crime) at which the aggravating and mitigating features of each particular case are considered. Such features relate not only to the offence but also to the character of the offender.

(2) There must be legislative guidance over what are "aggravating and mitigating" circumstances for the process of determining a sentence.

(3) The availability of review of this process on appeal must be specifically provided for in the statute.

In March 1978 Amnesty International understood that the constitutionality of the death penalty laws for the crime of murder applying in States of the Union was as follows:

*States that have enacted death penalty laws since the 1976 decision:* California, Delaware, Idaho, Illinois, Indiana, Kentucky, Louisiana, Maryland, Mississippi, Missouri, Montana, Nevada, New Hampshire, North Carolina, Oklahoma, South Carolina, Tennessee, Utah, Virginia, Washington and Wyoming.

*States that enacted death penalty laws after the 1972 decision but before the 1976 decision:* Alabama, Arizona, Arkansas, Colorado, Connecticut, Florida, Georgia, Nebraska, Ohio and Texas.

*States with death penalty laws which have been held unconstitutional and therefore invalid:* New Jersey, New Mexico, New York, Pennsylvania, Rhode Island and Vermont.

*States that have no death penalty laws in force:* Alaska, Hawaii, Iowa, Kansas, Massachusetts, Maine, Michigan, Minnesota, North Dakota, Oregon, South Dakota, West Virginia and Wisconsin.

*Non-State jurisdictions:* There is no death penalty in the territories of Guam, Puerto Rico, US Virgin Islands or the District of Columbia, but the Uniform Code of Military Justice retains the death penalty.

The federal jurisdiction provides the death penalty for piracy of an aircraft resulting in a death. It has yet to be determined whether the provision is constitutional, but so far no death sentences have been imposed for this crime.

Although the constitutionality of the death penalty for the following crimes is undecided, it exists in law in some States for certain types of treason; train-wrecking which results in death (California); deadly assault by a prisoner serving a life sentence; armed robbery; and illegal sale, for gain, of cocaine, heroin or methadone to a person who dies as a direct result of the use of the drug, provided at the time of the sale the seller was not dependent on drugs himself (Connecticut).

An important question is whether the Supreme Court has eliminated race as a factor in the outcome of a capital case by requiring legislative guidance for the process of determining sentence and by limiting the use of the death penalty essentially to murder cases. One result of this latter limitation is that rape is no longer to be punished by death and therefore any possible racial bias in the imposition of the death penalty in cases involving cross-racial rape is eliminated.

One of the few systematic inquiries into sentencing patterns under post-1972 guided-discretion statutes was undertaken in 1976 by Marc Riedel, the Director of the Center for Studies in Criminology & Criminal Law of the University of Pennsylvania. The primary conclusion of the study reads as follows: "There is no evidence to suggest that post-[1972] statutes have been successful in reducing the discretion which leads to a disproportionate number of nonwhite offenders being sentenced to death. If anything, the opposite is true; nationwide and especially in the western region of the United States, the proportion of nonwhite offenders is significantly higher in the post-[1972] period in comparison with the pre-[1972] period. It is only in the southern region that the proportion of nonwhite offenders is less in the post-[1972] period." ("Discrimination in the Imposition of the Death Penalty: A Comparison of the Characteristics of Offenders Sentenced Pre-Furman and Post-Furman", *Temple Law Quarterly* Vol. 49, 261, 282 (1976))

The execution of Gary Mark Gilmore on 17 January 1977 was the first to take place in the United States since 2 June 1967. However, although no other executions have taken place, sentences of death have continued to be passed. According to the NAACP Legal Defense and Educational Fund Inc. there were 446 people under sentence of death in 24 States on 15 February 1978.

The NAACP was quoted in the *New York Times* of 27 January 1978 as saying that

> *"... while more Blacks than Whites had drawn the death penalty throughout United States history, 183, or 44.96 per cent of those on Death Row under today's laws were Black and 202, or nearly 50 per cent, were White. Of the remainder, 14 were described as Spanish-surnamed, two as native Americans and six others as of unknown heritage.*
>
> *The percentage of Blacks among those facing execution remains far out of proportion to the 10 per cent of the population that is Black."*

According to the preliminary findings of a study covering three States–Georgia, Florida and Texas–which is currently being undertaken by the Center for Applied Social Research at Northeastern University in Boston, murderers of White people are said to be "far more likely to be sentenced to death than killers of Blacks". The Director of the Center, Dr William J. Bowers, is quoted as saying: "Now it appears that a new form of discrimination has emerged – not in who did the killing but who got killed."

Dr Bowers was reported in the *New York Times* of 6 March 1978 as saying that he had found that "the racial disparities between the percentages of those arrested for homicide and those on Death Row [were] at wide variance. Six per cent of those arrested for homicide were Blacks who allegedly killed Whites, compared with 45 per cent on Death Row. Fifty per cent of those arrested were Blacks who allegedly killed Blacks, compared with 5 per cent on Death Row. Forty per cent of those arrested were Whites who allegedly killed Whites, compared with 50 per cent on Death Row. Four per cent of those arrested were Whites who allegedly killed Blacks and none of those were on Death Row."

Clemency is normally the prerogative of the chief executive of the jurisdiction in question – the State Governor or the US President but the President has no jurisdiction to commute the sentence of a person condemned under State law. There is, however, a movement towards the sharing or delegation of the power to grant clemency. In 10 States it is exercised by the Board of Pardons, and in seven others it is the Governor who decides, on the recommendation of such a Board. In California, in cases when the condemned person has been sentenced to death on more than one occasion, it is the Governor who takes the decision whether to grant clemency, on the basis of a recommendation by the State Supreme Court. In the State of Rhode Island discretion lies with the Governor on the basis of a recommendation of the State Senate. In the remaining States discretion rests entirely with the Governor.

Methods of execution in the US vary from State to State. Those available in law include hanging, the electric chair, the gas chamber and firing squad. Gary Gilmore was executed in Utah by firing squad. Texas and Oklahoma have adopted legislation which provides for the death penalty to be carried out by simultaneous intravenous injection of an overdose of barbiturate to induce sleep, and a chemical paralytic to cause death, if it were not brought about by the barbiturate. Bills to this effect have also been introduced in other States.

## THE MIDDLE EAST

The Middle East here refers to the Arab countries from the Arabian Peninsula to Libya, and also includes Iran and Israel. The Maghreb countries (Morocco, Tunisia and Algeria) are dealt with in the section on Africa in this chapter.

None of the countries of the Middle East has abolished the death penalty. In almost all of them – especially those where the penal codes are based on Western codes of law – there is legislation providing for the death penalty for certain categories of murder and specific offences against the internal and external security of the State, such as treason, espionage, plotting to overthrow the government and political acts of sabotage. In some countries in the region, drug smuggling also is a capital offence, and in the People's Democratic Republic of Yemen (PDRY), a number of economic offences are considered to be crimes against the State and are punishable by death.

Detailed and reliable information on the imposition of death sentences and on executions in the Middle East is difficult to obtain. Executions for political offences are more likely to be publicized than those for non-political offences: for instance, although the death penalty is a discretionary punishment for certain categories of murder, reports of executions for non-political murder are rare, except in those countries where executions take place infrequently such as in Kuwait, where in May 1974 it was reported that a man was publicly hanged for murder, and that this was the fifth execution since the country's independence in 1961).

More widely publicized – and therefore better documented – are executions for political offences, such as political murder, political acts of sabotage, attempts to overthrow the government and espionage. However, in an area where, for the most part, the judiciary enjoys little or no independence, the frequency of the application of the death penalty tends to fluctuate in accordance with the country's internal political tensions.

In Syria and the Yemen Arab Republic, for example, almost all reported executions over the past three years have been for acts of sabotage. In Syria there have been 13, all carried out from 1975 to June 1977, a period when numerous acts of sabotage had taken place. In the Yemen Arab Republic, over 50 "saboteurs" were executed during 1973, when there were widespread acts of sabotage allegedly committed by South Yemeni infiltrators.

On the other hand, in Lebanon and Israel, despite internal political tension, external threat, and the existence of capital offences in the legislation, executions are rarely carried out. In Israel, under the Defence (Emergency) Regulations of 1945, military courts can impose the death penalty for acts of terrorism resulting in death, but although death sentences have been passed, they have been commuted on appeal. The only execution in Israel has been that of Adolf Eichmann in 1962. Eichmann was convicted of genocide committed outside Israel before and during the Second World War. In Lebanon, certain categories of murder, acts against the security of the state and terrorism are punishable by death, but all death sentences passed have been commuted. The last executions in the country took place in 1970 for murder, and before that in the early 1960s, again for murder. In Jordan, since 1973 only one execution is known to have been carried out – in December 1976, for sabotage.

In Libya, during the early years of Colonel Gaddafi's rule, when support for the Government was assured, attempts to overthrow it, although a capital offence, were, in practice, not punished by death. However, now that opposition has increased, executions take place. In the PDRY, on the other hand, offences such as espionage and opposition to the Government are, apparently, less likely to be punished by death now that the Government has consolidated its position.

Regular executions of spies in Egypt have been directly related to the country's "state of war" with Israel. Ten spies were executed over the period 1973–77. As far as the other countries in the front line of the Middle East conflict are concerned, in Israel and Syria, no executions for espionage are known to have been carried out during this period. In Jordan one death sentence for espionage has been passed, in July 1976, but Amnesty International does not know, at the time of writing, whether it was carried out or not. In the same country, it has been a capital offence since April 1973 to sell to the Israeli authorities land in territories occupied by Israel since 1967. Several death sentences for this offence have been passed, but all *in absentia*.

Given that governments often maintain that violence has been used by a person condemned to death, it is often difficult to identify precisely whether executions are, in fact, carried out for non-violent political offences, such as non-violent opposition to the government, or for membership of illegal political parties. In countries with a consistently high level of political executions during the period 1973–77 – Iran, Iraq, and to a lesser degree the PDRY – and where no internal opposition to the government in power is tolerated, most political executions are officially reported to be of persons convicted of, for example, acts of sabotage or espionage. However, these are also the countries where legal safeguards are notably inadequate. Political cases are usually tried in special courts – military courts, revolutionary courts, people's courts – in which the tribunal is composed of people other than representatives of the judiciary; trials and executions are usually held in secret and/or summarily; and the defendants have few legal rights, despite the guarantees which may be embodied in Constitutions and penal codes. In addition, penal legislation is often drafted extremely broadly, and all of these factors tend to cast doubt on the charges brought against people tried in special courts.

Specific legislation making membership of illegal parties a capital offence exists in certain countries. In Iraq, it is a capital offence for a member of the Ba'ath Party to conceal past or present political affiliations. In Libya, legislation was introduced in 1975, making membership of any party other than the Arab Socialist Union a capital offence. Two death sentences for this offence were passed in February 1977, but Amnesty International does not know, at the time of writing, whether they have been carried out.

In certain countries of the Middle East, justice is administered in accordance with Islamic law (*Sharia*). These countries are Saudi Arabia, Oman and the Yemen Arab Republic (although here, secular legislation is now being introduced). Although legislation in the other countries of the Middle East has for a long time been based on Western codes of law, there have been recent moves in some of them to reintroduce, in whole or in part, the tenets of Islam into the civil code. In Egypt such attempts have so far proved unsuccessful because of internal opposition; in Libya, Islamic law was reintroduced for certain offences in 1973 but has not so far been applied; in the Gulf States, where previously only matters of personal status, such as marriage, divorce and inheritance were governed by the *Sharia*, moves are now under way to widen its application; and in the United Arab Emirates, Islamic law was reintroduced at the end of 1977 and has already been applied in cases of rape.

The principles of Islamic law are based on the *Qur'an*, which Muslims believe to be divinely revealed, on the traditional pronouncements ascribed to the Prophet Muhammad, and on the interpretation of these two sources by various schools of Islamic law. Islamic law differs fundamentally from Western codes of law in that it is believed to be of divine origin, and its function is as much to preserve the moral standards of behaviour of the community as to enforce law and order.

Under Islamic law, wilful murder and, in some cases, lesser degrees of homicide constitute a capital offence. The penalty for such an offence is determined by the nearest relative of the victim, who traditionally is entitled to kill the culprit in retribution, or to accept "blood money" (this usually in the case of death by accident). In these days, the execution is carried out by an official executioner, and not by the family.

Amnesty International has received little information on death sentences imposed for murder for the past three years in the countries mentioned above. The only case given publicity has been that of Prince Faisal Ibn Musaed, who was executed on 18 June 1975, after being convicted of "the wilful and premeditated murder" of King Faisal of Saudi Arabia.

Certain cases of sexual immorality, such as adultery between two married people, fornication and sodomy, are punishable by death. The death sentence can only be imposed, however, if the offence is proved in accordance with stringent rules laid down by Islamic law (i.e., evidence from four eyewitnesses to the act, or confession by the accused). The traditional punishment in such cases is stoning to death for both men and women.

In March 1977 in Saudi Arabia, three married men who had confessed to kidnapping and raping a woman were executed in this way. The crime was considered particularly grave because it had been committed during the Muslim fasting month of *Ramadan*. Another man, though unmarried, was beheaded. In the previous month, on 25 February 1977, two men convicted of having kidnapped and indecently assaulted a young boy were beheaded. According to a Reuters report of November 1977, a youth was beheaded in public in Riyadh, the capital of Saudi Arabia, for kidnapping and raping a girl of seven. A report in January 1978 claimed that, in the previous November, a twenty-three-year-old Saudi princess and her Saudi husband had been executed in public in Jeddah (she was said to have been shot and he to have been beheaded). One report claimed that they had married in secret against the wishes of her family, were caught while trying to flee the country and were executed by order of her grandfather. If this were the case, the executions would have contravened Islamic law, since no offence under that law had been committed. However, another report claimed that the princess had previously been married and had therefore committed adultery, which, under Islamic law, is a capital offence.

In the Yemen Arab Republic, it would appear that offences involving sexual immorality are now punished by imprisonment, not death.

Highway robbery, robbery with violence, rape, acts of sabotage, and conspiring against the Muslim state are also capital offences. These are classed, in Islamic law, under the offence known as *hiraba*, which means, literally, "making war" and which is explained in the *Qur'an* as "those who make war against God and his Apostle, and go about to commit disorders in the earth" (*Sura* 5, verse 33, translation by Rodwell).

As many as 70 "saboteurs" were executed between May and December of 1973 in the Yemen Arab Republic. The executions happened after a series of sabotage incidents in the south of the country which, the Government claimed, had been instigated by South Yemeni infiltrators; the incidents included the assassination of a member of the Presidential Council. In Oman in June 1975 four men were executed for plotting assassination and armed revolution.

Another crime for which the death penalty applies is apostasy or rejection of the Islamic faith, although Amnesty International knows of no cases of people being executed for this offence.

The Muslim courts hear most cases concerning the offences listed above. The procedure is simple: the complainant and the defendant put forward their cases, and on the basis of the evidence presented by the complainant, defendant and witnesses, the judge gives his verdict and passes sentence. In the case of murder, however, the penalty is decided by the victim's family, and the role of the court is confined to announcing the family's decision.

Muslim judges are required to be well-versed in Islamic law, and to show fairness and impartiality: their task involves ensuring that the injured party obtains satisfaction. In general, they have wide discretionary powers in prescribing punishments, but no authority to alter punishments specified in the *Qur'an* (for murder, theft, adultery, *hiraba*, etc.). However, they are advised, in the tradition of the Prophet, to avoid applying the severest punishments if mitigating circumstances exist.

Offences against the State may, however, be dealt with by a special tribunal composed wholly or partly of representatives of the ruler, and not Muslim judges. In 1973, in the Yemen Arab Republic, a Supreme State Court with a military tribunal was set up within the Ministry of the Interior to try political saboteurs. At such times, the dossiers of those who are to be tried might be referred to the Muslim judges, who would be asked to evaluate the cases and to issue a *fatwa* (a formal legal opinion), specifying the punishment in accordance with Islamic law. On the basis of their *fatwa*, the military court would pass sentence after conviction. In the Yemen Arab Republic, Muslim judges issued a *fatwa* on the charges of sabotage, saying that "the laying and detonating of mines is found to come within the category of aggression and the disruption of public order, and is therefore a capital offence."

Since the end of the last century, under the influence of Western legal systems, defence counsel – in the Western legal sense – has been permitted in the Muslim courts in some countries. Usually, however, it is the defendant or a friend of the defendant who presents the case for the defence. There is no appeals machinery of the kind to be found in Western legal systems, though a convicted person, or his family, may appeal against a sentence, on the grounds of miscarriage of justice, to the *Qadi Muzalim*, who would be the ruler or his representative, and who is charged with hearing appeals. In political cases, the death sentence has to be approved by the head of state, who also has the authority to commute the sentence or grant pardon. A number of death sentences for political offences are known to have been commuted in the Yemen Arab Republic and Oman over the past three years.

In all Arab countries where Islamic law is no longer applied, death sentences have to be approved, as a formality, by the *Mufti*, the leading religious scholar in the community.

Execution is usually by beheading or by firing squad. Execution by firing squad is usual for murderers who shoot their victims. Traditionally, executions are public, and very often the body or the severed head is also displayed in public. Prince Faisal's head was displayed for 15 minutes after his execution, and in the Yemen Arab Republic some of the bodies of those executed were displayed for as long as two days.

The general acceptance in the Middle East of the death penalty as an appropriate and proper punishment, at least for murder and political acts of sabotage, is a result of deeply embedded Islamic tradition and customary practice. In one or two countries, the number of capital offences has increased in the past few years (e.g., Libya, Iraq); in some countries executions have been carried out for the first time for many years (e.g., Libya, and Bahrain, where three men were hanged for political murder in March 1977, the first executions since 1954). There are reports that, in Israel, the Government has been reconsidering its policy on the execution of terrorists convicted of murder.

On the other hand, there is also a growing trend among other Arab countries and among some inter-Arab organizations towards restricting the use of the death penalty. For example:

(a) in some countries where justice is administered according to Islamic law, the number of offences actually punished by death is gradually decreasing.

(b) the new penal code of the PDRY promulgated in March 1976 has reduced the number and range of political offences punishable by death, and has introduced restrictions in the application of the death sentence. In addition, there have been no reported executions in the country since 1975, and eight death sentences passed in early 1977 were commuted.

(c) the Arab League's Draft Declaration of Citizens' Rights in the Arab States and Countries stipulates that the death penalty should only be imposed for "an extremely grave crime", and never for a political crime.

(d) the Arab Lawyers Union was one of 26 non-governmental organizations to submit a joint statement to the Fifth United Nations Congress on the Prevention of Crime and the Treatment of Offenders held in Toronto in 1975, calling for the abolition of capital punishment (see Appendices).

The following sections on individual countries do not form an exhaustive survey; they deal only with the States about which Amnesty International has received reliable information on the imposition and execution of the death penalty.

***Egypt** (the Arab Republic of)*

As amended, the Egyptian Penal Code of 1937 provides for the death penalty as a punishment for certain offences against the State and against individuals.

Offences against the State are divided into those harmful to external security (e.g. joining the armed forces of a country at war with Egypt; espionage; conspiring with an enemy state to harm Egypt's defence or military operations–Articles 77a, b, c, 80, 82b), and those against internal security, a category which covers armed attacks against law enforcement authorities; forcible occupation, whilst armed, of a government or public building; the use of arms or explosives with the aim of overthrowing the government or changing the country's constitution; committing political murder; destroying public property (Articles 89, 90a, 91, 93, 102b). In addition, Article 83a provides the death penalty as a discretionary punishment for any offence against external security (Articles 77–85), if the intent of the person committing the offences has been to assist the enemy or harm the military operations of Egypt's armed forces. The death penalty as a discretionary punishment is available also for any offence against internal security (Articles 86–102), if the aim is to violate the country's independence or integrity; or if the offence takes place in time of war, its aim being to assist the enemy or harm military operations of the armed forces.

In the category of offences against the individual, the death penalty is provided for premeditated and deliberate murder, and murder by poisoning (Articles 230 and 233), murder in connection with other unspecified crimes (Article 234), for arson resulting in death (Article 257), and for exposing any means of public transport to danger if death results (Article 168). Article 235 provides the death penalty or life imprisonment with hard labour for accomplices to murder.

Other offences carrying the death penalty include: committing torture or ordering an employee of the State to torture someone to death (Article 126); and, if death results, exposing a child to danger by leaving it in a deserted place (Article 286). Article 295 provides the death penalty for giving false testimony leading to wrongful execution. In 1976, a new law was introduced, establishing the death penalty for hijacking.

Article 13 of the Penal Code provides that hanging be the method of execution, except in the case of a member of the armed forces, who would be executed by firing squad, in accordance with Article 106a of the Egyptian Military Code.

Article 62 states that there is no punishment for a person who is insane or mentally deficient, or under the influence of a drug not voluntarily taken. The same applies if the effect of a drug which has been taken is unforeseen. According to Article 245, there is no penalty for murder if the perpetrator is acting in self-defence. Article 476 of the Criminal Procedure Law, 1950, as amended, states that a pregnant woman may not be executed until two months after she has given birth. Other factors may be taken into consideration at the discretion of the judges, with whom rests the power to pass the death sentence.

According to Article 381 of the Criminal Procedure Law, the death sentence may only be passed when agreed unanimously by the three judges of the court. Before the sentence is passed, the dossier of the case must be passed to the *Mufti*, and if no reply is received within 10 days, the judges may then pass sentence. Appeals may be made to the Court of Cassation; an application for a retrial may also be made. After pronouncement of the death sentence, the dossier of the case must be passed by the Minister of Justice to the President (Article 470, Criminal Procedure Law), who has the power of executive clemency (Article 149, Constitution of 1971). If the President does not order a pardon or commutation of the death sentence within 14 days, the sentence may be carried out.

Relatives of the person sentenced to death may visit him on the day of execution (Article 472, the Criminal Procedure Law), which usually takes place inside the prison (Article 473), and is attended by a representative of the Prosecutor-General, the Director of the prison, the prison doctor or another doctor designated by the Prosecutor-General (Article 474). If no relatives offer to undertake burial, the State will do so. Burial takes place without "any ceremony" (Article 477).

The Egyptian military code of 1966 also lays down offences for which the death penalty is available. These include forms of collaboration with the enemy (Articles 130, 132, 133), such as facilitating the movement of enemy forces on to Egyptian territory, revealing defence secrets and offences concerning the capture of prisoners of war and maltreatment of the wounded (Articles 134, 135 and 136). Additional offences punishable by death concern sedition (Article 138); neglect of duties of service or supervision (Article 139) and looting, plundering and pillaging (Articles 140 and 141). The misuse of a position of power (Article 148), disobedience of orders (Article 151) and escape or desertion from the armed forces during combat (Article 154) also carry the death penalty.

Usually, during the period 1973–77, a period of at least one year elapsed between sentence and execution, and this has on occasion been extended to over two years. However, in March 1977, Amnesty International learned of the execution of an Egyptian man who had been sentenced to death in October 1976. He was convicted of exploding two bombs in a Government office block in Cairo, and having been in contact with Libya with the aim of harming Egyptian policies.

During the period 1973–77, Amnesty International received 27 reports of death sentences being passed (including two *in absentia*). Of these, 11 involved offences of espionage for, or collaboration with, Israel; three involved plotting the overthrow of the Government; seven involved planting bombs in public places, or membership of a bomb squad; one was for the attempted murder of a former Premier of the People's Democratic Republic of Yemen who was living in exile in Cairo; and five involved the kidnapping and murder of a former Egyptian minister. In the same period, 12 of these sentences are known to have been carried out: six for espionage, three for planting bombs, two for plotting the overthrow of the Government and one for the attempted assassination of the former PDRY Premier. An Egyptian student, who had been charged with attempting to overthrow the Government had his sentence commuted by the President to life imprisonment with hard labour. In January 1976, the President ordered the release of an Egyptian woman sentenced to death for espionage for Israel, so that she might be able to look after her children. Her Palestinian husband was executed for the same offence.

Although, in practice, the number of offences for which the death penalty is actually passed is fairly restricted, official Egyptian sources admit little possibility of the death penalty being abolished in Egypt while the country remains in a state of belligerency with Israel.

***Iran** (the Empire of)*

Articles 316–320 of the Iranian Military Penal Code and Procedures provide a mandatory death sentence for those convicted of participating in, or plotting, the assassination of the Shah or Crown Prince; causing or intending to cause any overthrow of the established Government, or disturbance of the hereditary Crown; or provoking the people to take up arms against the authority of the State.

The Military Penal Code provides the death penalty under Article 310 for those who take up arms against Iran; under Articles 311 and 312 for military personnel who cooperate with an enemy; and under Article 313 for espionage. There are other articles of the same code providing the death penalty for military personnel taking part in activities in infringement of military discipline. These include defection to the enemy, theft, destruction of army property, and certain specific cases of corruption.

The law governing the concepts of murder and assault appears in the Civil Penal Code. Premeditated murder (Article 170) is punishable by death, and so is assault with a deadly weapon, if death results. By Articles 202 and 203, kidnapping, if it results in death, carries the same punishment.

In 1956, a law designed to prevent the cultivation of poppies and the smoking of opium provided, in Article 4, that a producer or importer of narcotic drugs would, on second conviction for the same offence, be punished with death.

Armed robbery may be punished with a discretionary death sentence; a similar provision applies to armed resistance and armed attack on Government forces. This includes armed robbery on roads and highways outside city limits, but does not cover those who seek to use armed force for purely political reasons. Such a case would probably be prosecuted under Article 310 of the Military Code. The death penalty also exists for arms smuggling. It was the intention of an Act passed in 1959 to subject a wider spectrum of offences involving armed robbery and armed criminality to the death penalty.

On 24 November 1975, the Teheran newspaper, *Kayhan*, reported that: "According to statistics from the Criminal Court of Teheran, 20 per cent of murderers are executed." Drug smugglers and pedlars are frequently executed, and on 14 July 1974, the Iranian Government announced that in the two-and-a-half years then past, 239 drug smugglers and pedlars had been put to death.

Amnesty International does not have exact figures for the total number of executions in Iran in recent years, but at least 62 political prisoners have been executed since the beginning of 1972; 23 of these executions took place in 1976. This figure, based on official Government announcements, should be regarded as a minimum figure – the total number of executions in Iran since the beginning of 1972 is probably considerably in excess of 300.

In April 1977, six men were sentenced to death by the Isfahan High Criminal Court after having been convicted of the kidnapping and murder of four people, including a prominent religious leader, Ayatollah Shamsabadi.

During 1977, there were official announcements of three executions of people tried by military tribunals; two were alleged terrorists, one was convicted of espionage.

A person condemned to death has the right to appeal to a higher judicial authority and, after confirmation of the verdict, has the right further to petition for clemency. A judicial death sentence is not carried out until the procedures of appeal have been exhausted, after which it is further deferred until the results of the procedures of petition for reprieve or pardon have been announced.

It should be mentioned in this context that Iran has been criticized for deficiencies in legal safeguards. Facilities afforded the defence fall far short of the adequate minimum necessary to prepare a defence case properly.

### ***Iraq** (the Republic of)*

The Penal Code of 1969 provides the death penalty for 14 offences relating to the external security of the State, and nine relating to internal security. Ten offences in the former category and six offences in the latter carry a mandatory death penalty. Death is also a mandatory punishment for certain categories of murder and for arson resulting in death.

Any political activity by members of the armed forces, other than within the Ba'ath Party, is also punishable by death, in accordance with a directive by the Revolutionary Command Council of 10 November 1971.

In 1974, two additional laws were introduced providing the death penalty as a mandatory punishment for (1) Arab Socialist Ba'ath Party members who deliberately conceal previous political party membership or affiliation, or become affiliated to other political organizations or parties, or work in their interests (Second Amendment to the Penal Code); and (2) having any liaison whatsoever with foreign intelligence organizations (Law No. 141 of 1974).

It appears that a person condemned to death automatically has the right to have his case reviewed by the High Court, which has the authority to quash, amend, commute or confirm the sentence. However, there is no right of judicial appeal from the revolutionary court which is presided over by members of the Ba'ath Party and has jurisdiction over offences against the internal or external security of the State; a condemned person can petition only the President for clemency.

Article 228 of the law concerning judicial procedures provides that the death penalty should be carried out by hanging within a period of not less than 30 days after sentence. The execution should also take place in the presence of one of the judges of the Criminal Court, one member of the Public Prosecutor's Office and, if available, a representative of the Ministry of the Interior, the Prison Governor and the Prison Medical Officer or any other medical officer delegated by the Ministry of Health, as well as the condemned man's lawyer, if this is requested.

The actual use of the death penalty in Iraq is difficult to research because of the secrecy surrounding trials and executions. Amnesty International receives a considerable number of reports of death sentences and executions each year from diverse sources, but only a small proportion of these are ever officially made public or confirmed. It is also difficult to identify those offences actually punished by death in Iraq: official and unofficial sources of information differ sharply on the offences which people condemned to death are alleged to have committed. International observers, moreover, do not have access to Iraqi prisons or to trials, and members of the family of the accused are often in no better a position.

The majority of executions appear to be of members of political parties or groupings, all of which, apart from those comprising the ruling Progressive National Front, are illegal. The authorities maintain that such people are only condemned to death for having been engaged in, or having planned, acts "detrimental to the security of the State". On the other hand, the ruling Ba'ath Party, having existed clandestinely for many years before coming to power in a bloody *coup*, is itself a secretive organization, distrustful of any other secret organization which it sees as a potential threat. It therefore deals harshly with opposition.

Over the past several years, Amnesty International has received reports of the imposition of the death penalty on Maoists, Marxist-Leninists, members of the illegal Syrian wing of the Arab Socialist Ba'ath Party, and of the legal and illegal wings of the Iraqi Communist Party. The death penalty has also been imposed on a number of Shi'i religious leaders for their alleged membership of an illegal religious-political organization called the Islamic Mission; and on five elderly professional men who were connected with the Masonic Lodge in Baghdad before the revolution in 1958. These five sentences were commutted.

The largest number of reports, however, concern members of the illegal Kurdish Democratic Party, and other illegal Kurdish groupings. During the hostilities between the central authorities and the Kurdish revolutionary forces in 1974–75, Amnesty International received the names of at least 75 Kurds (not members of the Kurdish armed forces) executed during this period, including at least one woman. Only five of these cases, including a woman, were officially made public. During the first few months after the Iran–Iraq agreement of March 1975, bringing these hostilities to an end, Amnesty International received reports of at least 170 Kurds having been executed, although the names of only 25 were known. These included members of the Kurdish armed forces who surrendered to the Iraqi army in accordance with a declared amnesty, and Kurds who were in prison at the time of the agreement.

The death penalty has also been imposed for attempted *coup*, although the only incident publicly reported was that of July 1973, when 32 people were executed after an abortive attempt involving the former Head of Security. Since then there have been only vague rumours concerning groups of officers or Ba'ath Party members executed after equally vague rumours of *coup* attempts.

The death penalty has been imposed and carried out for espionage. The most widely documented case is that of Leon Aaronson, a Dutch male nurse convicted in late 1975 of spying for Israel and acting as an adviser to Mulla Mustapha Barzani, the Kurdish leader.

It is equally difficult to obtain definite information on actual legal procedures. People charged with political offences are tried by the Revolutionary Court; members of the armed forces are tried by military court. According to the Government's reply to a United Nations questionnaire, "The accused is entitled to a fair and public hearing by an independent tribunal ... and court hearings should be public unless the court decides otherwise" (3 September 1971). However, unofficial reports of trials in which people have been sentenced to death indicate that they are almost always held *in camera*, and are often summary; families are usually informed only after the event, and sometimes even after the execution. In the case of Leon Aaronson (see above), it was three months before the Iraqi authorities confirmed to his family and the Dutch authorities that he had been tried and executed.

Irregularities in legal procedure are also illustrated in the case of two Kurdish brothers, Lieutenant-Colonel Abdul Latif Barzanji and Captain Nazhat Barzanji. They were reported to have been arrested on 19 May 1975, tried on 20 May by a special military court on charges of being agents of the Kurdish revolution, acquitted due to lack of evidence but retried that same night by another court, which found them guilty and sentenced them to death. Their families were allowed to visit them on 21 May, and on 22 May they were executed by firing squad.

There are other instances of retrials: a number of Kurds arrested during the 1974–75 period of hostilities and sentenced to terms of imprisonment were reported to have been retried after the cessation of hostilities in March 1975, sentenced to death and executed. Amnesty International has also received two different reports of families being called to visit a prisoner for the first time, only to learn when they arrived that he was to be executed the next day.

Legal representation is permitted, but it is reported that prisoners have little opportunity of engaging a lawyer of their own choice or of meeting him before the trial. A defence lawyer is usually appointed by the court on the day of the trial, and is generally able only to plead for leniency, rather than to show the defendant's innocence.

There is no appeals machinery for a person condemned to death for a political offence. Only the President has the authority to commute a death sentence. The five former Freemasons mentioned earlier possibly had their sentences commuted to life imprisonment because they were elderly. In July 1973, Abdul Khaliq Samarrai, a member of the Revolutionary Command Council implicated in the *coup* attempt (also mentioned above), had his death sentence commuted to life imprisonment, and this was said to be because of his popularity.

Sometimes intervals of weeks or months elapse between the passing of the death sentence and the actual execution. Three Kurds, Shihab Nouri, Jaafar

Abdul Wahab and Anwar Zorab, were sentenced to death in July 1976 and executed on 24 November 1976. The reason for delay is not known, since there is no opportunity for a person condemned to death by a revolutionary court to appeal.

Executions are often carried out summarily. As has already been said, the two Barzanji brothers were executed the day after their trial. So were the 32 condemned to death in July 1973 for their part in the *coup* attempt.

Executions are usually carried out by hanging, except those of members of the armed forces, who are shot by firing squad.

Since the public execution in early 1969 of two groups of people (22 in all) accused of spying for Israel (predominantly Jews, but also Christians and Muslims) and the resulting international outcry, executions now – as far as is known to Amnesty International – are carried out inside the prison, and often without being officially made public. The bodies are usually, but not always, returned to the family for burial.

According to the Iraqi media, eight Iraqi Shi'is were sentenced to death by a specially constituted court on 25 February 1977. The charges were not specified but were connected with disturbances in the provinces of Najaf and Kerbala on 5/6 February during religious festivities. Unofficial sources claim that none of the defendants was present during the court hearing and that they had been killed, possibly under torture, before the trial.

On 24 September 1977, Butros Raed Zawaideh, a Jordanian student studying at Basra University in Iraq, was reported to have been hanged. He had been arrested on 14 May, tried in secret and found guilty of espionage. The Jordanian Embassy in Baghdad was not informed of the execution until 5 October, although the Iraqi authorities claim that the prisoner had been allowed visits from his family.

In September 1977, Kurdish sources claimed that 400 Kurds had been executed since the summer of 1975. They also claimed that over 50 of them had been executed since the beginning of 1977, 10 having been sentenced to death by a special court in Kirkuk on 3 April, after an attempt on the life of the Governor of Suleimaniya and the assassination of another Government official. They were charged collectively with "attending meetings to coordinate and carry out subversion, terror and assassination", although Kurdish sources maintain that those responsible for the acts had escaped to the mountains, and that a number of Kurds in Suleimaniya were arrested and tried in their place.

Kurdish sources also claimed that, in September 1977, 102 Kurds who had been arrested in May as members of illegal political organizations or sympathizers with the Kurdish resistance, were being held in Abu Ghraib Prison in Baghdad or in Mosul Prison and that they were under sentence of death. Fifty-two of those in Mosul Prison were believed to have been executed between 20 and 22 September 1977.

### ***Israel** (the State of) and the Occupied Territories*

The discretionary death penalty exists under Israeli law for genocide, crimes against humanity and crimes against the Jewish people. The last category includes crimes committed during the Second World War.

The only execution in Israel has been that of Adolf Eichmann who was hanged in 1962 after being convicted of genocide in Germany and territory under German occupation before and during the Second World War.

Military courts can impose the death penalty also for terrorist acts resulting in death, under the Defence (Emergency) Regulations 1945, but to date all death sentences passed by these courts have been commuted on appeal.

As far as murder committed or acquiesced in by Government is concerned, allegations have been made that the Israeli Secret Service (*Mossad*) has murdered members of the "Black September" and other Palestinian liberation movements regarded as having been involved in armed attacks against Israeli citizens. This type of action has allegedly taken place outside Israel and the Occupied Territories but, except on one occasion, has not been admitted by the Israeli Government. On 9 April 1973, three Palestinian Liberation Organization officials were shot by a joint *Mossad*-Israeli Defence Force unit in Beirut. On 10 April 1973, the then Prime Minister of Israel, Golda Meir, in a statement to the *Knesset* (the Israeli Parliament) acknowledged responsibility for the raid in Beirut the previous day.*

* Tinnin, David, *Hit Team*, Futura Publications Ltd (in association with Weidenfeld & Nicolson Ltd), 1977, p. 78.

### ***Jordan** (the Hashemite Kingdom of)*

The Jordanian Penal Code of 1961 provides the death penalty for the following offences against external State security: conspiring with an enemy, serving in the ranks of an enemy, or any attempt in wartime to paralyse national defence (Articles 110–113).

The Penal Code provides the death penalty for ten offences against internal State Security involving activities prejudicial to the monarchy and its constitutional authority, or designed to stir up civil war. The death penalty is prescribed also for the commission of terrorist acts resulting in death or destruction of an inhabitated building (Articles 135–139, 142 and 148).

Article 158 (clause 3) prescribes the death penalty for anyone who is party to a criminal conspiracy if he or she commits murder or torture. Article 328 provides the death penalty for murder if it was premeditated, committed to protect other criminals or facilitate a criminal act, or committed against one of the murderer's forebears.

In April 1973, the Council of Ministers decided on the introduction of the death penalty for the sale of land in territories occupied by Israel to the Israeli authoritites, as an act of high treason. Several death sentences were passed in 1976 for the sale of property to the Israeli authorities, all of them *in absentia*.

One death sentence was reported to have been passed in 1976 for espionage. A further death sentence was passed on 30 March 1977. Amnesty International was officially informed that it was subject to confirmation by the Army, the Prime Minister's Office and the King.

An execution by hanging which took place on 18 December 1976 was of one of four guerillas reported to have carried out an attack on the Intercontinental Hotel in Amman on 17 November 1976 (the other three had been killed during the attack). He was convicted by a military court of complicity in terrorist acts leading to the death of a number of civilians and soldiers. The execution took place nine days after the sentence was passed.

***Libya*** *(the Socialist People's Libyan Arab* Jamahiriya*)*

The Penal Code of 1956, together with a number of amendments introduced in August 1975 (Law No. 80 of 1975), provides the death penalty as a mandatory punishment for various offences against the integrity of the State, internal security, public safety, or the individual. Under the Penal Code, people under 18 may not be sentenced to death.

The offences against the integrity of the State include acts of treason, espionage and sabotage of the country's defences and economy, either in time of war or in circumstances leading to war or serious damage. Offences against internal security include attempts to change the Constitution or form of government. (This was first introduced as a capital offence in a Decree Law of 11 December 1969 entitled "Protection of the Revolution".) Also punishable by death is the promotion of activities against the constitutional order of the State, and forming or belonging to illegal political parties. This latter was first introduced as a capital offence by a decree of 30 May 1972.

The death penalty is also the punishment for wilful murder; for causing an epidemic by spreading germs; for polluting water or foodstuffs, if death results.

Amendments to the Penal Code in August 1975 increased the number of articles in which the death penalty is prescribed from 18 to 28. In some cases this resulted in a drastic increase in the severity of the penalty – for example, belonging to an illegal political party had formerly carried a sentence of five to ten years' imprisonment.

The decree of May 1972 on illegal political parties stipulates that the Revolutionary Command Council (RCC) decide on the composition of the courts and, moreover, that the sentences passed should be in line with the policy of the RCC, which has the authority to annul or reduce the sentences or refer the case to another court. There appears to be no higher court of appeal for political cases, although the RCC has the power to commute the sentence.

It is important to note the establishment in 1969 of the People's Court. It was created to try members of the Government overthrown by the *coup* in 1969 and people attempting to overthrow the new Government. The tribunal, generally composed of representatives of the Government and not of the judiciary, is in no way bound by normal Libyan trial procedures; all decisions have to be approved by the RCC, and there is no machinery for appeals.

Until the end of 1976, no execution had taken place in Libya under the Presidency of Colonel Gaddafi. However, the number of capital offences increased during his period of office (as a result of the amendments to the Penal Code introduced in August 1975). Furthermore, a number of death sentences have been passed, although, at the time of writing, they have not been carried out: the former King Idris was sentenced to death *in absentia* on 16 November 1971 by the People's Court, and his property confiscated. Five out of 18 officers convicted of planning a *coup* at the end of 1969 have been imprisoned and under sentence of death since their trial.

In early 1977, however, a number of executions were carried out, the first in Libya since 1954.

On 2 April 1977, 22 army officers convicted of planning a *coup* in August 1975 were executed. At their trial in December 1976, 23 out of a group of 75 were sentenced to death (one *in absentia*); at a second military (appeals) court, the number of death sentences was increased. (The total number is not known for certain. Some sources claim 33, others 45.) Amnesty International has received reports that a further 11 executions of members of the armed forces have taken place, but at the time of writing, this has not been officially confirmed.

On 7 April 1977, four civilians were officially reported to have been publicly executed in Benghazi at the scene of their crime. They had been convicted of "terrorist sabotage" by a People's Court. The trial had been held *in camera*, and no right of appeal was permitted.

In February 1977 death sentences were passed on two Libyans, Al Mabruk Abdul Mawla Al Zoul and Abdul Ghani Muhammad Khanfar; at the time of writing, their sentences have not been carried out. They and 38 others detained since April 1973 were tried *in camera* in January 1977 by a People's Court on charges of belonging to illegal political parties. Sentences of from four to 15 years' imprisonment were later amended by administrative decree to life imprisonment or, in the cases of the two named above, to death.

***Syria** (the Syrian Arab Republic)*

The Syrian Penal Code provides the death penalty for the following offences committed against external State security: bearing arms in the ranks of the enemy (Article 263); successfully conspiring or contacting any foreign country to encourage it to take hostile action against Syria (Article 264); conspiring with or contacting the enemy to bring about the defeat of the army (Article 265); undertaking any act with the intention of paralysing the country's defences in time of war or at the outbreak of war (Article 266).

The following offences against internal State security are punishable by the death penalty: causing civil or sectarian strife by arming the Syrian people or by arming some portion of the population against the rest; incitement to kill or to plunder premises (Article 298); commission of a terrorist act if it leads to death of a human being, or the partial or total destruction of a building if one or more persons are inside (Article 305).

In addition, Decree No. 6 of 7 January 1965, passed by Syria's first Ba'athist-led Government, introduced a mandatory death penalty for specified forms of collusion in any verbal or physical act hostile to the aims of the (Ba'athist) revolution, and for armed attack on any public or private establishment, incitement to disturbance or demonstrations, and for arson, robbery and pillage. It provided a discretionary death sentence for any deed, speech or writing incompatible with the socialist order and for all offences against legislative decrees connected with the socialist transformation.

Cases involving State security are tried by the Supreme State Security Court created by Legislative Decree No. 47 of 28 March 1968, which was amended by Decree No. 79 of 2 October 1971, whereby the President of the Republic was empowered to appoint the Court President, the bench and the prosecution staff (known as the "General Prosecution") all of whom may be either civilians or military personnel.

Verdicts by the Supreme State Security Court are not subject to appeal. They are not applied until ratified by the Head of State, who has the right to set aside the verdict and order a retrial or reduce the penalty. The Head of State may also "freeze the action", which has the effect of a total pardon. The decision of the Head of State is final (Article 8).

In the period since 1975, 13 people have been executed by hanging for crimes against internal State security. In addition, of four people sentenced to death for the same offence, three are reported to have had their sentences commuted to life imprisonment with hard labour; the fourth, according to report, was sentenced to 12 years in prison with hard labour, on the grounds that he was a minor. Three other people have been sentenced to death *in absentia.*

Of the executions carried out for crimes against State security, Amnesty International has reasonably detailed knowledge of the court procedure for one of the four trials reported. In July 1975, seven people, said to be members of the Arab Communist Organization, were sentenced to death for carrying out acts of terrorism and sabotage. The trial by the High Division of the Supreme State Security Court lasted for two days. Two days after the sentences were passed, they were confirmed by the President. It was officially reported that eight defence lawyers were present throughout the whole proceedings. However, Amnesty International has had reports indicating that lawyers were not allowed access to the defendants before the trial. Two of the death sentences were commuted to life imprisonment with hard labour on the grounds that the accused were "under age and repentant". The remaining five men were executed two days later in the Damascus Civilian Prison.

From 1975 to the time of writing, eight executions for offences against State security were carried out by means of public hanging. On 26 September 1976, three men were sentenced to death for carrying out a violent attack on the Semiramis Hotel, Damascus, during which four people were killed and between 30 and 40 injured. The sentence was passed by the Supreme State Security Court on the day of the attack itself, and confirmed by the President, also on the same day. The men were hanged in public at dawn the following morning in front of the Hotel. Three more public hangings took place on 6 January 1977, two in Aleppo and one in Damascus, for causing bomb explosions in Damascus and other cities.

On 2 June 1977, six death sentences were pronounced by the Supreme State Security Court, three of them passed *in absentia*, for complicity in numerous acts of violence, assassinations and collusion with a foreign State. One sentence was commuted to 12 years' imprisonment with hard labour on the grounds that the defendant was a minor. The remaining two defendants were executed by hanging in a central square in Damascus on 13 June 1977.

One other public hanging was reported to have taken place on 24 March 1977, of a person convicted of assaulting and murdering four minors. In all nine public executions, the bodies, draped in white with the sentence pinned at the neck, were left hanging on view for several hours.

Four executions by firing squad are reported to have taken place on 24 April 1977, following the killing of two Syrian soldiers in a Beirut suburb two days earlier.

From 1975 to the time of writing, there have been numerous unconfirmed reports of executions of members of the armed forces.

### ***Yemen** (the People's Democratic Republic of) (PDRY)*

The Penal Code promulgated in March 1976 provides the death penalty as a discretionary punishment for offences against the State (treason, espionage, terrorism, hijacking), against the economy (damaging public property, means of communication or polluting air or water), against the individual (wilful murder or rape), and for offences violating the international law of war. In the 15 relevant articles, the death penalty is usually specified in cases involving serious harm or death.

Generally, legal provisions relevant to offences against the State have been extremely broadly drafted. An example is Article 104a, which states that "whosoever commits an act designed to weaken the social national democratic system and the State system" can be sentenced to death. This also means that the responsibility for deciding upon the gravity of a particular case is formally left to the judge. At the same time, as will appear below, the judiciary in the PDRY has little or no independence.

The number and range of political offences punishable by death have been reduced by the current Penal Code. It specifically restricts the death penalty to "the most dangerous crimes", to be pronounced "only exceptionally when the security of society requires it, when there is no hope of reforming the offender" (Article 65a). The death penalty is not to be pronounced "on a woman pregnant at the time the crime was committed" (Article 65b).

The Penal Code provides for lesser sentences where there are mitigating circumstances. Thus, the death penalty is not imposed if the killing were committed unintentionally or in self-defence, or by a woman just before or after giving birth.

There is, however, no provision for any appeals machinery, other than that provided by Article 65c: this states that the death penalty shall not be carried out until it has been confirmed by the Presidential Council, which may grant pardons or commute penalties.

The application of the law is seriously hampered by an insufficiently manned judiciary. Many lawyers left the country following independence in 1967, or were deported, and only a handful of qualified members of the legal profession remain. At the time of writing, the only legal training being provided is at a recently established law institute, where after one year graduates may become legal clerks or rural magistrates. Members of the court usually have little or no training or experience. Thus, although "the defence of a person is guaranteed", a defendant may have extreme difficulty in finding a qualified lawyer, particularly in the country.

It is questionable to what extent the judiciary is independent of the executive. Its present small size inevitably reduces its strength and effectiveness. In 1972, for example, a magistrate, Tawfiq 'Az'azi, disappeared after he had refused to convict and sentence several political detainees, and had ordered their release because he claimed that they had committed no offences under the Penal Code.

Since the promulgation of the Penal Code in March 1976, Amnesty International has received only one report of the imposition of death sentences. Aden Radio announced in January 1977 that eight farmers had been sentenced to death for spreading hostile rumours, and for having demonstrated on 16 November 1976 against a Government decision to restrict the consumption, sale and purchase of *qat*, a narcotic made from a shrub. The sentences were later commuted to periods of imprisonment.

During the period 1972–74, Amnesty International received a considerable number of unofficial reports of executions in different parts of the PDRY of tribesmen, tribal leaders, landowners, religious leaders, graduates and others, all of them said to have opposed the Government or criticized its policies. In 1975, two Amnesty International delegates on a mission to Aden made inquiries about people named in these reports, and it was officially confirmed that at least 35 – including eight graduates – had been executed between 1972 and 1974, convicted under Law No. 11 of 1970 of sabotage, espionage or embezzlement.

During this same period, it was apparent that there was considerable opposition to Government policies; at the same time, the Government felt under serious threat of armed attack by militant South Yemeni exiles, infiltrating into PDRY across the Saudi and North Yemeni border. Local inhabitants suspected of collaborating with these exiles were sometimes executed.

In June 1975, Amnesty International learnt that two North Yemeni merchants had been sentenced to death in PDRY, allegedly for having illegally attempted to transport merchandise and money across the border, from PDRY to the Yemen Arab Republic. At the time of writing, it is not known whether these sentences were carried out, but the offence, if reported correctly, would appear to be punishable by imprisonment only, according to Article 16 of Law No. 11, 1970.

On the other hand, in July 1975, in a widely publicized trial, nine people were convicted of espionage and sabotage, both capital offences, but although the prosecution demanded the death penalty, the defendants were sentenced to periods of imprisonment of between five and 15 years.

It is probable that the number of death sentences and executions of which Amnesty International has been informed does not reflect the actual situation. First, not all death sentences are officially made public, and, of those that are, not all the reports reach Amnesty International. Often reports come from unofficial sources, and it is difficult for the organization to confirm their accuracy.

Second, most of the people arrested for political reasons in the PDRY appear never to be brought to trial. They are either held indefinitely without trial, or they simply disappear without trace and are presumed dead. Amnesty International has received the names of hundreds of such people. Sometimes it appears that they have been killed on the orders of officials in authority, able to use their positions to order arbitrary killings. In addition, there have been several cases of groups of prisoners being shot "while trying to escape", in circumstances which cast doubt on the accuracy of the Government's account of the incidents.

CHAPTER IV

# MURDER COMMITTED OR ACQUIESCED IN BY GOVERNMENT

In a number of countries, state authorities, or people for whom they are responsible, acquiesce in* or commit murder of individuals whom they see as a threat to their keeping political power. In certain countries the practice is known to occur on a wide scale. On occasion the victims are ordinary offenders, whose threat – whether real or apparent – is not a political one.

Murder committed or acquiesced in by government is sometimes referred to as "extra-judicial" or "extra-legal" execution. This *Report* does not use those terms because they carry the suggestion that there is an intermediate category of execution between the judicial form and ordinary murder. In Amnesty International's view, murder, whether committed by individuals or by governments, should be referred to by the proper legal term.

Murders in which governments acquiesce have characteristics which differentiate them from the death penalty: they are committed outside the framework of the law, without recourse to legally established judicial process and usually in violation of certain of the country's laws – those against murder itself and kidnapping, for example, which are included in almost every penal code. The death penalty, on the other hand, is imposed with the sanction of some form of legislation or state edict, after recourse to a legally established judicial process, however arbitrary and deficient that might be. In addition, it is carried out, directly or indirectly, "in the name of" the whole nation, or at all events that part of it from whom those in power derive – or claim to derive – their authority. As Chapter II shows, international law is decidedly less equivocal in condemning killings which have government approval than death penalties carried out under existing national law. Both forms of killing have been brought within the scope of this *Report* on the grounds that to single out one to the exclusion of the other would be to deal inadequately with the ways in which governments may put to death people under their jurisdiction or within their reach.

In some countries, certainly, the death penalty is carried out only with the sanction of laws and processes of justice lacking in what might be widely agreed to be "legitimacy". There are countries in which death penalties are imposed and executed with the sanction of laws which are no more than government *fiat*, applied inequitably for the political ends of those in power, through corrupt and subservient courts.

Governments that commit or acquiesce in murders usually deny that those murders have taken place. In general, they also try to conceal the killings in one

* The phrase "acquiesced in" is used in this chapter because it implies *unstated* agreement; it carries within it the sense of allowing something to happen – an event or a situation – simply by doing nothing to prevent it.

of a number of ways: by outright denial; by pretending that they were carried out according to legal process; by claiming that they resulted from armed combat or that they happened in the course of crime prevention; or even by grotesque efforts to hide or destroy the bodies of victims.

Killings to which a government gives approval – even tacitly – most often occur when its authority is challenged. They sometimes run parallel to the killing, by opposition groups, of people with government ties or in government favour. When those who oppose a régime use murder as a political weapon, they often try to give their killings a semblance of legitimacy by announcing them publicly and stating that their victims have been selected because of "past crimes" and "tried" before "execution". Such killings, like those committed or acquiesced in by governments, are murders.

Those who carry out the killings which have government acquiescence, and those who either order or abet their carrying out, are not, of course, normally apprehended, even when it would be within the capacity of a country's law enforcement agencies to see to it that they were.

Murder committed or acquiesced in by governments constitutes a breakdown of law and order wherever it occurs. Throughout the centuries, constitutional, legal and political theorists have argued that it is a function of the state to protect at least the lives of its citizens, both from foreign threat and internal lawlessness, but the government that orders or acquiesces in murder commits aggression against some part of the people. It denies the "freedom from fear" proclaimed in the Universal Declaration of Human Rights as being necessary to the "highest aspirations of the common people".

There follow studies of the use of murder with government acquiescence in Argentina, Ethiopia, Guatemala and Uganda. There are other countries in which such killings are carried out regularly, but a world-wide survey of the practice is beyond the scope of this *Report*.

***Argentina** (the Republic of)*

Although in Argentina the death penalty was re-introduced in 1976, shortly after the military *coup*, it has not since that date been imposed. The incidence of murder committed or acquiesced in by government, however, is high.

From 1974 onwards, violence had become increasingly prominent in Argentina's political life. In rural areas such as the province of Tucumán, the People's Revolutionary Army (the *ERP*, a Marxist-Leninist group) intensified its operations; and in the major cities the *Montoneros* (a left-wing Peronist guerilla group) also stepped up its activities. There were two responses to this increase in violence. The Government introduced a State of Siege; and extreme right-wing para-military groups, such as the AAA (*Alianza Anti-Comunista Argentina*), began to abduct and kill people they suspected of having left-wing sympathies. In a single year, 1974, the *AAA* is believed to have been responsible for the murder of 300 people. Yet at no time has anyone been arrested or tried for any of these crimes.

Ever since the 1976 *coup* the most horrifying aspect of the repression has been the sheer number of *los desaparecidos* – "those who have disappeared". In the past three years, thousands of people have vanished after they have been arrested or abducted by military or security agents. The Government has repeatedly denied all knowledge of the disappeared people and also that they have ever been detained. But from the testimonies of detainees who have subsequently been released (and who have usually been warned by officials not to speak about their detention), Amnesty International has been able to piece together a characteristic train of events in the lives of the *desaparecidos.*

During their captivity they are kept hooded or blindfolded; as a result, they have great difficulty in recognizing their place of detention. (Nevertheless, a number of prisons have been clearly located throughout the country. During 1977, perhaps as many as 60 secret camps, often military barracks or garrisons, were being used as prisons.) The *desaparecidos* are also handcuffed and chained. They are usually subjected to torture and physical abuse. From the statements of those who have been released, it is clear that the camps vary in size; sometimes there are few other prisoners, sometimes there are several hundred. It is also clear that in these camps not only is systematic torture inflicted, but also summary execution.

Amnesty International believes that its main task is to establish an accurate estimate of the number of the disappeared. About 4,000 well-documented cases have already been recorded. The three human rights organizations which collect information within Argentina (*Asamblea permanente por los Derechos Humanos; Movimiento Ecuménico por los Derechos Humanos; Liga Argentina por los Derechos del Hombre*) have petitioned the Supreme Court on behalf of the families of 3,000 *desaparecidos.* In reply the Court has simply declared that the matter is outside its competence.

Amnesty International and the human rights organizations within Argentina believe that the number of written complaints received (often accompanied by *habeas corpus* documents) is far below the real figure of people missing after arrest. The limitation of the figures is partly the result of fear (relatives and friends are apprehensive in case their complaints should make things worse for the person who has disappeared) and is partly due to ignorance of formal procedures. Furthermore, since support for human rights is widely regarded as subversive, not much genuine information is published about the actions of those who complain. A sample inquiry, carried out by the organizations within Argentina, covering 20 towns whose size made it possible for every disappearance to be discovered, suggested that the number of registered disappearances would have to be multiplied by at least five. Since these organizations have a register of 3,000, it is likely that the real number of people missing after arrest or abduction is as large as 15,000.

On three occasions the Argentinian Government has published lists of people who, it claims, were thought to be missing but have since been "found" (12 April 1978 – 232 people; 7 August 1978 – 201 people; 14 December 1978 – 159 people). It is strange that no names on such Government lists have ever corresponded to the cases known to Amnesty International.

There is, then, in Argentina a very large number of disappeared persons. The question that naturally arises is how many of these people have been killed or have died while in detention. In September 1977, the Army Chief of Staff, General Roberto Viola, stated that since the March 1976 *coup*, 8,000 "subversives" had been killed or captured. In the same year the Minister of the Interior estimated the number of official detainees at about 3,700. It would appear from lists issued by the Ministry of the Interior (of prisoners, releases and arrests) that the number of people officially in detention has remained at about 4,000. It follows that if the figures are correct, at least 4,000 people have been killed. This would be the case even if, after September 1977, no further arrests or killings had occurred. But, in fact, since that date Amnesty International has received continual reports of more killings, arrests and abductions. Thus, the total number of those killed is likely to be much greater than 4,000.

When pressed about the human rights violations in Argentina, the Government usually speaks in terms of isolated excesses by over-zealous officers and claims that it has insufficient control of the various security forces. While there may be some truth in these explanations, they cannot be accepted as entirely adequate. Firstly, exceptional use of violence and insufficient official control could hardly account for the vast numbers of people who have been abducted or killed. And, on the other hand, since the *coup*, most anti-subversive operations have been of an illegal and unconstitutional nature. As previously mentioned, the death penalty has never been officially applied; nor have other severe penalties been inflicted in the civil courts (in the case of military tribunals the evidence on this point is harder to come by). Most people who have been abducted or arrested have not even been charged or tried at all. Yet, during this period, military commanders have frequently made reference in speeches to the fact that subversives are irredeemable ("*irrecuperables*") and should be eliminated. General Videla himself, speaking in Montevideo in October 1975 (five months before he became President), asserted that "As many people will die in Argentina as necessary to restore order."

It was, perhaps, through the influence of statements like this that a system of repression sprang up, involving cells of security officers who were able not only to abduct any suspects, but also to imprison and torture and kill them. Even if the Government has not had complete control of this system, it has certainly allowed it to flourish with impunity. No security officer has yet been punished (or even indicted) for the "excesses" that have been committed.

The evidence which Amnesty International has that a large number of people in Argentina have been put to death by security forces goes beyond deductions from Government statistics. Since the 1976 *coup*, dead bodies (sometimes mutilated) have been discovered throughout the country: washed up on the seashore or on river banks, discovered at the bottom of lakes or in mass shallow graves. These bodies are seldom identified. There is also eye-witness evidence that people held in detention have been killed. Prisoners who have been released have given accounts, with corroborative detail, of how other prisoners have died under torture or have been shot in the secret camps. From 1976 to 1977 a number of officially recognized prisoners (*reconocidos*) were killed, according to official statements, in transit, "while attempting to escape". But Amnesty International believes that there is evidence – from the weakness of some of the official statements themselves as well as from the testimony of other prisoners – that these accounts of the killings are highly dubious.

Three of the most notorious political murders occurred in late May and early June 1976 when the prominent exiled Uruguayan politicians, Zelmar Michelini and Héctor Gutiérrez Ruiz and the former President of Bolivia, Juan José Torres, were assassinated. In the cases of the Uruguayans at least, there are several factors which offer firm proof that the Argentine police and security forces were accomplices in this crime. Another Uruguayan senator, Wilson Ferreira Aldunate, wrote to President Videla on 24 May 1976, only hours before seeking diplomatic asylum, drawing attention to the anomalous behaviour of the Argentine authorities

He pointed out that although the abduction of Gutiérrez Ruiz and Zelmar Michelini had occurred in central Buenos Aires, the abductors had taken no precautions to conceal what they were doing and that, despite the nearness of members of the police and military guarding embassy and telecommunications buildings close to the two men's apartments, no attempt had been made to prevent the kidnappings; only once, at Hector Gutiérrez Ruiz' house, had the kidnappers been challenged: a guard on duty outside the home of the Brazilian military attaché had checked their credentials and then gone away. Finally, the police refused to register the kidnappings or to initiate any inquiry when relatives tried to report the incident. The three men were later found shot dead.

Many summary executions have been carried out by the police and army. As a matter of common practice, they are usually officially explained – and often condoned – by reference to "counter-subversion". On 15 June 1977, Amnesty International protested about the death of Elizabeth Käsemann, a German sociology student who had lived in Argentina for eight years. The organization had firm information that she had been held since 9 March 1977 in an unofficial detention center, where it is believed that she was subjected to torture. On 1 June 1977, the Argentine newspapers named her as one of 16 guerillas killed by the army in Monte Grande on 23 May 1977. Another person named by the authorities as having been killed in the same confrontation was Luís Fabri, who disappeared in February 1977. In the week of Elizabeth Käsemann's death, about 50 people were reported to have died in similar anti-subversive operations. Elizabeth Käsemann's relatives have rejected the official explanation of her death as "absolute nonsense". On 20 June 1977, the West German Foreign Office stressed the Argentine Government's responsibility in this case. Her body was returned to West Germany and on 12 June 1977, an autopsy was carried out. The results revealed gunshot wounds in the back and two surface wounds made by a machine-gun at the back of the neck and around the heart.

Amnesty International has received many reports of the deaths in dubious circumstances of officially recognized political prisoners. On 26 January 1977, Angel Alberto Georgiadis Otero was removed by ambulance from La Plata Prison, Buenos Aires Province, and was never seen alive again. The testimony of his wife contradicts official reports of "suicide". On 4 February 1977, Mrs Georgiadis received an official telegram from Buenos Aires Province Police Department: "Your husband Angel Alberto Georgiadis Otero was removed from Unit 9 by military personnel on 1 February 1977 for interrogation under military jurisdiction, Operations Area 113, and inflicted on himself injuries which caused his death."

The official death certificate states that death was due to "acute anaemia and *external* haemorrhage". However, in a copy of the burial certificate, filed at a police station, the reason stated was "acute anaemia and internal haemorrhage". Although an autopsy would have revealed the real cause of death, the authorities refused to permit one to be held. Mrs Georgiadis had tried to locate her husband before his death but had been warned by a judge that she should leave everything "in the hands of the law". Otherwise, she was told, she too might disappear. After her husband's death, she tried unsuccessfully to obtain an autopsy, an investigation, or permission to identify the body. All requests were denied and finally, fearing for her own life, she left the country.

Georgiadis and other prisoners had denounced the killings of Dardo Cabo and another prisoner who had been removed from La Plata prison on 4 January 1977 and were found dead a few days later.

The number of reports in Amnesty International's possession, the wide variety of the sources, the detailed descriptions provided by the witnesses – all these things point to the inevitable conclusion that the Argentine Government has acquiesced or taken part in the murder of numerous opponents, real or imaginary, of its political régime. In Argentina there are thousands of missing people who have never, officially, been detained. Likewise, with no formal death sentences, there are thousands of people dead.

### *Ethiopia*

Killing carried out for political reasons by Government officers without recourse to any legal process is extremely common in Ethiopia under military rule – since 1974. It is evident that in several situations it is Government policy to order alleged political opponents to be killed, either by official security forces, members of the civilian militia or armed guards attached to factories, peasants' associations or associations of urban-dwellers (*kebelle*). Speeches by leaders of the Provisional Military Administration Council (*Derg*) commonly use the slogan "revolutionary Motherland or death" and, since early 1977, openly encourage their armed supporters to administer "revolutionary justice" in order to eliminate "counter-revolutionaries". A "revolutionary measure", such as that taken against the Vice-Chairman of the *Derg*, Lieutenant-Colonel Atnafu Abate, on 11 November 1977, entails being killed on the orders of *Derg* leaders, for political reasons and without trial. Lieutenant-Colonel Abate was later accused of various "counter-revolutionary" activities and opinions. After taking this "revolutionary measure" the *Derg* urged its armed supporters not to hold demonstrations but to take action – "spread revolutionary Red Terror". The extent of the killings which took place in the following months far surpassed the mass killings of April–May 1977.

The murders fall into different categories:

(a) *Officially announced executions where there has been no trial:*
This was the case of 60 prominent people "executed" on 23 November 1974, including the Head of State, Brigadier Aman Andom, relatives of the deposed Emperor Haile Selassie, many senior officials and military officers who served under the former Government, Eritreans, some *Derg* members and others. Since then, at least 20 high-ranking military officers have been "executed" on political grounds: one example is Major Sissay Habte (10 July 1976). The next Ethiopian Head of State, Brigadier-General Teferi Bante, was reported to have been "executed" on 3 February 1977, but, in fact, he was killed in a gun battle within the *Derg* headquarters, in which six leading members of opposing factions within the *Derg* were also killed.

(b) *Secret killings of detainees in custody:*
Emperor Haile Selassie was almost certainly killed in custody despite the *Derg's* announcement that he died on 27 August 1975 as a result of complications following surgery. Killings of detainees suspected of belonging to the illegal Ethiopian People's Revolutionary Party (EPRP) became extremely common during 1977: for example, 44 students are said to have been killed on the outskirts of Addis Ababa on 26 February 1977 after they had been held at the Third Police Station. Abebech Bekelle, an Ethiopian Women's Coordinating

Committee leader, was said to have been murdered at about the same time. Killings of this nature have taken place both inside and outside prison throughout Ethiopia. There are many cases of prisoners' families being given back their relative's clothes, or being told not to bring food again – a sure sign that the detainees have been killed. In no cases are the bodies of detainees who have disappeared given back to their relatives for burial.

(c) *Killings by security officers, militias and kebelle guards during house-to-house searches:*
There have been many killings by the security forces during searches for illegal weapons or publications and for wanted people. Searchers sometimes act upon lists of names of people suspected of anti-Government opinions or activities, based on information supplied in confidence by informers and other sources. Amnesty International has had accounts of people being shot dead during these searches, either without even being asked their identity, or for not complying fully with orders, or even as substitute for an absent relative wanted by the authorities. After searches (such as those of September 1976, 23–27 March 1977 or 7–9 May 1977, when all traffic was prohibited without special permit, and other regulations forced people to stay at home at night), radio reports gave the number of weapons seized, and stated that people were "shot resisting arrest" and that "counter-revolutionaries were liquidated". The declared purpose of the March 1977 search was "to cleanse the city of Addis Ababa of the last remaining hideout of reactionaries, of anti-people, anti-revolutionary and anti-Ethiopian forces". People in these categories were said to have been "liquidated by speedy and determined revolutionary measures" (Radio Addis Ababa, 29 March 1977). It is not known how many people were killed in these searches. Rumours continually circulated in Addis Ababa during 1977 that a new final sweep was about to be carried out to get rid of all remaining opponents of the régime.

(d) *Killings after demonstrations against the military régime:*
Soldiers shot to kill in Addis Ababa during May Day demonstrations in 1975 and 1976, in July 1976 and on 22 September 1976, when anti-Government feeling was expressed. In December 1976, at least 30 were shot dead during a rally at Gondar. The killing of people circulating or possessing illegal publications also took place during the Adowa Day rally in Addis Ababa on 2 March 1977. The worst such incident happened just before the May Day rally in May 1977, when, on the night of 29 April, soldiers and militia in Addis Ababa launched a massive attack on a demonstration of students who opposed the régime. It is estimated that about 500 were killed. The *Derg* totally denied this massacre, dismissing accounts of it as "imperialist propaganda". Amnesty International is satisfied that the reports of several foreign journalists and diplomats, based on the count of bodies of people recently shot, in hospitals, mortuaries, and in the streets, were not exaggerated.

Killings went on for some days after the actual massacre. On 16 May 1977, the Secretary-General of the Swedish Save the Children Fund said that "... about 3,000 children have been massacred in Addis Ababa and their bodies, lying in the streets, are ravaged by roving hyenas ... The bodies of murdered children, mostly aged eleven to thirteen years, can be seen heaped at the roadside when one leaves Addis Ababa." He claimed that between 100 and 150 children were being slaughtered nightly, according to official Swedish sources (reported in the *Daily Telegraph* and *The Times*, London, 16 and 17 May 1977). There were killings in Nazareth and Debre Zeit also, mainly of young people and students.

(e) *Killing in Eritrea and the rural areas:*
The killing of suspected supporters of the armed movements fighting for the independence of Eritrea is arbitrary and on a large scale. Any expression of opposition to the régime is likely to lead to death. Arbitrary massacres have often been carried out in reprisal for such incidents as the assassination of a military officer in October 1975. Eritreans living in other parts of Ethiopia are constantly liable to arbitrary arrest and killing. It is not clear whether the frequent reports on Ethiopia Radio of the "liquidation" of "bandits", "outlaws", "infiltrators" and other "anti-revolutionaries" in different parts of Ethiopia refer to activities of the kind just described or to military-type operations. For example, Ethiopia Radio reported that deaths of this kind in Gondar, Sidamo, Wollo, Bale, Harrar and elsewhere, during the first half of May 1977, totalled 1,713. This indicates either grave unrest in rural areas, armed conflict, or murder on a large scale by – or on behalf of – the Government.

The number of people killed by the Ethiopian security forces in these various ways cannot be estimated accurately. A Reuters report on 7 March 1977 gauged that 2,000 were killed during the month between the *Derg* killings of 3 February 1977 and early March. There can be no doubt that, since 1974, several thousand people have been killed for political reasons without trial, by the military régime: the former Secretary-General of the banned Ethiopian Teachers' Association, who fled from Ethiopia in 1977, has claimed that the figure is about 30,000. The level of political violence is very high indeed, both in Eritrea and many rural areas, where several movements are in armed conflict with the régime. It is high, too, in Addis Ababa and other towns, where EPRP "assassination squads" killed possibly as many as 100 members and supporters of the *Derg* in the second half of 1977. One of the people assassinated was Tewodros Bekelle, Chairman of the All-Ethiopia Labour Union, created by the *Derg*, which replaced the banned Confederation of Ethiopian Labour Unions. At his funeral on 26 February 1977, a *Derg* leader promised revenge "by liquidating 1,000 reactionaries" by means of armed "revolutionary defence squads" (Radio Addis Ababa). While condemning these murders by opposition groups, Amnesty International considers that the mass killing by the Government of suspected political opponents, labelled variously "counter-revolutionaries", "anarchists", "feudalists", "bandits" and so on, cannot under any circumstances be justified.

### ***Guatemala*** *(the Republic of)*

Amnesty International estimates that the total number of deaths and disappearances in Guatemala attributable to the activities of official and semi-official bodies since 1966 would be likely to exceed 20,000. This figure is based on reports from the Guatemalan and international press, from Government and opposition statements, and from Amnesty International's own statistical findings. Before 1972, Amnesty International had on record the names of over 1,000 Guatemalans reported to have been executed or to have "disappeared". From the beginning of 1972 until April 1976, a total of 1,105 individual executions and disappearances were documented. Of this total, 786 were abducted before "disappearance" or before being found dead, while 320 were shot outright.

Charts 1, 2, and 3 illustrate characteristics of the total of 1,105 deaths and disappearances which occurred between 1972 and April 1976 where Amnesty International considered official or semi-official forces responsible for abduction and/or murder.

The largest group within the 1,105 cases documented in the period from 1972 until April 1976 were victims whose dead bodies could not be identified, and those who were identified only by name. In their case, the only other information

**Chart 1: Disappearances and probable murder by official agencies, 1972 - 30 April 1976**

(Source: Amnesty International case dossier)

***(a) Yearly numerical totals: categories of victim***

| | 1972 | 1973 | 1974 | 1975 | to 30 April 1976 |
|---|---|---|---|---|---|
| Peasants | 30 | 151 | 25 | 52 | 24 |
| Members of political opposition | 39 | 34 | 10 | 29 | 12 |
| Unidentified bodies | 80 | 57 | 44 | 12 | 35 |
| Bodies identified by name only | 147 | 167 | 56 | 57 | 44 |
| | 296 | 409 | 135 | 150 | 115 |

Total: 1,105. (This figure does not include an estimated but unconfirmed 200 shot dead in the aftermath of the earthquake of February 1976.)

***(b) Percentage totals: categories of victim***

The unidentified—and those identified by name only—are generally considered to have been peasants or poor urban residents. The figures for members of the political opposition include journalists, students, trade unionists, teachers, as well as members and leaders of opposition parties

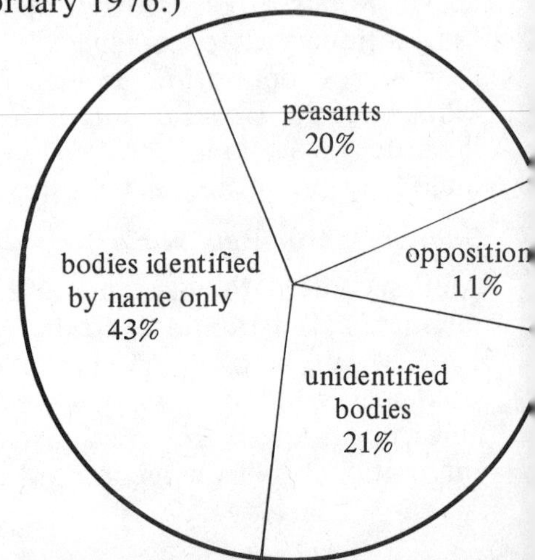

**Chart 2: Geographic distribution of disappearances and probable murder by official agencies. 1972 – 30 April 1976**

(Source: Amnesty International case dossiers)

| | Central Highlands | North | Guatemala City | Pacific Coast | East |
|---|---|---|---|---|---|
| 1972 | 22% | 6% | 33% | 14% | 25% |
| 1973 | 20% | 4% | 28% | 22% | 26% |
| 1974 | 26% | 5% | 25% | 24% | 20% |
| 1975 | 26% | 22% | 22% | 15% | 15% |
| 1976 to 30 April | 13% | 28% | 33% | 15% | 11% |

Central Highlands: San Marcos, Huehuetenango, Sololá, Sacatepequez, Quetzaltenango, Totonicapan, Baja Verapaz, El Progreso, Chimaltenango
North: Peten, Alta Verapaz, Quiche
Pacific Coast: Santa Rosa, Escuintla, Retalhuleu, Suchitepequez
East: Jalapa, Jutiapa, Chiquimula, Zacapa, Izabal

**Chart 3: Disappearances and probable murders by official agencies in the North (Peten, Alta Verapaz, Quiche) 1972 - 30 April 1976**

(Percentages are calculated on the basis of the totals in Chart 2)

1972 XXXXXX

1973 XXXX

1974 XXXXX

1975 XXXXXXXXXXXXXXXXXXXXXX

1976 to 30 April XXXXXXXXXXXXXXXXXXXXXXXXXXXX

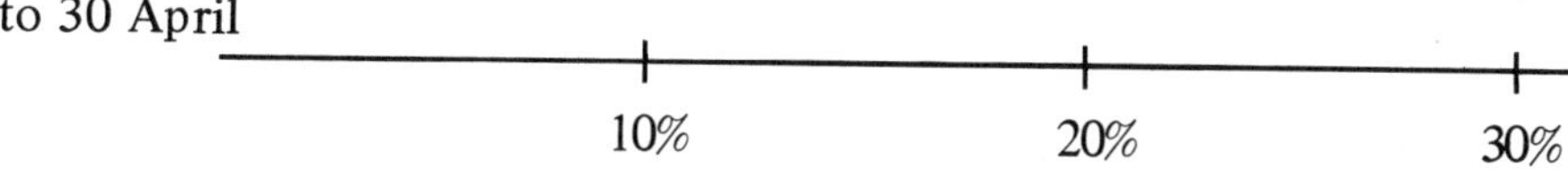


available dealt with the method used in the abduction and murder, and with the physical state of the corpse. Amnesty International believes that most of the victims come from the peasantry or the urban poor. Many were probably suspected petty criminals.

The second largest group of victims were clearly identified as peasants (*campesinos, agricultores*). Others included leaders and members of opposition parties, trade unionists, journalists, students and teachers. Among the victims were a relatively small number of businessmen and some people working for municipal governments and Government development agencies.

For the same period (1972–April 1976), Guatemala City newspapers reported a high incidence of what was apparently left-wing violence, including 149 murders of members of security forces, other Governmental personnel, businessmen, and large landowners and their employees.

The vast majority of those who have disappeared, when they are located, are found to have died by violence. Many bodies, bearing signs of torture or mutilation, are discovered along roadsides or in ravines, floating in plastic bags in lakes and rivers, or buried in mass graves in the countryside. Other victims have been shot in their homes or in the street. The disappearances represent not only a major human rights problem, but also a social one: a volunteer organization exists to care for the destitute families of people who have disappeared.

From mid 1966, the *Movimiento de Liberación Nacional* (Movement of National Liberation: *MLN*), a party formed by the participants in the successful 1954 coup, supported the organization of armed groups of civilians to fight "subversion". A manifesto published by the *MLN* on 27 September 1966 noted that "the Government should not consider it strange that citizens organize to take justice into their own hands ..." In June 1966 the first leaflets appeared from a new para-military group calling itself *MANO – Movimiento Anticomunista Nacional Organizado* (National Organized Anti-Communist Movement), its symbol a white hand in a red circle. The leaflets threatened all "communists" with death. The group soon became known as the *Mano Blanca* (White Hand). By 1967, some 20 similar groups had emerged, publicly claiming responsibility for killings.

Administrative provisions for internal security, established in 1966 and still in operation, provide for large numbers of armed civilians to function legally as agents of law enforcement at the local level, or as special security agents. The largely unregulated selection and supervision of semi-official security forces provided a pool of men, legally armed and acting with some official authority. This can be seen as an important contributing factor in the formation of para-military groups and their persistence today.

The use of "counter-terror" against left-wing opposition was justified by Licenciado Mario Sandoval Alarcón, now Vice-President and Secretary-General of the *MLN* Party, who has also claimed responsibility for the formation of *Mano Blanca*. In 1967, he was quoted as maintaining that:

> *"The Army was demoralized by the guerillas last year until we organized the White Hand... In the systematic elimination of the guerillas, a series of injustices have been committed... Several hundred persons have been killed, but between January and March (1967) the guerillas have been almost completely eliminated from the Guatemalan Oriente. The terrorism of the guerillas... has forced the Government to adopt a completely illegal plan, but this has brought results."* (Norman Gall "Guatemalan Slaughter", *New York Review of Books*, 20 May 1971)

The para-military groups did not limit their operations to the largely rural guerillas or their supporters. From late 1966, right-wing groups claimed responsibility for the increasing number of tortured and mutilated corpses discovered in and around Guatemala City. Most of the bodies were so badly mutilated that identification was difficult. Many were accompanied by notes stating that the particular individual had been killed because of communist sympathies. At times, several different groups claimed "credit" for a single killing.

One study, which appears to point to the beginning of official murders on a large scale in 1966 and 1967, and to their increase under the State of Siege from November 1970 to October 1971, was undertaken by the Guatemala City magazine, *Domingo*. Using the official register of one of Guatemala's principal cemeteries, *La Verbena*, the report compiled statistics for burials of unidentified bodies from 1966 to 1972. It noted that most of the bodies were recovered from places in which it could be assumed that they would go unnoticed – "sandpits, ravines or heavy brush" and that most of them showed "signs of violence". (Of the 797 unidentified bodies buried in *La Verbena* in the seven-year period, 23 were women.) Analysis of the numbers of burials in each year covered by the survey, indicated peaks coinciding with reported intensifications of violence on the part of the Government and Government-sanctioned para-military groups.

In July 1974, Kjell Laugerud García, formerly Minister of Defence and Chief of the General Staff of the Army, took office as President. Although there was a general lessening of political violence in the period before the elections in March 1974, a rash of political killings by para-military groups began once they were over. The earthquake of February 1976, which killed some 22,000 Guatemalans, was followed by another increase in the number of murders by Government and para-military groups: over 200 people alleged to be common criminals, were killed by these groups, according to reports in the Guatemalan press. In March 1976, General Leonel Vassaux Martínez, then Minister of the Interior (*Ministerio de Gobernación*) justified the summary executions, saying that the patrols of citizens responsible for the killings were vitally important in protecting lives and property, and that their existence had resulted in an improvement in the "control (exercised) by police authorities". When asked whether members of the opposition were not also victimized by these groups, he answered that such allegations "could not be proved".

The Government of General Laugerud has been notable in the support it has shown for cooperatives of small farmers. However, Vice-President Sandoval, and former President Arana, have repeatedly labelled these agrarian cooperatives communist-inspired, and under the present Government, security forces have been instrumental, on a number of occasions, in the detention and subsequent disappearance of some of their leaders and members. In July 1975, over 30 peasant farmers were abducted by uniformed paratroopers in the region of Ixcan Grande. In January 1976, four cooperative leaders in the area of Chisec were summarily executed by four men in civilian clothes, later identified as members of the *Guardia de Hacienda* (Border Patrol), an authorized, official security force.

In 1975, Amnesty International presented, to both the Government of Guatemala and to the Inter-American Commission on Human Rights, a survey of cases of political violence reported in the Guatemala City press: 134 cases of political murder and disappearance were documented between 1 July 1974 and 31 January 1975. The survey examined cases of probable official or semi-official abuse of human rights within the overall context of political violence in the country. It covered the deaths and disappearances reported in the press during that period which appeared to have political overtones regardless of the victim's political orientation. The survey was, however, intended to give only an indication of the scope and character of political violence; the actual number of victims was considered to be higher than press reports showed, especially when isolated rural areas were taken into account.

The survey found that 30 of the 134 reported victims of political violence could be grouped as members of police or military bodies, officials of the Government or of the ruling political parties, or businessmen and large landowners and their employees. All but one of the 30 were killed outright by being shot in the street, at home or at work; only one was abducted before being murdered. None of the 30 was reported to have been tortured.

Of the remaining 104 victims:
- 39 were identified as peasants;
- 4 were identified as students;
- 3 were identified as leaders or members of opposition parties;
- 3 were named as guerillas or violent criminals;
- 21 were identified by name only, and were probably people from the towns and peasants.

Of these 104 victims:
- 30 were shot dead;
- 5 were reported killed in armed encounters;
- 69 were reported "disappeared" or found dead after abduction. (Of those found dead, 29 were said to bear marks of severe torture.)

While the social and political background of the victims appeared to remain relatively unchanged during the period 1972–30 April 1976, the geographical regions in which the greater numbers of killings occurred showed some variation. Guatemala City and its immediate surroundings consistently represented over 20 per cent and as much as 33 per cent of the total cases (with an average of 28 per cent). This is in part explained by the fact that nearly one-sixth of Guatemala's total population is concentrated in the area, and that it has a predominant place in both the political and economic life of the nation.

The most striking finding of the survey is that cases in the departments considered together as the North, the most sparsely-populated area of the country, rose from an average of 4 per cent in 1972, 1973 and 1974, to 22 per cent in 1975 and 28 per cent in 1976, with a resulting relative decline in deaths and disappearances in the Central Highlands and in the East. Most of the individuals killed or "disappeared" in the North have been peasant farmers. The high figures are in part due to large-scale detentions and disappearances in the northern part of Quiché Department, where observers suggest that the situation has been affected by the rapid increase in the value of the land – at present occupied largely by peasant smallholders organized in cooperatives. The increase is due to the planned construction of a major highway into the area, linking agricultural land with national markets, and to the discovery of petroleum deposits in the region (see Chart 3). Over 30 peasant members of cooperatives were detained by uniformed paratroopers in July 1975 and subsequently disappeared.

Further large-scale disappearances have occurred in the Quiché region more recently. Seventeen Indian peasants of the area of San Fernando Cotzal, in El

Quiché Department, were the subject of Amnesty International inquiry after their arrest in March 1976, after a dispute over land tenure went unacknowledged by authorities. The 17 were later reported by reliable sources to have been released, but trade union, church and press sources alleged that over 60 other peasant farmers from the region have been detained and have "disappeared" since the beginning of 1977.

***Uganda** (the Republic of)*

Since 1971, a very large number of people in Uganda have "disappeared" following their arrest by the security forces. Although a few have managed to flee the country on hearing that they are to be arrested, the vast majority of those arrested on suspicion of having committed a political offence are rarely seen alive again. Only very few "political detainees" survive the initial period of detention and torture, and there is seldom any genuine judicial investigation of their cases leading to a court appearance. Nearly all are severely tortured, and either die under torture or are killed in other ways. One common method of killing is by hammers: detainees are lined up, the second man in line is ordered to hammer the first man's head to kill him, and the second man is then killed in the same way by the third, until the whole line is killed, the last survivor being shot by a soldier supervising the killings. Such killings have been carried out by various branches of the security forces, who normally take victims to their headquarters. These various security agencies are as follows:

(a) *The Police:* Although the police were in the past a fairly well-disciplined body, people have been tortured and killed at Kampala Central Police Station – although possibly not by police officers.

(b) *The Army:* Army barracks, in all towns in Uganda, have been the scene of mass killings of soldiers and police officers, especially from the Acholi and Lango tribes in 1971, 1972, 1973 and 1977. Members of other tribes, such as Lugbara and Teso, have suffered a similar fate on other occasions. Civilians have also been tortured and killed in army barracks – for example, at Bugolobi Marine Commando Barracks during 1976–77.

(c) *The Military Police:* Their headquarters is at Makindye Barracks in Kampala, where numerous atrocities took place in 1972–73, and to a lesser extent thereafter, although torture and killings are still carried out in the barracks.

(d) *The Public Safety Unit (PSU):* A police unit, both uniformed and plainclothes, set up in 1972 to deal with armed robbers (*kondos*). PSU night patrols regularly shoot on sight, supposedly at suspected *kondos*, or people allegedly "resisting arrest". These deaths are not normally reported, nor are inquiries made into them. The PSU headquarters at Naguru Barracks (Kampala) has been the worst center of torture and killing since 1972.

(e) *The Bureau of State Research:* The much-feared State intelligence agency, whose powers override those of other security agencies, is directly under the control of the President. Its headquarters are at Nakasero (Kampala), where many people have been tortured and killed since 1976, with few survivors.

Victims of State Research officers have also been tortured and summarily killed in isolated places in the bush, and in various private houses used for the purpose.

The dead bodies of people killed by the various branches of the security forces have been seen in such places as the Sezibwa River, Namanve Forest, Mabira Forest, Nandere Forest and Murchison Bay graveyard.

Amnesty International has not been able to compile a list of those killed, because most names are known only to close relatives and associates. Examples are given here of prominent people killed, to illustrate the range of the killings. (Mention is not made of Asians killed during the forced exodus in 1972, of which there is an account in other publications, for example, *Uganda and Human Rights*, International Commission of Jurists, Geneva, 1977). It is commonly alleged that prominent individuals are killed on "orders from above"; this is not necessarily the case for people less well known. (It is impossible to assess the accuracy of this allegation.) Categories of people known to have been killed, especially in 1977, include:

(a) *Politicians:* large numbers of former politicians of the civilian government overthrown in January 1971, and of former political parties have been killed. They range from members of the former President Obote's Cabinet to several members serving as ministers under President Amin, such as Mr Charles Oboth-Ofumbi and Lieutenant-Colonel Wilson Oryema, both killed on 16 February 1977. All the members of President Amin's original Cabinet have been killed, or have fled into exile. A former Minister of Agriculture, Justus Byagagaire, was shot and seriously wounded by soldiers near Mbarara in May 1977.

(b) *Religious Leaders:* the killing of the Rt Rev. Janani Luwum, Archbishop of the Church of Uganda, Rwanda, Burundi and Boga-Zaire, is a well-documented example. He was murdered on 16 February 1977 by security officers after being accused of conspiring to overthrow President Amin. An attempt was made by the Uganda authorities to disguise the killing as a car accident. Other leading churchmen (but no other bishops) have been killed since that incident, and there are reports of ordinary church people being arrested or shot for contributing to the church's centenary celebrations, or for wearing a centenary badge (*Sunday Times*, London, 6 March 1977). Several soldiers were reported to have been shot for attending mass at Jinja at Christmas 1976. Between October and November 1977, about 400 Christians in Masaka region – mainly Catholics, including 37 catechists – were arbitrarily killed by soldiers. At first this was thought to be revenge for the murder of a Muslim trader, but one reliable source states that he was, in fact, murdered by soldiers to create a pretext for eliminating people engaged in passive resistance to the régime.

(c) *Civil Servants:* many senior civil servants, especially of the Acholi and Lango tribes, have almost certainly been killed, following arrest in February 1977. They include: Y. Engur, the former Minister of Culture and Ambassador to the USSR, Jeremiah Angulu, Under-Secretary at the Ministry of Public Administration and Ben Emor, a member of the East African Legislative Assembly.

(d) *Academics, Teachers and Students:* several Acholi and Langi academics and students from Makerere University have either been arrested and killed, or have fled, since February 1977. Many headmasters and secondary school teachers are reported to have been killed in the north about this time.

(e) *Businessmen:* it is alleged that nearly all managers of former foreign companies have been killed, such as a business partner of a West German firm, arrested in August 1976 (*Kenya Daily Nation*, 9 August 1976). Acholi and Langi businessmen have suffered most in recent months: an example is Ben Ongom, who was among those publicly executed in September 1977. Mr Kasule, a supplier of food to Makerere University, was arrested in February 1977 and is feared dead.

(f) *Writers:* the Editor of the Catholic newspaper, *MUNNO*, Father Clement Kiggundu, was killed in 1975. Byron Kawadwa, a well-known playwright and director of the National Theatre, was killed with four or five other theatre workers in February 1977. He had been rehearsing a play about the first Ugandan martyr, St Charles Lwanga, for the Church of Uganda's forthcoming centenary celebrations.

(g) *Soldiers and Policemen:* very large numbers of Acholi and Langi soldiers and police officers have been killed since February 1977. The former Commissioner of Prisons, Leonard Kigoonya, was killed in April 1977 (*Kenya Daily Nation,* 19 April 1977).

(h) *Wives and Families of well-known People:* cases have been reported of the relatives of murdered prominent people themselves being killed, such as Mrs Bataringaya, the wife of the former Interior Minister, who was himself murdered in April 1977. More than one source states that about 200 wives and children of murdered Acholi and Langi soldiers from Mubende and Mbarara Barracks were also killed on their return to the north in February 1977.

(i) *Foreigners:* citizens of other nations, including Kenya, Tanzania, Somalia, Ghana, Zaire, the United Kingdom and the United States have been arbitrarily killed. They include Mrs Dora Bloch, the British-Israeli hostage abducted and murdered by security officials after the Israeli military operation at Entebbe Airport on 4 July 1976. At least nine of the 245 Kenyans arrested in August 1976 after the same incident were also killed. A South African, Solly May, "disappeared" at the same time.* Available evidence leads almost inevitably to the conclusion that Robert Scanlon, a British-born businessman with Uganda citizenship, arrested in June 1977, was hammered to death on 14 September with other detainees held in a private house at Kololo, in Kampala. The detention and killing of many of the above have followed a systematic pattern, for example, the elimination of Acholi and Langi soldiers in the army in 1972–73 and 1977. Reports state that there was a "Death List", planned in advance and organized on a country-wide basis in February 1977, of all Acholi and Langi prominent in the professions and the Civil Service. This numbered 7,000 in some accounts (*Irish Times*, 5 March 1977), and, in others, covered all Acholi and Langi males between the ages of 15 and 50. It is certain that soldiers went to government offices, Makerere University, other educational institutions, hospitals and other similar places, with lists of names of people to be taken into custody. Although a number managed to flee the country, very many were arrested and are believed to be dead.

Arbitrary and random arrests and killings take place in all parts of the country, especially after any "crisis" thought to affect the security of the régime – the numerous *coup* and assassination attempts, the circulation of anti-Government leaflets (as in August 1976), students' demonstrations and demonstrations of

* He was released from detention in 1978.

popular support for the churches. Some sources report that Roman Catholics organizing the welcome for the Archbishop of Kampala, Cardinal Nsubuga, on his return from Rome in mid 1976 were arrested and killed. Many people have been arrested and killed simply because a security official or soldier decided to take their wife, house, car, property or shop, cattle, coffee crop, etc., or because of a secret report from an informer. This happens as frequently in the towns to wealthier Ugandans as in the countryside to peasants. A reported escalation of killings during April and May 1977, was undertaken by new "death squads" (also called "clearance squads" – *Sunday Times*, London, 1 May 1977), consisting of organized gangs of soldiers or Public Safety Unit officers in civilian clothes.

Killings by the security forces are the most serious human rights violation in Uganda. Estimates of those who have "disappeared" and been murdered vary between 50,000 and 300,000. Amnesty International is unable to verify them. Relatives and friends of the victims commonly refuse to speak out for fear of reprisals. Those who have fled the country have been openly warned not to speak out publicly against the régime, lest their relatives inside Uganda suffer for it (*Kenya Standard*, 2 February 1975, and Uganda Radio, 22 January 1977). Examples of reprisals are the torture and killing of relatives of the former Minister for Economic Affairs, Wanaume Kibedi, and the former Finance Minister Emmanuel Wakhweya, following their flight and public denunciation of the military régime (*Uganda and Human Rights*, the International Commission of Jurists, Geneva, 1977).

APPENDIX A

## Amnesty International Conference on the Abolition of the Death Penalty

## DECLARATION OF STOCKHOLM

## 11 December 1977

The Stockholm Conference on the Abolition of the Death Penalty, composed of more than 200 delegates and participants from Asia, Africa, Europe, the Middle East, North and South America and the Caribbean region,

**RECALLS THAT:**

- The death penalty is the ultimate cruel, inhuman and degrading punishment and violates the right to life.

**CONSIDERS THAT:**

- The death penalty is frequently used as an instrument of repression against opposition, racial, ethnic, religious and under-privileged groups,
- Execution is an act of violence, and violence tends to provoke violence,
- The imposition and infliction of the death penalty is brutalizing to all who are involved in the process,
- The death penalty has never been shown to have a special deterrent effect,
- The death penalty is increasingly taking the form of unexplained disappearances, extra-judicial executions and political murders,
- Execution is irrevocable and can be inflicted on the innocent.

**AFFIRMS THAT:**

- It is the duty of the state to protect the life of all persons within its jurisdiction without exception,
- Executions for the purposes of political coercion, whether by government agencies or others, are equally unacceptable,
- Abolition of the death penalty is imperative for the achievement of declared international standards.

**DECLARES:**

- Its total and unconditional opposition to the death penalty,
- Its condemnation of all executions, in whatever form, committed or condoned by governments,
- Its commitment to work for the universal abolition of the death penalty.

**CALLS UPON:**

- Non-governmental organizations, both national and international, to work collectively and individually to provide public information materials directed towards the abolition of the death penalty,
- All governments to bring about the immediate and total abolition of the death penalty,
- The United Nations unambiguously to declare that the death penalty is contrary to international law.

APPENDIX B

## United Nations General Assembly Resolution 32/61 of 8 December 1977 on Capital Punishment

*The General Assembly,*

HAVING REGARD to article 3 of the Universal Declaration of Human Rights,[20] which affirms everyone's right to life, and article 6 of the International Covenant on Civil and Political Rights,[21] which also affirms the right to life as inherent to every human being,

RECALLING its resolution 1396 (XIV) of 20 November 1959, 2393 (XXIII) of 26 November 1968, 2857 (XXVI) of 20 December 1971 and 3011 (XXVII) of 18 December 1972 as well as Economic and Social Council resolutions 934 (XXXV) of 9 April 1963, 1574 (L) of 20 May 1971, 1656 (LII) of 1 June 1972, 1745 (LIV) of 16 May 1973 and 1930 (LVIII) of 6 May 1975, which confirm the continuing interest of the United Nations in the study of the question of capital punishment with a view to promoting full respect for everyone's right to life,

CONCERNED at the fact that only 32 Governments responded to the questionnaire on capital punishment addressed to them for the preparation of the first five-year report of 1975 on capital punishment,[22] submitted in accordance with General Assembly resolution 1745 (LIV),

NOTING WITH CONCERN that, notwithstanding the limited progress mentioned in the first five-year report of the Secretary-General of 1975 on capital punishment, it remains extremely doubtful whether there is any progression towards the restriction of the use of the death penalty, thus justifying the conclusions drawn by the Secretary-General in the aforementioned report,

CONSIDERING that the Sixth United Nations Congress on the Prevention of Crime and the Treatment of Offenders is to be held in 1980,

TAKING NOTE of the request of the Economic and Social Council, in its resolution 1930 (LVIII), to the Secretary-General, in accordance with General Assembly resolution 2857 (XXVI), to proceed with the report on practices and statutory rules which may govern the right of a person sentenced to capital punishment to petition for pardon, commutation or reprieve, and to report on these questions to the Council at the latest at its sixty-eighth session, together with the basic report of 1980 on capital punishment,

EXPRESSING the desirability of continuing and expanding the consideration of the question of capital punishment by the United Nations,

1. REAFFIRMS that, as established by the General Assembly in resolution 2857 (XXVI) and by the Economic and Social Council in resolutions 1574 (L), 1745 (LIV) and 1930 (LVIII), the main objective to be pursued in the field of capital punishment is that of progressively restricting the number of offences for which the death penalty may be imposed with a view to the desirability of abolishing this punishment;

20 General Assembly resolution 217 A (III).
21 General Assembly resolution 2200 A (XXI), annex.
22 E/5616 and Corr. 1 and 2 and Add. 1.

2. URGES Member States to provide the Secretary-General with relevant information for his preparation of the second five-year report of 1980 on capital punishment and of the report on practices and statutory rules which may govern the right of a person sentenced to capital punishment to petition for pardon, commutation or reprieve;

3. INVITES the Economic and Social Council to report to the General Assembly at its thirty-fifth session on its deliberation and recommendations on the basis of the aforementioned reports of the Secretary-General and of the study to be submitted by the Committee on Crime Prevention and Control in accordance with Council resolution 1930 (LVIII);

4. CALLS UPON the Sixth United Nations Congress on the Prevention of Crime and the Treatment of Offenders to discuss the various aspects of the use of capital punishment and the possible restriction thereof, including a more generous application of rules relating to pardon, commutation or reprieve, and to report thereon, with recommendations, to the General Assembly at its thirty-fifth session;

5. REQUESTS the Committee on Crime Prevention and Control to give consideration to the appropriate place on the agenda of the Sixth Congress of the issue mentioned in paragraph 4 above, and to prepare documentation on the question;

6. DECIDES to consider, with high priority, at its thirty-fifth session the question of capital punishment.

APPENDIX C

## Fifth United Nations Congress on the Prevention of Crime and the Treatment of Offenders
## Toronto 1-15 September 1975

## ABOLITION OF THE DEATH PENALTY

***A Joint Statement by International Non-Governmental Organizations Concerned with Human Rights in Consultative Status with the Economic and Social Council***

The resolution which follows has been accepted by the international non-governmental organizations listed below, all of whom are members of the Special NGO Committee on Human Rights. It is submitted by them to this Congress in the hope that the Congress, composed of experts rather than politicians, will itself adopt the proposals it advocates. This would provide a sorely needed momentum to a humanitarian movement whose objectives have seen little realization in recent years. It is suggested that the Congress may wish to deal with the matter under item 2 of its agenda: *The role of criminal legislation, judicial procedures and social controls in the prevention of crime.*

***The Undersigned International Non-Governmental Organizations Concerned with Human Rights,***

***Affirming* their unswerving commitment to the protection of the right to life of every human being,**

***Re-iterating* their total opposition to any form of cruel, inhuman or degrading treatment or punishment,**

***Considering* that the death penalty is in violation of both the above principles,**

**1. *Call on* all governments that retain capital punishment to cease employing it;**

**2. *Call on* the General Assembly of the United Nations to promulgate a declaration that would urge its total worldwide abolition;**

**3. *Call on* all non-governmental organizations concerned with human rights to make every effort at the national and international level to secure the abolition of capital punishment.**

Amnesty International
Arab Lawyers Union
Commission of the Churches on International Affairs of the World Council of Churches
Friends World Committee for Consultation (Quakers)
International Association of Democratic Lawyers
International Confederation of Free Trade Unions
International Council of Jewish Women
International Council of Social Democratic Women
International Council of Women
International Federation of Free Journalists
International Federation of Human Rights
International Federation of Women Lawyers
International League for the Rights of Man
International Movement for Fraternal Union among Races and Peoples
International Peace Bureau
International Social Service
International Youth and Student Movement for the United Nations
Pax Romana

Womens International League for Peace and Freedom
Womens International Zionist Organization
World Assembly of Youth
World Confederation of Labour
World Federation of United Nations Associations
World Jewish Congress
World Muslim Congress
World Student Christian Federation

APPENDIX D

## Amnesty International Conference on the Abolition of the Death Penalty
## THE PREPARATORY SEMINARS

The four seminars convened by Amnesty International in Colombo, Hamburg, New York and Paris were allotted two or three agenda items of the ten which the series of seminars as a whole was designed to consider. The Ibadan and Port-of-Spain seminars, both of which constituted the first occasion on which the subject of the death penalty was considered at a regional seminar in the respective areas, had agendas of a somewhat wider nature.

***Paris: 18 June 1977***

(1) The Psychology of Individuals Involved in and Affected by Death Sentences (Juror, Judge, Executioner and Condemned Person)
(2) Alternatives to the Death Penalty

***Hamburg: 9–10 July 1977***

(3) Conventional Arguments on the Death Penalty
(4) Theological Attitudes to the Death Penalty
(5) The Death Penalty and Discrimination

***New York: 22 July 1977***

(6) The Death Penalty in International Law and Organization: Norms and Standards of International Conduct
(7) Murder Committed or Acquiesced in by Government: the Death Penalty Without Process of Law

***Colombo (Sri Lanka): 2–4 September 1977***

(8) Public Opinion and the Death Penalty
(9) The Mass Media and the Death Penalty
(10) The Influence of Cultural Factors on Attitudes towards the Death Penalty

***Ibadan (Nigeria): 3–8 October 1977***

(a) Trends and Issues in Capital Punishment
(b) The Death Penalty and Public Opinion in Africa
(c) International Norms Affecting the Death Penalty
(d) Some Moral and Ethical Implications of Capital Punishment
(e) The Death Sentence in Times of National Emergency
(f) Human Rights vis-à-vis the Death Penalty
(g) The Dilemma of the Death Penalty in Africa
(h) The Death Penalty in States with Minority Régimes
(i) The Death Penalty and its Alternatives
(j) Deterrent and non-Deterrent Value of Capital Punishment

***Port-of-Spain (Trinidad): 7–8 November 1977***

The aims of this seminar were:

(a) to provide for the presentation and exchange of basic information relating to the question of the death penalty
(b) to provide for an exchange of views on the problems likely to confront the abolitionist movements in the region and the elaboration of strategies to deal with them

(c) to establish appropriate regional instruments for the implementation of such strategies
(d) to consider any theoretical problems which might emerge unavoidably from (a), (b) and (c) above. (As a result, the seminar discussed the nature of those factors, operating in legal systems in the region, which promote possible miscarriages of justice and judicial error. The seminar also considered whether there was any need for an abolitionist movement to propose alternatives to the death penalty.)

## AMNESTY INTERNATIONAL PUBLICATIONS

**Report on Allegations of Torture in Brazil,** A5, 108 pages, first edition September 1972, re-set with updated preface March 1976: £1.20
* **Report on an Amnesty International Mission to Spain,** A5, 24 pages, September 1975: 35 pence
**Prisoners of Conscience in the USSR: Their Treatment and Conditions,** A5, 154 pages, November 1975: £1.00
**AI in Quotes,** A5 24 pages, Day 1976: 25 pence
**Amnesty International 1961–1976: A Chronology,** May 1976: 20 pence
**Professional Codes of Ethics,** A5, 32 pages, October 1976: 40 pence
**Report of an Amnesty International Mission to Sri Lanka,** A4, 52 pages, second edition December 1976: 75 pence
* **Los Abogados Contra La Tortura,** A4, 31 pages, first published in Spanish, January 1977: 60 pesetas, 50 pence
* **Report of an Amnesty International Mission to the Republic of the Philippines,** A5, 60 pages, first published September 1976, second (updated) edition March 1977: £1.00
* **Dossier on Political Prisoners Held in Secret Detention Camps in Chile,** A4, March 1977: £1.45
* **Report of an Amnesty International Mission to Argentina,** A4, 92 pages, March 1977: £1.00
* **Torture in Greece: The First Torturers' Trial 1975,** A5, 98 pages, April 1977: 85 pence
**Islamic Republic of Pakistan. An Amnesty International Report including the findings of a Mission,** A4, 96 pages, May 1977: 75 pence
* **Evidence of Torture: Studies by the Amnesty International Danish Medical Group,** A5, 40 pages, June 1977: 50 pence
**Report of an Amnesty International Mission to the Republic of Korea,** A4, 46 pages, first published April 1976, second edition June 1977: 75 pence
* **The Republic of Nicaragua. An Amnesty International Report, including the findings of a Mission to Nicaragua 10–15 May 1976,** A4, 75 pages, July 1977: 75 pence
** **Indonesia. An Amnesty International Report,** A5, 148 pages, October 1977:£2.00
* **Amnesty International Report 1977,** A5, 352 pages, December 1977: £2.00
**Political Imprisonment in South Africa,** A5, 105 pages, January 1978: £1.00
**Political Imprisonment in the People's Republic of China,** A5, 192 pages, November 1978, £1.50. Soon to be available in Spanish.
* **Amnesty International Report 1978,** 320 pages, January 1979: £2.50

*also available in Spanish
**also available in Indonesian

In addition to these major reports, Amnesty International also publishes a monthly **Newsletter**, an annual **Report** and a series of **Amnesty International Briefing Papers**:

**Amnesty International Newsletter and annual Report**: The **Newsletter** is an eight-page monthly account of Amnesty International's work for human rights in countries throughout the world and includes a one-page bulletin on the work of the Campaign for the Abolition of Torture. The annual **Report** gives a country- by-country survey of human rights violations which have come to the attention of Amnesty International. Yearly subscription £6.00 (US $15.00) inclusive.

**Amnesty International Briefing Papers:** a series of human rights reference booklet on individual countries, averaging between 12 and 16 pages in A5 format. Briefing Papers Numbers 1–15:

**Singapore**
**Paraguay***
**Iran****
**Namibia**
**Rhodesia/Zimbabwe**
**Malawi**
**Guatemala***
**Turkey**
**People's Democratic Republic of Yemen**
**Taiwan (Republic of China)**
**Czechoslovakia***
**German Democratic Republic (GDR)***
**Morocco**
**Guinea***
**Peru***

*also available in Spanish
**also available in Farsi

Subscription price for series of 10 Briefing Papers: £6.00 (US $15.00). Price includes postage and packing. Single copies 40 pence (US $1.00), plus 20 pence (50 cents) for postage and handling.

**AMNESTY INTERNATIONAL PUBLICATIONS** may be obtained from the following national sections:

**Australia**: Amnesty International, Box X2258, GPO Perth, Western Australia 6001
Branch Addresses:
*New South Wales:* Amnesty International, New South Wales Branch, PO Box. 2598, GPO Sydney, New South Wales 2001
*Queensland:* Amnesty International, Queensland Branch, PO Box 87, Clayfield, Brisbane, Queensland 4011
*South Australia:* Ms Margaret Illman, 16 Tester Drive, Blackwood, South Australia 5051
*Tasmania:* Mrs B.E.G. Rolls, 194 Waterworks Road, Hobart, Tasmania 7005
*Victoria:* Amnesty International, Victoria Branch, PO Box 28, St Kilda, 3182 Victoria
*Western Australia:* Mrs G. Graham, Box X2258, GPO Perth, Western Australia 6001

**Austria**: Amnesty International, Austrian Section, Esslinggasse 15/4, A-1010 Wien

**Bangladesh**: Amnesty Bangladesh, GPO Box 2095, Dacca

**Belgium**: *(Dutch/Flemish-speaking)* Amnesty International, Blijde Inkomststraat 98, 3000 Leuven
*(French-speaking)* Amnesty International Belgique, 145 Boulevard Leopold 2, 1080 Bruxelles

**Canada**: *(English-speaking)* Amnesty International, Canadian Section, PO Box 6033, 2101 Algonquin Avenue, Ottawa, Ontario K2A 1T1
*(French-speaking)* Amnistie Internationale, Section Canadienne (Francophone), 1800 Ouest, Boulevard Dorchester, 4ème étage, Montreal, Quebec H3H 2H2

**Costa Rica**: Apartado Postal 72, Centro Colon, San José

**Denmark**: Amnesty International, Frederiksbörggade 1, 1360 København K

**Faroe Islands**: Anette Wang, Tróndargøta 47, Post Box 23, 3800 Tórshavn

**Finland**: Amnesty International, Finnish Section, Laivasillankatu 10A, Helsinki 14

**France**: Amnesty International, Section française, 18 rue de Varenne, 75007 Paris

**Germany, Federal Republic of**: Amnesty International, Section of the Federal Republic of Germany, Heerstrasse 178, 5300 Bonn
**Ghana**: Dr I.S. Ephson, Ilen Chambers, PO Box 6354, Accra
**Greece**: Amnesty International, Greek Section, 22 Kleitomachou Street, Athens 502
**Iceland**: Amnesty International, Icelandic Section, Hafnarstraeti 15, PO Box 7124, 127 Reykjavik
**India**: Amnesty International, Indian Section, D-19 Annexe, Gulmohar Park, New Delhi 110049
**Ireland**: Amnesty International, Irish Section, 39 Dartry Road, Dublin 6
**Israel**: Amnesty International, Israel National Section, PO Box 37638, Tel Aviv
**Italy**: Amnesty International, Italian Section, Via della Penna 51, Rome
**Japan**: Amnesty International, Japanese Section, Room 74, 3-18 Nishi-Waseda 2-chome, Shinjuku-ku, Tokyo 160
**Korea, Republic of**: Amnesty Korean Committee, Fifth floor, Donhwamoon Building, 64-1 Kwonnongdong, Chongnoku, Seoul
**Luxembourg**: Amnesty International Luxembourg, Boîte Postale 1914, Luxembourg-Gare
**Mexico**: Amnistía Internacional, Sección Mexicana, Apartado Postal No. 20-217, México 20DF
**Nepal**: Amnesty International, Nepal Section, GPO Box 890, 21/242A Dillibazar, Kathmandu
**Netherlands**: Amnesty International, Dutch Section, 3$^{e}$ Hugo de Grootstraat 7, Amsterdam
**New Zealand**: Amnesty International, New Zealand Section, PO Box 3597, Wellington
**Nigeria**: Amnesty International, Nigerian Section, 15 Onayade Street, Fadeyi-Yaba, Lagos
**Norway**: Amnesty International, Norwegian Section, Akersgaten 39 II, Oslo 1
**Pakistan**: Amnesty International, Pakistan Section, 615 Muhammadi House, I.I. Chundrigar Road, Karachi
**Peru**: Jirón Pachitea 279, Oficina 500, Lima
**Spain**: *Secretariat:* Columela 2, 1° dcha., Madrid 1
*Barcelona:* Rambla de Prat 21 1°, Barcelona 12
*San Sebastián:* Apartado 1109, San Sebastián
**Sri Lanka**: E.A.G. de Silva, 79/15 Dr C.W.W. Kannangara Mawatha, Colombo 7
**Sweden**: Amnesty International, Smalandsgatan 2, 114 34 Stockholm
**Switzerland**: Amnesty International, Swiss Section, PO Box 1051, CH-3001 Bern
**Turkey**: Uluslararasi Af Örgütü, Türkiye Ulusal Subesi, Izmir Caddesi, Ihlamur Sk 6 (Tugay Han, 1/30), Ankara
**USA**: *New York:* Amnesty International USA, 2112 Broadway, New York NY 10023
*San Francisco:* Amnesty International USA, Western Region Office, 3618 Sacramento Street, San Francisco CA 94118
**United Kingdom**: Amnesty International, British Section, 8-14 Southampton Street, London WC2E 7HF
**Venezuela**: Amnesty International, Venezuelan Section, Apartado 51184, Caracas 105

# THE DEATH PENALTY
## addenda and update to the Amnesty International report published 26 September 1979

**The Amnesty International report *The Death Penalty* mainly concentrates on the period from 1973 to 1976. It also takes into account major trends up to the end of 1977.**

**The information contained in this addenda and update covers significant developments from the end of 1977 up to mid-1979. Mention is made only of countries in which Amnesty International is aware of changes in legislation affecting the death penalty, or new patterns in its use.**

### *International and regional initiatives*

On 8 April 1979 the International Executive Committee of Amnesty International cabled United Nations Secretary General Dr Kurt Waldheim requesting him to convene an emergency meeting of the United Nations Security Council to halt the resurgence of executions and political killings throughout the world. At the same time Amnesty International publicly called for an international moratorium on executions.

Thomas Hammarberg, Chairperson of the organization's International Executive Committee, stated: "We are urging the UN Security Council to take emergency action for two reasons. We want the death toll to stop. And we are appalled by the fact that death sentences have been carried out or handed down in the face of an unprecedented expresssion of world opinion on behalf of the victims."

"We unequivocally condemn each death sentence and each killing as a denial of the purposes of the Charter of the United Nations and a violation of the human rights and fundamental freedoms proclaimed in the Universal Declaration of Human Rights," he said.

The Amnesty International statement drew attention to people in 12 countries who had been sentenced to death, executed, assassinated or found dead in the previous week. The dead included the former Prime Ministers of Iran and Pakistan, 10 political prisoners in Mozambique, five blacks in South Africa, five Nigerians, and individuals executed in Trinidad, the Soviet Union and the United States of America.

Amnesty International said it also opposed political murders committed by government agencies or opposition groups. Recent victims of political murders had included:

– British member of parliament Airey Neave, the Conservative Party spokesman

on Northern Ireland, who was assassinated by a bomb in his car at the House of Commons in London;
- Salvadorean industrialist Ernesto Liebes, the Honorary Consul of Israel, killed by the guerrilla organization FARN in El Salvador;
- a Guatemalan trade union leader and four other victims of assassination whose bodies were found in Guatemala City on 6 April. All the corpses bore marks of torture and knife wounds.

## Council of Europe

Since the writing of the Amnesty International report, there have been significant trends within the Council of Europe towards complete abolition of the death penalty throughout the European Community. During the meeting of the Council's Legal Affairs Committee in June 1979, a Swedish member of parliament, Carl Lidbom, submitted a report recommending that the Council take a stand on the issue of the death penalty. No vote was taken at the meeting but after the discussion the committee chairman, British member of parliament, Percy Grieve, said that "there had been a clear majority for abolition".

The Legal Affairs Committee will meet again in September 1979 and is expected to prepare a draft resolution on the question of the death penalty for submission to the Parliamentary Assembly meeting in October.

During the past 10 years the death penalty has been completely abolished in Denmark, Finland, Luxembourg, Norway, Portugal, Sweden and abolished for peace time offences in Malta, Spain and Switzerland. To Amnesty International's knowledge the death penalty has not been re-introduced in any country of Western Europe except Belgium where the number of offences punishable by death has been increased. The practice of executions in Western Europe shows a similar downward trend and is now limited to only three countries: France, Greece and Turkey.

## ***Afghanistan*** *(the Democratic Republic of)*

On 27 April 1978, the People's Democratic Party government led by President Noor Mohammad Taraki came to power through a takeover in which several hundred people died. Sardar Mohammed Daud, who had been President of Afghanistan since 1973, and 16 members of his family were killed during these events. Kabul Radio announced that Sayed Abdullah (the Vice President), Ghulam Haider Rasooli (the Defence Minister), Abdul Kadir Nuristani (the Minister of the Interior) and General Mohammed Musa (Chief of the Air Force), had been executed in the days following the government takeover. Three more army officials, General Abdul Khaliq, General Rokay Soleiman and General Yahya Nawrooz were reported to have been summarily executed in the Ministry of Defence on 28 April 1978. Amnesty International has also been reliably informed that Wahid Abdullah, (former Minister of Foreign Affairs), was executed on or around 30 April 1978. As far as Amnesty International is aware, none of those executed in the days following the 27 April 1978 government takeover had been tried by a court of law.

In Afghanistan the death penalty cannot be imposed for criminal offences.

However, there have been several reports in the international press quoting opposition sources as stating that, in late 1978 and early 1979 "scores of political prisoners" were being summarily executed by firing squad, after having been taken away from Kabul prisons (*Sunday Telegraph*, London, 4 January 1979).

Amnesty International has not been able to assess whether such general reports are accurate. However, Amnesty International has the names of more than 10 political prisoners whom it believes have been killed or summarily executed without any form of trial while in the custody of the government. Among them are a former Minister of Justice in President Daud's government, a Professor of Anthropology at Kabul University, and former Prime Minister Mohammed Moosa Shafiq, all of whom were arrested after 27 April 1978. Amnesty International has also received dozens of reports of family members of other political prisoners from whom no news has been received since their arrest last year, and whom family members fear to have been killed while in custody.

### ***Angola*** *(People's Republic of)*

On at least three occasions in December 1978, Angolan radio announced that supporters of two opposition movements, UNITA (*União Nacional para a Independencia Total de Angola*) and FLEC (*Frente de Libertacão do Enclabe de Cabinda*), had been paraded at public rallies and sentenced to death by acclaim. On the first occasion, five alleged UNITA members were condemned to death by firing squad at a mass rally held in Lobito on 3 December 1978. A week later, other UNITA members were condemned at a rally in Huambo and in Cabinda a crowd sentenced a group of five FLEC supporters to be shot.

### ***Argentina*** *(the Republic of)*

Although in Argentina the death penalty was re-introduced in 1976 (by decrees passed in March and June), it was never formally applied until March 1979, when a court sentenced to death by firing squad a man accused of a double murder. (In this case an appeal has been lodged.) This is the first death sentence to be officially imposed in Argentina since the 1930s; it concerns a *crime passionel* that has no political connotations.

### ***China*** *(People's Republic of)*

New legislation was adopted on 1 July 1979 by the Fifth National People's Congress (China's parliament) which discussed and approved a revision of the laws for the first time since the 1960s. Article 43 of the new Criminal Law states: "the death penalty is imposed only for the most heinous crimes. In the case of an offender who should be given the death penalty, if immediate execution of the death penalty is not mandatory, a two-year reprieve may be pronounced simultaneously with the death sentence. . ." The new Law on Criminal Procedure also specifies that a death sentence shall be approved by the Supreme People's Court and carried out within seven days after the Supreme People's Court issues an order to that effect.

Commentaries published in the Chinese official press about the new legislation stressed the importance of distinguishing between people who are "reactionary in political thinking" and those guilty of criminal acts, implying that the first category should not be executed. In connection with this, a woman named Zhang Zhixin, who was executed in 1975 on political grounds, was portrayed as a heroine in the Chinese media. Zhang Zhixin, who was 45 when she was executed, was arrested in 1969 for criticizing the former Defence Minister Lin Piao (who disappeared later in 1971) and the "gang of four". She was executed six years later for refusing to recant. The press stressed that "even if she was a 'counter-revolutionary', she did not murder anyone, she did not commit arson, nor did she incite or organize people to make trouble . . . what she did . . . was honestly express her political viewpoint". The *People's Daily* of 13 July 1979 also commented on the "red terror" of the Cultural Revolution: "What was the result? Facts prove that many of those who were attacked or killed were innocent Party members, cadres or people".

### ***Djibouti*** *(the Republic of)*

Djibouti, which gained independence from France in 1977, is a retentionist jurisdiction, though Amnesty International knows of no instance of executions since independence.

On 29 March 1979, Amnesty International called on President Hassan Gouled Aptidon to conduct an inquiry into the death under torture of Omar Mohammed, a soldier who died earlier that month while in pre-trial detention.

### ***Ethiopia***

There has been no new legislation since 1977 affecting the use of the death penalty. However, the practice appears to have changed. From about June 1978 or earlier the powers given to tribunals of urban dwellers associations (*kebelles*) and peasant associations to impose the death penalty for counter-revolutionary offences were administratively withdrawn. The state thus restored to itself the exclusive judicial power to impose and carry out the death penalty through civilian and military courts. The number of executions by these processes is not known. Nevertheless there were continuing reports during 1978 and 1979 of killings outside the framework of law carried out by the security forces against political opponents of the government, though at a reduced rate relative to late 1977 and early 1978.

### ***Indonesia*** *(the Republic of)*

On 14 September 1978, the first execution of a common murderer in Indonesia was carried out by firing squad. The executed man, Husin bin Umar, had been convicted and sentenced to death in 1967. There are 41 persons at present known to be under sentence of death in Indonesia. Of these, nine are under sentence of death on criminal charges, 31 because of their alleged involvement in the 1965 *coup* and one for alleged activities on behalf of the Moslem *Kommando Jihad* (Holy War Command).

The maximum penalty for murder in Indonesia is death. This corrects the statement on page 82 of the report that "The maximum penalty for murder remains life imprisonment".

***Iran** (the Islamic Republic of)*

After the revolution of February 1979 special courts known as "Islamic Revolutionary Tribunals" were established in Iranian cities to try persons who had held positions of authority under the Shah. Charges related not only to the torture and killing of dissenters and demonstrators, but also to being actively involved in the running of the country under the Imperial government. By 1 May 1979 approximately 160 people had been reported executed by firing squad.

The indictments made reference not only to secular offences, but also included religious concepts of Islamic law, such as "corruption on earth" *Mofsed-e-Fel'Arz*. *Sura* 5 verse 36 of the *Qu'ran* (translation by Abdullah Yusuf Ali) reveals that "the punishment of those who wage war against God and His Apostle and strive with might and main for mischief through the land is execution . . . or exile from the land. . . ."

In come cases however defendants were only charged with "corruption on earth" as "their crimes [were] well enough known". (*Ettela'at* newspaper, Teheran, 13 March 1979). Examples included the cases of 12 people among whom were an army and police officer, a "theoretician of the previous regime" and a torturer. They were executed on 13 March.

The tribunals, which were created by the Islamic Revolutionary Council, initially operated without specific procedural rules. On 5 April 1979 a set of regulations was promulgated under which they were given jurisdiction to try "civil and political offences such as murder, torture, imprisonment of innocent Iranians, [acts undertaken to strengthen] the influence of foreigners [in Iran] or the disgraceful Pahlavi regime . . . ruining the economy . . . taking part in armed attacks . . . implementing programs against the national and public interest . . . or any [similar] abuse against the people". The tribunals also exercise jurisdiction over sexual offences such as homosexual rape.

The three-member tribunals are chaired by a religious judge whose word on all questions is apparently final. Many trials have been summary in nature and no adequate opportunity is afforded to prepare a defence. The sentences, none of which are stated in the regulations to be mandatory, include the death penalty. Acquittals have occurred.

Although the trials are normally carried out in secret, some foreign journalists have very occasionally gained access to trials in Teheran and the provinces. Local correspondents reported on 13 March that the chief government spokesman, Vice Premier Abbas Amir-Entezam had said that the trials were held *in camera* "for security reasons", and to preclude the "secrets revealed doing any damage". However, some trials are extensively covered by the local media.

No appeal is allowed from the sentences of the revolutionary court though one case is of particular note: on 22 April 1979 local correspondents reported the case of a condemned conscript in Kermanshah which, according to *Kayhan*, was sent to Qom for review by Ayatollah Khomeini after fellow conscripts physically prevented the prisoner from being transferred to the place of execution and threatened to take hostages in an attempt to publicize what in their view was an erroneous verdict. Amnesty International knows of no similar cases but the concern that the procedures being applied could result in the execution of persons guilty of no crime even under present standards is not infrequently voiced.

Regulation 33 provides that sentences pronounced by the revolutionary tribunals prior to the coming into force of the regulations themselves remain valid. Illustrative of this are the cases of two persons convicted of murder by the Isfahan Revolutionary Tribunal. The three men, identified as an internal security chief, a SAVAK interrogator and a constable, were sentenced to death on 17, 18 and 22 March respectively. The regulations were promulgated on 5 April, the sentences were then confirmed by the Chief Revolutionary Protector in Teheran and the men taken to the firing squad on 6 April (*Kayhan* 7 April).

### ***Iraq** (the Republic of)*

Two new capital offences were introduced in mid-1978. It became a capital offence for any serviceman who retired from, or left, the armed forces for any reason after 17 July 1968 to join or work for any party or political grouping other than the Ba'ath Party.

It also became a capital offence for anyone to enlist to another party or political grouping anyone with an organizational relation with the Ba'ath Party while knowing of his previous relation with that party. This is an amendment to article 200 of the penal code. There have been two previous amendments to this article, one in 1974 (see Report) and one in 1976 which makes it a capital offence for anyone who leaves the Ba'ath Party to join or work for another party or political grouping.

There is no information available as to whether anyone has been sentenced to death or executed under this new legislation.

### ***Israel** (the State of)*

On 29 April 1979, in the aftermath of several violent incidents which followed the signing of the Israel-Egypt peace treaty, the Israeli cabinet sanctioned the use of the death penalty for "acts of inhuman cruelty". This overturned a 1967 Labour government decision that the death penalty would no longer be carried out, despite remaining in force under several provisions of the Defence Emergency Regulations, the Nazi and Nazi Collaboration Law (1950), the Crime of Genocide Law (1950) and for the crime of treason under the Penal Law (1957).

### ***Luxembourg** (the Grand Duchy of)*

In the spring of 1979 the death penalty was abolished in law for all crimes in time of peace and war. The death penalty is still retained under the constitution, which will be amended to bring it in line with the law.

### ***Madagascar** (the Democratic Republic of)*

Amnesty International knows of no executions in Madagascar during the period under review but in November 1977 special tribunals were created to deal with bandits, and were empowered to impose the death penalty. Defendants' legal rights are restricted and they have no right of judicial appeal.

### *Malawi (the Republic of)*

According to information received by Amnesty International at least 35 people were hanged in Malawi during the first four months of 1979.

### *Malaysia (the Federation of)*

In December 1978 the Privy Council in London granted an appeal against the validity of the Essential (Security Cases) Regulations based on the contention that they were subsidiary to the Emergency (Essential Powers) Ordinance of 1969 which should have lapsed once Parliament reconvened in 1971. In January 1979, Parliament passed the Emergency (Essential Powers) Act enacting the 1969 Ordinance and all subsidiary legislation including the 1975 Regulations. The President of the Malayan Bar Council, which had advised its members to refuse to handle cases tried under the 1975 Regulations, called the retrospective legislation "ill-advised". In December 1978, 44 persons were reportedly in prison sentenced to death under the 1975 Regulations.

### *Mozambique (the People's Republic of)*

The Mozambique government introduced the death penalty in February 1979 following sporadic acts of sabotage in Maputo and other towns. Under the new criminal code issued on 28 February, crimes such as treason and acts of terrorism or sabotage involving loss of life were made capital offences. The first executions under the new law were carried out in Maputo on 1 April 1979 when 10 people convicted of espionage and treason before a Revolutionary Military Tribunal were shot by firing squad. Another 13 executions had been carried out by the end of May 1979.

### *Nigeria (the Federal Republic of)*

The death penalty is retained in the new constitution due to come into force on 1 October 1979, the date of the planned return to civilian rule.

Public executions of those convicted under the Armed Robbery Decree were suspended in October 1978, but resumed in March 1979, after a public outcry against a new wave of violent crime in the capital Lagos.

### *Norway (the Kingdom of)*

In May 1979 Norway abolished the death penalty for all crimes in time of peace. and war.

### *Pakistan (the Islamic Republic of)*

On 4 April 1979 former Prime Minister Z.A. Bhutto was hanged in Rawalpindi Jail despite the findings of three of the seven judges of Pakistan's Supreme Court that the prosecution had "failed to prove guilt beyond reasonable doubt" in his case. Execution of the death sentence under such circumstances is, as far as Amnesty International is aware, unprecedented in Pakistan.

An Amnesty International delegation, which had attended Mr Bhutto's review petition before the Supreme Court found there were legal grounds for commutation of the death sentence that were particularly strong in Mr Bhutto's case, as he had been convicted on the basis of unconvincing evidence. (He had been convicted solely on evidence supplied by accomplices, which is normally not sufficient for conviction without substantial corroboration.)

Mr Bhutto was executed soon after all legal remedies had been exhausted, whereas the clemency petitions of his four co-accused, who had been sentenced to death with him, were "still being reviewed" by the government as of the time of writing (May 1979).* Considering the unsatisfactory nature of Mr Bhutto's trial, and the evidence produced against him, there will always remain a strong suspicion that political factors only were responsible for the decision by President Zia-ul-Haq to execute Mr Bhutto, and that a miscarriage of justice occurred.

Mr Bhutto's execution was one of around 800 which, according to the then Law Minister A.K. Brohi, occur in Pakistan every year (*Dawn* 8 February 1979). This figure puts Pakistan among the countries with the highest number of yearly executions in Asia, and reports in the international press of February 1979 stated that President Zia-ul-Haq had dismissed all clemency petitions in death penalty cases since assuming office. Of particular concern to Amnesty International is the fact that among the hundreds of executions being carried out in Pakistan every year, many are those of civilians who are tried and convicted by military courts. These courts apply summary rules of evidence and many of the civilians accused cannot appeal to ordinary courts of law against a death sentence.

On 22 March 1978 three civilians were hanged outside Camp Jail Lahore, after having been found guilty by a military court of charges of kidnapping and murder. The executions were carried out publicly and were the first public hangings to occur for many years in Pakistan. They were also the first to occur under the present government.

### *Peru (the Republic of)*

In a 307-article constitution drafted and approved by Peru's Constituent Assembly during its final session in the second week of July 1979, the death penalty was abolished for all offences in peace time. The penalty has been retained solely for cases of people convicted of treason in time of war. The new constitution will come into force in July 1980 when a civilian government takes over from the current military administration.

### *Rhodesia [Zimbabwe]*

In September 1978 the Transitional Government introduced martial law throughout much of Rhodesia. The regulations which were introduced made provision for the establishment of special courts martial with jurisdiction to try any person charged with offences relating to the guerrilla war. These courts martial were empowered to impose any sentence—including the death penalty—so long as it did not exceed the maximum sentence which could have been imposed by the high court. A Review Authority was also set up to review all death sentences

---

* On 24 July 1979 the four men convicted with Mr Bhutto were hanged—two in Rawalpindi District Jail and the others in prisons in Lahore and Faisalabad.

imposed by special courts martial. However, the composition and membership of the Review Authority is not known and its meetings are held *in camera*. Martial Law Regulations have subsequently prohibited judicial review of death sentences imposed by special courts martial.

No official figures are available to indicate how many people have been sentenced to death and executed since the introduction of martial law. In practice it is known that most defendants appearing before special courts martial are not legally represented, and it is widely suspected that the courts martial tend to impose more severe sentences than the high court would have done. It is known also that gross irregularities have occurred during the trials of a number of people sentenced to death by special courts martial, and such irregularities are thought to have been caused largely by a lack of legal training on the part of those military and other officials who preside at the courts martial.

Following the conclusion of the internal settlement agreement on 3 March 1978, it was widely reported that Bishop Abel Muzorewa and Reverend Ndabaningi Sithole had intervened effectively to end political executions in Rhodesia. However, further executions are known to have taken place within a short time of the 3 March 1978 agreement. Executions have also been carried out since Bishop Muzorewa became Prime Minister in June 1979.

### ***Rwanda*** *(the Rwandese Republic)*

President Juvenal Habyalimana commuted all death sentences on 8 January 1979 to mark the formation of a new government and his re-election as president after a national referendum.

### ***Singapore*** *(the Republic of)*

In 1978 death sentences against persons convicted under the amended Misuse of Drugs Act were carried out for the first time. Teh Sin Tong and Teo Hock Seng were hanged in April and August 1978 respectively. Both had been convicted on drug trafficking charges. At least 20 persons had been sentenced to death under the Drugs Act as of May 1979. Among them was Siti Aminah Binto Jaffar, a 19-year-old Malay girl, who was found guilty in August 1978 of abetting her boy-friend in the trafficking of heroin.

On 11 May 1979 three men convicted of armed robbery were hanged. The three were sentenced to death for illegal use of firearms–a capital offence in Singapore–although no injuries were sustained during the robbery.

### ***Somalia*** *(the Somali Democratic Republic)*

Seventeen people were executed on 26 October 1978 after being convicted by the National Security Court of "endangering the unity, freedom and security of the nation". They were originally charged with attempting to overthrow the government during the abortive *coup* attempt of 9 April 1978, in which 28 people were killed. All except one of those condemned were military officers. They were permitted legal representation, and had access to their relatives. They were executed in public in Mogadishu, the capital, six weeks after the verdicts were given, following confirmation of verdict by the Head of State.

### ***Spain*** *(the Spanish State)*

In December 1978 the death penalty was abolished in Spain for all crimes committed in time of peace. It was retained under military justice for specific offences committed in time of war. The death penalty had previously been abolished only under civilian law in the new constitution introduced in July 1978.

### ***South Africa*** *(the Republic of)*

On 16 January 1979 the Minister of Justice reported in parliament that a total of 132 executions had been carried out in South Africa during 1978. One of those executed was white. All those executed were people who had been convicted of criminal offences.

On 6 April 1979 the execution of Solomon Mahlangu took place at Pretoria Central Prison. Mahlangu, 22, was convicted and sentenced to death in March 1978 on charges of murder and on charges under the Terrorism Act. These charges arose out of his participation in an incident in Johannesburg in June 1977 which resulted in the death of two white civilians. The execution of Mahlangu was the first execution for a politically-related offence since the mid-1960s.

### ***Taiwan*** *(the Republic of China)*

At the end of May 1979 Wu Chun-fa (alias Wu Tai-an), an alleged "communist spy", was executed in Taipei by firing squad. He was sentenced to death in April on conviction of "plotting to overthrow the government by violent means". This was the first political execution known to have been carried out in Taiwan in the past five years.

### ***Tanzania*** *(the Union Republic of)*

On 30 March 1978 Vice President Jumbe commuted three death sentences imposed in the 1973–74 Zanzibar treason trial. All remaining prisoners convicted at that time were freed in December 1978 after serving sentence, with full remission for good conduct. Death penalties imposed *in absentia* on four other Zanzibaris who were held under administrative detention on mainland Tanzania since 1972 were not formally commuted, although these four and other detainees were freed in April 1978 by President Nyerere. It is believed however that the ruling Zanzibar Revolutionary Council does not intend to proceed with these sentences if the persons concerned were to return to Zanzibar.

### ***Uganda*** *(the Republic of)*

On 12 April 1979 the new government of President Yusuf Lule was sworn into office by the new Chief Justice, after the capture of the capital Kampala by the Tanzanian army and Ugandan exile force. The new government repealed decrees of President Amin creating special military tribunals empowered to impose the death penalty for a wide range of security and economic offences. Many people are believed to have been executed after summary trial by these tribunals during 1978 and 1979, including civilians refusing to be conscripted to fight the liberation forces. In April 1979 all surviving prisoners, political and non-political, were freed by the liberation forces, including a number of convicted murderers.

The new government has stated its desire to retain the death penalty for the same offences as under previous civilian rule. It has also announced its intention to prosecute through the civil courts those members of the security forces and other officials of the previous administration against whom it has sufficient evidence to charge them with specific offences under the Uganda penal code. The government has sought the extradition of several former officials who had fled the country to face charges of murder.

### *United Kingdom of Great Britain and Northern Ireland (the)*

On 19 July 1979 the House of Commons, in a free vote, defeated a motion introduced by Conservative member of parliament Eldon Griffiths that "the sentence of capital punishment should again be available to the courts". The motion was defeated by 362 votes to 243 votes.

### *United States of America*

On 1 May 1979 the laws of the following states provided for the death penalty for aggravated murder: Alabama, Arizona, Arkansas, California, Connecticut, Delaware, Florida, Georgia, Idaho, Illinois, Indiana, Kentucky, Louisiana, Maryland, Mississippi, Missouri, Montana, Nebraska, Nevada, New Hampshire, New Mexico, New York, North Carolina, Oklahoma, Oregon, Pennsylvania, South Carolina, South Dakota, Tennessee, Texas, Utah, Vermont, Virginia, Washington, Wyoming.

The following states were without death penalty statutes: Alaska, Colorado, Hawaii, Iowa, Kansas, Maine, Massachusetts, Michigan, Minneapolis, New Jersey, North Dakota, Ohio, Rhode Island, West Virginia, Wisconsin. In some of these states the legislature is considering re-introducing the death penalty.

On 20 April 1979, 494 persons, nearly half of whom are members of racial minorities, were under sentence of death in 23 states. This figure included five women. Over 80 per cent of these prisoners had been sentenced in the courts of the 11 southern states of the old Confederacy: the largest death row populations being in Florida (125), Texas (108), Georgia (76) and Alabama (41).

Two further states have now provided that the death penalty be carried out by lethal injection: Idaho and New Mexico; bills to this effect have also been introduced elsewhere.

The execution of Mr John Evans in Alabama scheduled for 6 April 1979 was stayed at the last moment by US Supreme Court Justice William Rehnquist and legal proceedings in the case are continuing. In Florida Mr John Spenkelink, after having exhausted all avenues of appeal against the death sentence imposed on him in 1973, was executed in the electric chair on 25 May 1979. Immediately after the execution an Amnesty International mission to the United States pleaded with Florida state officials for the commutation of death sentences facing more than 130 prisoners on death row.

The US Congress continues to consider proposed federal legislation re-introducing the death penalty for a larger range of offences of homicide.

To Amnesty International's knowledge, as of 30 May 1979, the following countries had abolished the death penalty for all offences:

| | | |
|---|---|---|
| **Austria** | **Ecuador** | **Luxembourg** |
| **Brazil** | **Fiji** | **Norway** |
| **Colombia** | **Finland** | **Portugal** |
| **Costa Rica** | **Federal Republic of Germany** | **Sweden** |
| **Denmark** | **Honduras** | **Uruguay** |
| **Dominican Republic** | **Iceland** | **Venezuela** |

*Note:* Legislation on the death penalty in both **Australia** and the **United States of America** is under the jurisdiction of individual states. In both countries, some states are abolitionist, others retentionist.

To Amnesty International's knowledge, as of 30 May 1979, the following countries had abolished the death penalty in time of peace, but retained it for specific offences committed in time of war.

| | | |
|---|---|---|
| **Canada** | **Netherlands** | **Spain** |
| **Italy** | **Panama** | **Switzerland** |
| **Malta** | **Peru** | |

To Amnesty International's knowledge, as of 30 May 1979, the following states retained the death penalty but were believed not to have conducted executions in the period under review because of government policy:

| | | |
|---|---|---|
| **Algeria** | **Guyana** | **Upper Volta** |
| **Belgium** | **Ivory Coast** | |
| **Greece** | **Seychelles** | |

AI Index: ACT 05/03/79